WINGS
OF
EMPIRE

WINGS
OF
EMPIRE

THE FORGOTTEN WARS OF THE ROYAL AIR FORCE, 1919–1939

BARRY RENFREW

For Margaret

First published 2015

The History Press
The Mill, Brimscombe Port
Stroud, Gloucestershire, GL5 2QG
www.thehistorypress.co.uk

British Library Cataloguing in Publication Data.
A catalogue record for this book is available from the British Library.

ISBN 978 0 7509 6507 1

Typesetting and origination by The History Press
Printed and bound in Great Britain by TJ International

CONTENTS

ACKNOWLEDGEMENTS

I chanced on the subject of Air Control while researching British colonial campaigns during the interwar period for another book. Little has been written about the subject despite the scale of the operations and the elaborate theories that underlay them. My efforts to find out more led to the writing of this narrative history. I benefited greatly from the studies of Charles Townshend, David Omissi and R.A. Beaumont.

The book is based on research at a number of museums and libraries, including the Royal Air Force Museum, the Imperial War Museum, the National Army Museum, and the National Archives at Kew. My thanks to the many remarkable and dedicated people who work at all of these fine places.

A small group of friends played a much bigger role than they probably realised in getting the book aloft with their unfailing help and encouragement. They include Jim Donna, Mike McHenry, Mark Shields, Bill Cranston, Donald Somerville and Wendell Hollis. I hope they will not be disappointed by the result.

I owe a special debt to Field Marshal Sir John Chapple. He has selflessly given of his time, experience and knowledge to inspire and assist people around the world in the study of military history.

My thanks to Michael Leventhal at History Press for taking on the book. Andrew Latimer and Lauren Newby did an excellent job of handling the manuscript.

And above all my thanks to Margaret, who inspired all that is good in these pages.

PROLOGUE – POLICE BOMBING

A solitary aeroplane with a 19-year-old English pilot at the controls raced down a crude runway hacked out of the Sudanese desert in the spring of 1916 as the first red flush of dawn peeled the darkness from the land. Lieutenant John Slessor flew west over the empty wastes, buffeted by low clouds and the desert wind. He wasn't sure how long he had been flying when he spotted a black smudge in the distance. As Slessor nosed lower, what at first looked like shadows cast by the clouds were transformed into a spectacle from the Crusades.

An army of Muslim horsemen arrayed in long, serried ranks stood in the desert below. Sunlight glinted on the riders' steel helmets, gleaming breast-plates and the tips of their lances; the wind ruffled their white robes; and green and black war flags emblazoned with verses from the Koran fluttered over their heads. It reminded Slessor of the toy soldiers he had played with as a child. For the rest of his life he never forgot the tragic beauty of that doomed army.

Few, if any, of the horsemen had seen an aeroplane before; some pointed and shouted in panic or astonishment, while others stared mutely as it roared over them. For a moment, Slessor was convinced he must seem like a winged god soaring across the sky. Shaking the distracting conceit from his mind, the young aviator began dropping bombs into the heart of the formation. Each blast tore gaping holes in the packed ranks of men and animals. Within minutes the army fractured into a terrified mob as thousands of men and animals bolted in every direction. Although barely noticed by a world transfixed by the titanic battles of the First World War, the defeat of a native army by a single aeroplane was the start of a revolution in British colonial warfare.

Aircraft were only added at the last minute when an expeditionary force was sent in 1916 against the Dervish sultanate of Darfur after it challenged British control of the Sudan. Such a thing had not been done before in British colonial warfare, but a senior official thought that it would terrify natives who had never seen an aeroplane.

Ground operations were already under way in the Sudan when the Royal Flying Corps' (RFC) 17 Squadron in Egypt received an order on 29 March to provide a flight of four BE2c aircraft. The little wood and canvas planes were far too flimsy to fly the hundreds of miles to Darfur. Each machine had to be dismantled and packed in wooden crates to be transported by ship and then train. Along with them went a little contingent of nine officers and fifty-six men.[1]

An airbase was built just inside Darfur at El Hilla, with an advance landing strip 50 miles further west at Abiad Wells. The landing strips were just bare earth cleared of rocks and shrub by gangs of Sudanese labourers with wooden tools and their hands. The only shelter against the sun and desert winds, which could warp or crack the planes' wooden frames if left in the open for even a few hours, were two RFC canvas hangars and a marquee borrowed from the army.

Each tent had just enough space to house a single plane. Teams of mechanics and fitters worked for up to twelve hours at a time in the gloomy, stifling interiors. Poison was smeared on the canvas walls to keep out ants that could devour every part of an aeroplane except the engines and other metal components.

The 40 tons of fuel, weapons and spare parts needed for two weeks of operations had to be taken by camel over the last 100 miles to the airstrip at El Hilla. It took twenty-eight camels to transport the parts that made up each of the canvas hangars, and most collapsed and died after just a day or two.

At dawn on 11 May the first two planes, flown by Lieutenants F. Bellamy and Slessor, touched down at El Hilla. Watching Sudanese soldiers were awed. A British officer wrote in his diary:

> For the first time astonished troops saw the beautiful sight of an aeroplane gleaming against a gold sunshine as it turned in a downward circle to land on the prepared stretch of ground. The ship of the air brought down the house. 'By God! Our General is very clever,' murmured the marvelling soldiery.[2]

The pilots had little time to appreciate such veneration; flying over the western Sudan was difficult and dangerous. Severe turbulence buffeted the frail aircraft and sandstorms, towering thousands of feet, appeared without warning and easily outraced the lumbering planes. Navigation over the desert was mostly guesswork: there were no reliable maps, and few hills or other natural features on the dun-hued landscape to steer by. Huge arrows of white calico cloth, 25ft long and 3ft wide, were positioned every 30 miles across the desert to stop crews going off course.

Slessor was guided on one flight by the sergeant major of a native camel unit, a hulking 6ft 4in Sudanese. The man had never seen an aeroplane before, but he climbed calmly into the front cockpit and unerringly guided Slessor over the empty desert with confident sweeps of his great hand.[3]

The air contingent made a dramatic debut in the campaign on 12 May when a plane flew over El Fasher, the capital of Darfur, roaring above the palace of Sultan Ali Dinar. In a gesture from an older, courtly era of warfare, the pilot tossed down a challenge demanding the sultan's surrender. In elaborate Arabic, it said that Ali Dinar did not possess 'the character, the knowledge, nor any other quality of an enlightened ruler'.[4] Ali Dinar's reply was tossed into the British camp a few nights later. He derided the aeroplane as a 'disguised horseman', and said the commander of the English force would be tortured 'in the worst possible manner' and his severed head displayed in El Fasher's public market 'as an example to people of understanding'.[5]

Such exploits were novel and exhilarating, but the army saw them as mere antics and the flyers were relegated to scouting and conveying messages as the soldiers set out to win the war with tactics that had barely changed in a century. The force of 3,000 mostly Sudanese and Egyptian infantry advanced in pageant-like splendour across the desert in a huge, bristling square of men and weapons. The flags of the battalions flapped in the desert breeze, and the sun glanced off the steel cannons and the long lines of bayonet-tipped rifles, as bugle calls and the bark of drums pierced the air. Marching lines of infantry formed the living walls of the square, their ranks shielding the horse-drawn guns, supply wagons and more than 2,000 pack camels in the centre. Cavalry and mounted scouts reconnoitred ahead and guarded the flanks. At the end of each day, the formation was transformed into the lines of a camp simply by halting.

British scouts on 22 May found a force of 3,000 Dervish warriors about 13 miles from El Fasher. Poor weather had grounded the air contingent and it would play no part in what was to come. A company of camel troops went forward to goad the Dervishes into abandoning their positions and attacking. What followed was more like a ritual than a battle, a one-sided choreographed slaughter at which British armies had become adept in colonial campaigns.

Screaming warriors, most on foot and armed only with swords and spears, lunged across the intervening stretch of sand, a wave of half-naked bodies in a frantic race to reach the distant lines of riflemen, machine guns and cannons. There must have been some apprehension in the British ranks – Dervish spearmen had done the seemingly impossible before and broken a British square.

The Dervishes were still hundreds of yards away when the British opened fire with artillery, machine guns and rifle volleys. For forty minutes the warriors hurled themselves at the square, trying to force their way through a wall of exploding shells and bullets with their bodies. Several times they were halted by the withering fire, only to regroup and surge forward again.

The charging men, their lungs and hearts pounding with fear, strain and desperation, had to leap over the shattered and bleeding bodies of dead and wounded companions. A few got to within 10 yards of the British lines before being cut down, and then the Dervishes' determination snapped and the survivors turned and fled. More than 1,000 dead and wounded littered the ground, their blood-splattered white and brown robes fluttering in the morning breeze. Among the mangled corpses were many boy soldiers.

Ali Dinar was waiting for the British outside El Fasher the following day with 2,000 cavalry who were the cream of his army. The airmen were desperate to play a role in the final battle and demonstrate the potential of air power. Flying conditions were still bad, but a single plane piloted by Slessor got into the sky. He spotted the Dervish cavalry and attacked while the British ground force was still miles away. His BE2c had a single machine gun and could only carry four 20lb bombs in the desert conditions, but it was a formidable arsenal against men armed mostly with swords. He zoomed over the horsemen, releasing on each pass a single bomb that bowled over clumps of riders and animals.

With one bomb left, Slessor glimpsed a figure on a white camel ringed by guards in the centre of the Dervish Army. He realised it must be Ali Dinar, and released the last bomb. Its blast tore the camel to bits, hurling the sultan to the ground and killing two of his guards. Ali Dinar was led away by his servants as his army disintegrated and fled. Slessor had little time to watch the rout: a bullet smashed through the plane's canvas side, slamming into his thigh. Battling to fly back to the airstrip through a sandstorm and the searing pain of the wound, Slessor had no time to think about the momentous implications of what he had just done.

★★★

Histories of the British armed forces invariably treat the decades between 1918 and 1939 as little more than a footnote between the two world wars. Accounts of the Royal Air Force, in particular, skip over the interwar years, fast-forwarding to the rapid expansion of the later 1930s to meet the threat of Nazi Germany and the development of iconic aircraft such as the Spitfire and Hurricane.

Almost forgotten is how the RAF in the interwar years waged one of the most extraordinary conflicts in the history of the British Empire. With British power crumbling in the wake of the First World War, a ragtag band of visionaries and aviators set out to show that the aeroplane, the wonder weapon of the age, would save the empire. A generation of young airmen in primitive wood and canvas biplanes fought a series of campaigns over Iraq, Afghanistan, Somalia and other battlefields where, almost a century later, the West is still locked in a battle for power and beliefs.

The airmen derided the army and navy as redundant, able only to crawl across the face of the earth like slugs. Air power alone, with its speed, force and flexibility, they argued, could hold down vast stretches of territory and the warlike people who inhabited them. This doctrine of replacing ground forces with aircraft was called Air Control, or more tellingly, 'police bombing', and would be used to control huge swathes of the Middle East, Asia and Africa. Aircraft and bombing were employed for everything from frontier wars to enforcing tax collections. Air power became so crucial that the bomber, rather than the battleship, was hailed by some as the true symbol of British imperial power.

Air Control was pivotal in saving the newly-formed RAF from being disbanded after the First World War. Prime ministers, Cabinet ministers and civil servants wanted to scrap the air force to save money. A population eager for peace believed the force served no useful purpose, and was even a threat to stability; and the navy and army were determined to break up what they saw as a bunch of uncouth upstarts and regain their duopoly of military aviation.

The air force lived under 'suspended sentence' of death for years, one minister said.[6] If the RAF had not proved its worth over the Khyber Pass and the deserts of Iraq in the 1920s, its opponents at home might have succeeded in destroying it. Britain's fate in the Second World War might have been very different if the country had lacked a strong air force in 1940.

Colonial conflicts preoccupied the British military during the interwar era to an extent not understood today because we are blinkered by the knowledge of what was to come in the Second World War. There was barely a year between 1919 and 1939 when British forces were not locked in a colonial campaign somewhere in the empire. These wars were far from negligible, despite being dismissed as so-called 'small wars'. The military's losses in these campaigns exceeded the casualties their modern counterparts have suffered in Iraq and Afghanistan – a single Indian frontier campaign in the late 1930s saw the army sustain 312 dead and 893 wounded in a few months, a toll rivalling British losses in a decade of fighting in Afghanistan in this century.[7]

Until the early 1930s, many in Britain's military establishment were more concerned about the threat posed by tribes of the North-West Frontier of India than the possibility of another world war. In these years, the RAF focused on strategies to suppress 'primitive' tribesmen rather than future bomber offensives in Europe. These colonial air campaigns helped prop up the British Empire in its twilight years. They also inaugurated a new type of warfare in which poorly armed, but skilled and zealous opponents in some of the most remote places on earth were fought at a distance with the latest Western military technology: the use of drones and satellites to kill militants in such places as Afghanistan and Yemen, some of them the grandchildren and great-grandchildren of those the RAF bombed, is the descendant of the campaigns of almost a century ago.

These colonial campaigns were formative in shaping the young RAF. This first generation of career airmen formed the bedrock on which the force was built, and colonial service did much to shape its enduring professionalism, fighting spirit and dedication. Many of the outstanding British air commanders of the Second World War, including Harris, Dowding, Portal and Slessor, were pivotal figures in the Air Control saga, and many of their key subordinates learned their trade on colonial service. It is quite remarkable how so many of the young men who figure in these pages as pilots and junior commanders rose to the highest ranks during and after the Second World War.

Air Control was based on the premise that aircraft would end small wars and unrest by keeping constant watch, like a giant eye, over the wilder parts of the empire, instantly detecting and crushing any sign of unrest or rebellion. It was claimed that even the fiercest tribe or warlord would submit to a weapon that struck from the heavens like divine wrath, and against which they would be defenceless.

Employing technology to win wars and master hostile territory was hardly new. Superior military technology and organisation always played a key role in the triumph of Western colonialism; the aeroplane was the latest step in a progression that included the repeating rifle, the machine gun and the gunboat. The architects of Air Control tried to go much further than mere bombing, however, and some of the keenest minds in the RAF spent much of the interwar era trying to develop a complex strategy of colonial control, drawing on everything from psychology to economics.

More beguilingly for British officials and taxpayers, air power was cheap; air policing promised success for a fraction of the cost in money and British lives consumed every year by colonial land campaigns. Unlike the extravagantly expensive warplanes of the jet age, military aircraft in the 1920s were built from wood, canvas and wire, and cost a few hundred pounds. The RAF received just a tenth of the military budget in the 1920s, but its contribution to imperial firepower was out of all proportion to its paltry share of defence spending. Historian R.A. Beaumont calculated that the RAF could carry out colonial operations for just 5 per cent of what it cost the army to do the same work.[8]

Advocates said colonial air power also meant 'control without occupation', reducing the need for expensive garrisons.[9] Air Control was touted as the modern equivalent of alchemy, but instead of turning lead into gold it would increase British military power while drastically slashing its costs. Inspired by this lethal bargain, Britain, more than any other Western colonial power, was to rely on the bomber as a means of imperial control.

Ultimately, Air Control depended on bombing largely defenceless people and villages with the most destructive and terrifying weapon of the age. Thousands of men, women and children were killed and injured in British colonial operations between 1919 and 1939. Further immense suffering was inflicted by the destruction of the homes, farms, crops, orchards, irrigation systems and herds that these primitive societies depended on for their meagre survival. Inspired by the possibilities of scientific warfare, some in the RAF advocated the use of poison gas, early forms of napalm and other innovations to subdue some of the most primitive people in the world.

The air force and its supporters insisted that Air Control was humane, claiming that it saved lives because it prevented or shortened wars and rebellions, and the use of lethal force was limited. Above all, the RAF argued that Air Control worked because it broke opponents' morale rather than their bodies; the moral effect, they said, was out of all proportion to the physical damage. The airmen liked to compare themselves to the kindly neighbourhood bobby. But George Orwell, who had been a colonial police officer, used the Stalinist purges of the 1930s and Air Control in one of his most famous essays as examples of how language was used to distort or conceal truth.

'Defenceless villages are bombarded from the air, the inhabitants driven out into the countryside, the cattle machine-gunned, the huts set on fire with incendiary bullets: this is called pacification,' he wrote.[10]

There is no way to calculate the casualty toll from two decades of bombing: most of the raids were in inaccessible areas on backward, mostly illiterate communities that had no way of compiling such figures. While there is no overall figure for the number of bombs dropped in colonial policing operations either, it far exceeded the 8,000 tons that British aircraft dropped during the entire course of the First World War, and matched the level of bombing witnessed in the early stages of the Second World War.[11]

The scale and intensity of colonial bombing steadily increased during the interwar era as planes and technology improved. The 20 tons of bombs dropped in a two-day 1921 operation in Kurdish areas of northern Iraq was a major attack by the early standards of Air Control.[12] By the summer of 1930, a fairly routine operation against a handful of villages on the North-West Frontier of India saw the use of 23,826 bombs, weighing a total of 583 tons, 80,853 incendiaries and millions of machine gun bullets.[13] By comparison, German bombers and airships dropped some 269 tons of bombs on Britain during the entire course of the First World War.[14]

Some senior British military commanders and government officials anguished over the human cost of the bombing raids, but air power seemed a panacea for the empire's ills, and no one was willing to abandon it. Instead, the military and successive governments attempted to conceal the extent of the bombing. Air force and other government files from the interwar period are filled with memos warning that details of raids must be played down or omitted; colonial squadrons were constantly instructed to strip unsettling details from any reports that might be seen by the public. Government ministers were especially anxious to remove anything on the killing of farm animals or wildlife for fear of offending a British public that could be far more sentimental about animals than natives.

Air Control was more than a monotonous chronicle of destruction and heavy-handed colonial control. The RAF protected peaceful tribes and villages from hostile neighbours, and in many areas imposed a rough form of law and order. It defeated an army of Wahabi fanatics decades before the world had heard of Osama bin Laden and it reduced British casualties. But Air Control never came close to achieving the predictions of its architects that it would end all resistance to British rule and usher in a golden age of peace and prosperity across the empire.

Its greatest success was enabling Britain to retain control of Iraq and other parts of the Middle East in the 1920s; it was the only time in history that an air force commanded the defence and policing of large territories. Air Control did less well in the 1930s as opponents, particularly the Pathan tribes of north-west India and better-trained Arab forces, lost their fear of air attack and found many, often brilliantly simple ways to counter the British technological advantage. Whether Air Control could have delayed the end of British imperial rule, as some hoped, is moot; the deluge of the Second World War swept away Western colonialism.

Air Control reinforced the RAF's belief that air power alone, above all bombing, would win wars. It is possible to see the colonial campaigns as a precursor of the attempt to bomb Nazi Germany into submission; both hinged on the notion of destroying an opponent's morale and economy. The RAF's colonial experience reinforced its disinclination to work closely with the other services, and it took several years to develop effective ground support methods to aid the army during the Second World War. In 1939 the RAF had very few planes and pilots suited for close support operations, despite twenty years of ostensibly working with the army on colonial campaigns.

★★★

This book is not an attack on the men who tried to rule the empire from the sky. Air crews could be happy or heedless killers, who talked about machine-gunning a village as nonchalantly as they recounted shooting a buck or a bird on a hunting trip. They were also mostly admirable, honourable and idealistic young men, among the best of their generation, who believed they were serving their country, the greater good and even those they bombed. The use of weapons ranging from bombs to incendiary devices to chastise primitive people in the name of civilisation, however, is not a comfortable subject. Modern readers are likely to cringe at the prejudice and callousness that imbued the empire's rulers.

Many airmen, soldiers and colonial administrators argued with complete sincerity that people regarded as savages could only be subdued with savage methods. Such attitudes were as much a part of the RAF's armoury as the bombs slung under the wings of its aircraft; indeed, Air Control would have been inconceivable without such assumptions. At the same time, Britain and other Western powers saw no contradiction in insisting that it would be barbaric to bomb their own populations. In the later 1930s, the British

Government led an international campaign for a global ban on bombing – except in its own colonies.

Military history tends to be written from the standpoint of one side, but any account of the RAF's colonial campaigns is unavoidably skewed. The voices of the people who lived under the shadow of Air Control were almost never recorded. The few snippets that exist come mostly from British files and the memoirs of airmen, where the natives are usually portrayed as amiable ruffians who regarded the bombing of their villages as a fair price for their own naughty escapades. Air Control is not always a comfortable or uplifting saga, but it is a vital part of British military and colonial history, not least for the insights it provides into the conflicts of the early twenty-first century.

1

SMALL WARS

The British Empire reached its zenith after the First World War with the acquisition of vast swathes of the Middle East and Africa from the wreckage of the Ottoman and German empires. Lord Curzon, one of the grandest of the empire's proconsuls, caught the pride and assurance of the moment by declaring:

> The British flag never flew over more powerful or united an Empire than now; Britons never had better cause to look the world in the face; never did our voice count for more in the councils of the nations, or in determining the future destinies of mankind.[1]

It seemed that the empire would last for ever. Virtually no one saw that the war which had enlarged this vast realm had also unleashed or accelerated the political and economic forces that would tear it down in just a few decades.

The British preferred to forget or play down that the empire had been conquered, and that large parts of it were held by force rather than the gratitude of their subjects. Garrisoning the empire was a staggering global commitment; British forces had to watch over almost a quarter of the world's land mass and hundreds of millions of people. Now there was a string of former Ottoman and German territories to be pacified and guarded.

People in Britain, while proud of the empire, wanted the government to improve their living standards rather than spend money on distant colonies. There was considerable grumbling about the costs of some of the newly acquired tracts of desert in the Middle East. 'Mesopotamia and "Mess-up-at-home-here"' was a popular anti-government slogan in the early post-war years.[2]

Winston Churchill, the new secretary of state for war, was faced with the twin challenges of drastically slashing the armed forces and finding more troops to garrison the expanded empire. He summed up the dilemma when he told the House of Commons in December 1919:

> Odd as it may seem on the morrow of unheard-of-victories, we have all those dependencies and possessions in our hands which existed before the war, and in addition, we have large promises of new responsibilities to be placed upon us.[3]

Prime Minister David Lloyd George had given Churchill oversight of the newly formed RAF as well as the army after eliminating the post of air minister. (There was no Ministry of Defence at the time; the three armed services came under their own ministries.) There were suggestions at the time that Lloyd George wanted to disband the RAF and included it in Churchill's portfolio as a first step to scrapping the service. The air force's future appeared highly doubtful. Many people in Britain questioned why the country needed an air force after winning what was proclaimed as the war to end all wars, and there were loud calls to get rid of the service. The army and navy, in particular, were determined to destroy a rival that threatened their centuries-old control of military affairs. It seemed to many that the RAF would not last another year. 'Its chances of survival around its first anniversary in the spring of 1919 were minimal,' recalled Maurice Dean, a senior official at the Air Ministry. '… In the early years the Royal Air Force was miniscule, a breeze could have blown it away and nearly did so on several occasions.'[4]

The air force was a rich target for a government and populace eager to drastically slash military spending after the world war. The Royal Flying Corps (RFC), formed in 1912 as the army's aviation wing, had just a few dozen planes when war erupted in 1914. Aviation and warfare transformed each other over the next four bloody years, and by the end of the conflict Britain had the world's largest air force with 22,000 planes, 263 squadrons and 290,000 men. Air power's importance was recognised when the Royal Air Force was created on 1 April 1918 by combining the army and navy air wings to form an independent service. Peace changed everything. The RAF was singled out for some of the deepest cuts after the war; its ranks were reduced by 90 per cent, dozens of airbases were closed and the number of squadrons dwindled to just twenty-four by early 1920.

Whatever Lloyd George or others thought, Churchill had no intention of abolishing a service that appealed to his enthusiasm for innovation, daring and romance, and might also solve the conundrum of policing the expanded empire while cutting military costs. He favoured keeping the territories that had been seized during the war, particularly the Middle East acquisitions, but knew that it had to be at a price which the country could afford and public opinion would stomach. Within weeks of taking charge at the War Office, Churchill was considering how to save the RAF by using it to police the new territories.

Sir Frederick Sykes, head of the RAF after the war, wrote the first formal proposal on a colonial role for the air force. Aircraft, with their speed, striking power and low cost, were ideal for imperial police work, he wrote, and would be of particular value in the Middle East. But Churchill was not impressed by Sykes or his proposal for a peacetime air force of 150 squadrons. The politician knew that such grandiose plans would never be accepted in the political climate of the day. He wanted a man who could run the RAF and help control the world's largest empire on a shoestring; his search for a candidate led him to a complex, prickly, former army officer named Hugh Trenchard.

Trenchard was a towering figure in every sense. He stood 6ft 3in with piercing blue eyes and a formidable moustache that announced his fearsome personality. He was nicknamed 'Boom' because of the power of his voice when animated or angry, which he often was. Trenchard was a masterly administrator; an autocratic, if inspired, manager of men rather than a dashing leader; a tireless worker with a superb grasp of detail; a brilliant politician, with a deft sense of the public mood and a ferocious antagonist. He possessed the necessary combination of vision, practical skill and belligerence needed to save the infant air force from being throttled by the older armed services, penny-pinching civil servants and indifferent politicians in the early years after the First World War.

Trenchard has been celebrated as the father of the RAF ever since. His many admirers saw him as a giant towering over pygmy rivals in the military and political establishments. Some of his most ardent supporters were not obvious friends of authority or the professional military. T.E. Lawrence, whose adventures in Arabia made him a far bigger legend than Trenchard, wrote, 'Trenchard spells out confidence in the RAF ... He knows; and by virtue of this pole-star of knowledge he steers through all the ingenuity and cleverness and hesitations of the little men who help or hinder him.'[5] The professorial author of the RAF's First World War history described Trenchard in similarly Olympian terms, 'The power which Nature made his own, and which attends him like his shadow, is the power given him by his single-ness [*sic*] of purpose and faith in the men whom he commands.'[6]

Trenchard could inspire loathing as well as adulation, but did not seem to care which, as long as he got his way. He was a man of strong emotions, aggressive and quick-tempered, who frequently and needlessly personalised disagreements over official issues. Trenchard's detractors, including more than a few in the air force, saw him as domineering, opinionated, divisive and self-righteous. Even admirers, who downplayed his flaws as the quirks of an endearing ogre, admitted he excelled at needlessly provoking people. Weary friends and aides said that Trenchard believed he must be doing something right if everyone disagreed with him. And yet even many of those who disliked him conceded the importance of the man's achievements.

Born in 1873, there was little in Trenchard's early life to suggest the commanding figure of later years. Trenchard's father was a struggling country lawyer in Somerset, and his upbringing had the feel of penny-pinching Dickensian shabbiness. Young Hugh was an unexceptional child who was happiest roaming the countryside around the family's rural home. He disliked school, his handwriting was indecipherable and he enraged teachers with his atrocious spelling. Part of the later Trenchard legend was his inability to express his ideas clearly. To get around this, Trenchard would toss out rambling, disconnected thoughts to aides he called his 'English merchants', who would then rewrite them until their master announced they had got it right. 'I can't write what I mean, I can't say what I mean,' he once told an aide, 'but I expect you to know what I mean!'[7]

His parents' plan for a career as a navy officer had to be abandoned when Trenchard failed the entrance exam. It was decided to put the boy into the army if he could get through the less demanding entry tests. At the age of 13 Trenchard was sent to a crammer, an educational battery farm designed to force youths through entrance exams without necessarily imparting any learning. His father's legal practice collapsed, meanwhile, and the family was left bankrupt. Trenchard was to become good at skimping, something that would endear him later to government cost cutters.

Frugality did not boost his academic abilities, however, and Trenchard twice failed the test for the regular army. The British establishment, with plenty of sons and few suitable careers for gentlemen, had other ways of getting around obstacles like mere entrance exams. Trenchard scraped his way through the exam for the militia, or part-time army, which was a backdoor into the regular army for the dullest scholars. It was enough to get the 20-year-old Trenchard a commission with the Royal Scots Fusiliers, who were then in India.

Soldiering, with its practical, outdoors life, suited Trenchard. Contemporaries remembered him as a good, if unexceptional, platoon officer, although he was awkward and uncomfortable with the social routine that was an important part of the peacetime army; he was dubbed 'the camel' in the officers' mess because he rarely drank anything stronger than water. Even as a young man Trenchard was noted for being prickly, and in the army he did not hide his contempt for anyone he disliked, including superior officers. He occupied most of his spare time running the regimental polo team, with freelance horse dealing to supplement his pay because, unlike many officers, he did not have independent means. Nobody seems to have thought that he was destined for great things.

Trenchard's lacklustre career picked up with the outbreak of the Boer War. He fought in the mounted infantry until he was shot in the left lung attacking a Boer post, made a spectacular recovery, and was promoted to major and given a job shaking up units that had not done well on the battlefield.

Whether because he had developed a taste for active service or for Africa, Trenchard obtained a post in 1903 as deputy commander of the Southern Nigeria Regiment. Britain's African colonies were mostly garrisoned by black troops led by regular British officers on temporary contracts. Such postings were popular because they were a chance for active soldiering and paid well. They attracted some of the best and some of the least savoury characters in the army. Trenchard walked into the mess at breakfast shortly after his arrival to find the officers lounging about unshaved and in pyjamas; most of the conversation was about drink, sex with native women and gambling. It was an appalling revelation for a man who was a natural puritan. Trenchard promptly banned drunkenness, illicit sex and gambling, and officers who failed to meet his strict sense of decorum were sent home.

Britain was still imposing its control on the more remote regions of its West African possessions, and colonial forces freely employed harsh tactics. Trenchard led columns deep into the bush on sweeps lasting weeks. The formations trudged through the jungle for weeks in search of elusive opponents, enduring searing heat, intense humidity and hungry insects that wracked men's bodies with infected bites.

Initially, Trenchard employed the traditional, heavy-handed tactics of burning villages and whipping captured natives. Questions were asked in Parliament following press reports that a column led by Trenchard had burned six villages. A government spokesman said such tactics were necessary to end lawlessness and open 'backward' areas to trade. As he learned more about the people and the country, Trenchard later claimed he used different methods, offering the natives a choice between punishment or peacefully accepting British rule.

Trenchard returned home in 1910. Africa had been exciting, but had not done much for his career. Now 37, he was just another nondescript major facing an impoverished retirement. Attempts to get postings with colonial cavalry units in Australia, New Zealand and South Africa were unsuccessful, as was an application to the Macedonian Gendarmerie. And then in 1912 a fellow officer breezily suggested that Trenchard learn to fly with the army's new aviation wing. 'Come and see men like ants crawling,' was the offhand suggestion.[8]

It was a startling idea; flying was for the young and unconventional with a good chance of death or crippling injuries in the notoriously unstable and dangerous machines of the day. Trenchard was 39, and the cut-off age for entry to the army's tiny aviation wing was 40. He gave himself a week to earn the flying licence required for admission to the RFC. The qualifying exam was mainly a question of staying alive – Trenchard's test consisted of taking off solo, climbing to 1,000ft, flying a figure of eight over the airfield and landing.[9]

In view of his age and experience, the newly qualified pilot was given a staff position rather than an active flying role. The coming of the First World War saw Trenchard rise rapidly, and he was commanding the RFC on the Western Front by 1915 with the rank of major general. He was still an army man, however, and shared the dogmatic belief of the General Staff that victory would only be achieved by breaking the Germans with massive ground attacks on the Western Front. In the same spirit, Trenchard hurled his crews at the enemy despite inadequate resources, lack of training and heavy losses in the early years. Critics, including some of his officers, accused him of throwing away lives; he replied that casualties were the price of success.

It is the supreme irony of the early history of the RAF that the man who ensured its survival had vehemently opposed its creation. Trenchard was highly critical of the decision to form an independent air force; he believed the air squadrons should be part of the army like the artillery or the engineers. Despite his opposition, Trenchard was picked to head the new service, but quickly fell out with Lord Rothermere, the bombastic press baron who was air minister, and resigned. Rothermere later said sourly of his former subordinate, 'He was a man who tried to strangle the infant [the RAF] at birth though he got credit for the grown man.'[10]

After several weeks mostly spent brooding on a London park bench, Trenchard was given command of an independent bomber force to attack

Germany, a role he took on with his usual drive. He left France a few days after the war ended, sure that his military career was behind him until he was summoned to see Churchill. The two men met in early February 1919 and talked about the RAF's future. Impressed by what he heard, Churchill told Trenchard to write a memo on restructuring the service. That evening Trenchard jotted down in 700 words a plan for a barebones air force. His thinking had undergone a total turnabout: he now believed that the aeroplane had transformed warfare, making ground and sea forces largely redundant, and that Britain's and the empire's security depended on an independent air force.

No one was thinking about the possibility of another war, however, and Trenchard had to make the RAF indispensable there and then to ensure its survival. The only realistic way was to show that an independent air force could police the empire more effectively and, above all, more cheaply than the older services. The brief plan that Trenchard gave Churchill envisaged a small, robust air force for colonial defence and policing that could also serve as a foundation which could be expanded, if needed, in the future. Although sparse in details, the scheme was the pragmatic, cut-rate approach that Churchill was looking for, and he insisted Trenchard replace Sykes as head of the air force. Churchill was soon telling colleagues that the RAF would transform imperial defence. 'The first duty of the Royal Air Force,' he told the House of Commons, 'is to garrison the British Empire.'[11]

Taking command of the embattled RAF, Trenchard promptly staked its future on the empire, allocating nineteen of its twenty-four squadrons to colonial stations with just two for home defence, while the remainder were given naval or training roles.

For a century, the British Army had spent much of its time fighting 'small wars' across the empire, conflicts which a leading military handbook defined as 'expeditions against savages and semi-civilized races by disciplined soldiers' or wars against non-white opponents.[12] Most of these wars were never-ending pacification campaigns on the wild fringes of the empire in Asia and Africa, where imperial authority petered out amid the deserts and the mountains with their impenetrable terrain, implacable climates and ferocious inhabitants. Military columns would be sent out when the tribes became too troublesome, to inflict what the army euphemistically termed 'havoc', killing tribesmen, destroying villages and burning crops – army veterans sardonically summed it up as 'butcher and bolt'. Such methods, which were justified on the grounds that 'savages' did not respect the rules of war, rarely brought more than a temporary, sullen truce, however, forcing the British to mount endless campaigns.

Most air force leaders in 1919 were ex-army officers who had served on the Indian frontier or in the jungles of Africa, where they experienced the brutal reality of colonial warfare and the maddening difficulty of subduing far weaker opponents. They and others saw that the aeroplane, with its ability to vanquish the obstacles of terrain, climate and even time, could revolutionise colonial warfare. It is not clear who came up with the term 'Air Control', but it was widely adopted sometime around 1919, and expressed the RAF's emerging belief that air power would revolutionise the control of the empire by halting the seemingly endless cycle of small wars.

The army justified its methods by arguing that a short, savage dose of punishment broke the morale of belligerent tribes, and avoided more protracted wars and the casualties that went with them. That reverberated with the RAF, which claimed that aerial bombing worked primarily by 'moral effect', breaking an opponent's will to fight or resist, rather than by inflicting massive damage. 'The moral effect of bombing stands to the material in a proportion of 20 to 1,' was one of the cardinal tenets of the young RAF.[13]

Surely, the airmen said, such methods would be even more effective against 'backward' and 'ignorant' savages. Nor were there qualms about using bombers, the most advanced and destructive weapon of the day, to suppress 'backward' people. The British military had always been more willing to try out new weapons against primitive tribes. Veterans of African wars dryly noted that the army saw the machine gun as an excellent way to stop 'wild rushes of savages' while showing 'a good deal of prejudice' over its use against white troops.[14] Or as Robert Graves, the novelist and poet, archly commented, 'There had always been a tacit understanding that a different code might be used by European nations against savages who would not appreciate the civilized courtesies of war.'[15]

Air Control was used interchangeably to refer to both the underlying doctrine and actual operations during the interwar period. It would take several years after 1918 to develop and refine the basic idea of aircraft controlling territory and tribes into a fully-fledged strategy. Aircraft and air war were only a few years old, and while the airmen saw limitless possibilities they still had to learn what was practical.

At first, many British airmen naively or lazily believed that the mere sight of a flying machine would reduce even the most warlike tribes to jabbering wrecks. This was followed by schemes of early aerial surveillance to prevent unrest and, if that did not work, bombing raids to isolate and subdue troublemakers. Some of the more visionary RAF theorists worked on ways to control native societies with a form of collective mind control. But whether it was done with psychological pressure, economic warfare or mass bombing, instilling terror and a sense of helplessness was at the heart of Air Control.

Wing Commander R.A. Chamier, in a 1921 talk entitled 'The Use of Air Power for Replacing Military Garrisons', candidly stated:

> ... the Air Force must, if called upon to administer punishment, do it with all its might and in the proper manner. The attack with bombs and machine guns must be relentless and unremitting and carried on continuously by day and night, on houses, inhabitants, crops and cattle ... This sounds brutal, I know, but it must be made brutal to start with.[16]

Trenchard and the RAF had no doubts that air power could pacify the empire's lawless fringes for a pittance compared to the huge quantities of men and money the army consumed annually for often imperfect results. 'Air Control will go far to prevent the occurrence of what for years has been described as a "chronic disease of the British Empire", in the shape of long drawn-out frontier wars and recurrent punitive expeditions,' an air theorist wrote.[17] Having found a role for the RAF, Trenchard now had to ensure it would meet the challenge.

2

THE CINDERELLA SERVICE

Unlike the navy and the army, the RAF did not have a peacetime establishment or traditions to fall back on after the war. When S.E. Towson enlisted in the force, all of the non-commissioned officers at the training depot were army veterans of the Boer War, and lectures on the air force's history were extremely short.[1] To Trenchard it was an ideal chance to build a visionary service that would transform the empire's defences.

Trenchard's vision rested on creating a new type of warrior. He proclaimed that the air was the new dimension of warfare, totally distinct from the land and the sea. It could only be mastered by a new breed of officers who were brainy as well as brawny, able to control the most complex technology, fight wars scientifically and command the heavens. Many of the RAF's rougher wartime veterans were replaced by better-educated recruits who fitted the new template, although it took time. A 19-year-old Geoffrey Tuttle began his career in 1925 in a squadron where breakfast consisted of pink gins in the pilots' mess.[2]

With its need for talent, the air force was willing to overlook humble origins for real ability. Sydney Ubee, a future air vice marshal who served in Iraq and India in the 1930s, worked as a labourer and a car salesman before being accepted as an officer cadet, while Francis Long, a future test pilot and air vice marshal, was a factory apprentice.[3] It all lent the service an image of being less rigid, more meritocratic and more in tune with the progressive spirit of the times than the older services. This did not mean the RAF was free of the class divisions and snobbery that were still a hallmark of many parts of British life, and the armed forces in particular; very few air force officers saw a mirror image of themselves in the lower ranks. Still, there was not much room for class barriers in a two-man plane crewed by an officer and an enlisted man over the Khyber Pass or the Iraqi desert.

Trenchard also insisted that the RAF improve its social standing and reputation. Pilots had been idolised as knights of the air during the war, but were also notorious for wild excesses and flouting convention. The service's official history of the war said aviators should be judged by their courage rather than their manners.[4] An element of disrepute dogged the little force after the war. Fairly or not, air force officers had a reputation for being too friendly with other peoples' wives, not paying their bills or being light-fingered with official funds. 'We tended to look over our shoulders at the other services and it worried us that it so often seemed to be an officer of the Royal Air Force whose cheque bounced or who was mixed up in a scandal,' recalled T.C. Traill, yet another future air vice marshal who shot down eight enemy aircraft during the war.[5]

The country's powerful upper classes were suspicious of a service filled with officers from humble backgrounds or the colonies; such men did not fit the traditional image of an officer as a man of impeccable breeding and social graces. A government minister complained that 'the calibre of young [RAF] officers who are taken in now is very low, worse even than many of those who were taken in during the war, and we know what their standard was'.[6]

Much of the business of government was still done in the salons and country houses of the establishment. Such doors were often closed to the air force in the early post-war years, and its leaders complained of what they called the service's lack of 'dining out power'. Trenchard and his senior lieutenants worked tirelessly to charm politicians, society matrons, newspaper editors and other potential backers, but it took years to finally transform the service's reputation. Tuttle, who would rise to be vice chief of the Air Staff in the 1950s, said it was difficult to get car insurance in the 1920s because insurers lumped RAF officers, actors and Jews together as the worst risks.[7]

The RAF did not want for recruits, even when it seemed that the force might not survive. Most young men were drawn by the power and romance of the aeroplane, the ultimate symbol of the technological revolution that was transforming the world. Flying had a novelty and glamour in the interwar era that is hard to comprehend in modern times. Aviators were among the leading celebrities of the day along with film stars, royalty and business moguls; anyone associated with aircraft, no matter how humbly, was touched by the magic of flight.

RAF leaders knew that one of the service's strongest advantages was its image of spearheading the future. An article in the *RAF Quarterly* declared:

> To the ardent youngster who wants to see the world in a novel and romantic guise the Royal Air Force offers far more. This is a mechanical age, an age of ever increasing speed, and an age of rapid scientific development, and where can the rising generation enjoy all these to anything like the same extent as in the Royal Air Force?[8]

A generation of schoolboys, who had grown up making model aeroplanes and reading about heroic pilots, provided a steady pool of eager recruits. Working-class youths who could not expect to be officers and pilots aspired to be the mechanics and fitters who kept the great machines flying. In the post-war years, the RAF provided excellent technical training at a time when educational opportunities and good jobs for the lower classes were scarce.

Gilbert Smith, who served in India in the 1930s, joined the RAF apprentice system at 16 to learn electrical engineering. The three-year course – with its tri-part program of general education, technical instruction, and military training – was gruelling. Apprentices spent long days in classrooms and workshops, often working late into the evening, but graduates were keenly sought by civilian companies after they left the service.[9]

Travel was the other great enticement to join the air force in an age when few people could expect to go far from home. RAF recruiting campaigns played up the service's numerous foreign stations and the opportunity to travel and see the empire. Richard Brooks was an 18-year-old office boy in the mid-1920s when he saw an RAF poster with a painting of a desert oasis and palm trees that brought back all of his boyhood dreams of foreign adventure; he walked into the recruiting office and soon found himself in southern Iraq.[10] Religion still had a strong hold on British society, and the RAF's numerous stations in the Middle East attracted plenty of young men who wanted to see the places they had read about in the Bible as children.[11]

Even the lowest-ranking airmen could see a lot of the world if they saved their pay and made the best use of leave time overseas. Sydney Sills, a wireless operator in the 1930s, visited the ruins of Babylon and Ur, the palaces of Baghdad, the Taj Mahal, the temples of Rangoon and Singapore's Tiger Balm Gardens.[12] Spencer Viles, an air gunner in Iraq in the early 1930s, managed to travel across almost the entire country.[13]

New officers and men learned about the benefits and drawbacks of foreign posts through a service grapevine: Egypt and Malta were seen as the best postings because of the climate and comfortable lifestyle; Singapore and Hong Kong became popular after the RAF established bases in the Far East; but Iraq and Aden had hideous reputations.

Colonial postings were also a chance for officers and enlisted men to taste the privileges and comforts of the empire. For the lower ranks it was a chance to be the masters for once. 'In those days the Raj was definitely supreme so if you were white you were a top dog,' recalled Smith, who served in India. 'Even as AC2 [aircraftman second class] you were still a *burra sahib* and you had everything done for you because you had batmen, you had waiters, you had bearers.'[14]

Stanley Eastmead, who served in an RAF armoured car company in Iraq in the mid-1930s, said a firm belief in British superiority over the rest of the human race saturated the ranks. 'You always had the sort of feeling then that if you were British you were bloody good and the rest of the world, well, they were definitely second-class citizens. That was the attitude we had, we had this instilled into us.'[15]

All ranks took it as a fact of nature that black people were inferior and must defer to the British rulers. One young officer, G.V. Howard, was furious when he went to a Baghdad nightclub and found Arabs being served alongside British officers and officials. 'I consider it is damn bad for British prestige,' he wrote home.[16] Howard believed Arab labourers and servants should be kept in their place with a taste of the riding crop, although officers should delegate such tasks. 'I think it is rather undignified to do it yourself, besides being unpleasant,' he noted.[17] Squadron Leader E. Brewerton, a languid young fighter pilot, had no reservations about dirtying his hands. He and another officer had a disagreement with 'two dirty Indians' over the cost of rowing them ashore in Karachi in 1920 during a port call; they tossed one of the boatmen into the water, after which 'they agreed to take us in for our price'.[18]

Not everyone who joined the RAF was drawn by dreams of flying or foreign adventures. Some men and boys enlisted for the same reasons or compulsions that had pushed men into the forces for generations: poverty and the lack of work, or the need to find a haven or obscurity for personal reasons. Patriotism, a sense of service and idealism motivated some to enlist, while others joined because they had been too young to serve in the war and did not want to spend their lives wondering what they had missed. More than a few recruits joined because they had nothing better to do.

John Buckley, at the age of 19, faced a choice between the armed forces or a life in the coal mines of his native Wales. He and two friends were given railway tickets to the RAF recruiting office in Liverpool, the start of a journey that within a few months took him to the deserts of Iraq.[19] Samuel Wentworth, an unemployed chauffer, was walking along a street when he saw an RAF poster with the slogan 'Come and be one of us'; he promptly enlisted in the ranks despite knowing almost nothing about the air force, and ended up spending almost five years in Iraq and Palestine.[20]

It was not a promising start. He spent the first few days at an RAF depot wearing his civilian serge suit, while the man next to him on parade was dressed in pinstripe trousers and a bowler hat. The food slopped on the men's plates in the shabby canteen was barely edible, and recruits grumbled about foregoing bread one day a week for economy reasons. Still, men who had served in the army said that life in the RAF was easier, with less bullying and mind-numbing routine. Alfred Griffin, who had experienced the Spartan lifestyle of the army during the world war, was astonished to be given pyjamas and sheets when he joined the air force in 1919 as a dispatch rider.[21]

★★★

The RAF would spend the interwar years fighting the empire's enemies and feuding with the other British armed services. Many army officers had little enthusiasm for modern weapons like the aeroplane and the tank despite the bloody lessons of the recent war. Military dinosaurs agitated after the conflict to bring back red tunics for the infantry, and a committee was working on an improved cavalry lance as late as 1928.

Conventional army thinking was summed up in a well-respected 1934 textbook on colonial policing by Major General Charles Gwynn, who wrote that the aeroplane was 'of great value' for transport '... but infantry still remains the chief offensive agent' and the bayonet was often the best weapon – 'the sight of cold steel has a calming effect' on rebels and troublemakers.[22] Soldiering was still seen by too many army officers as a gentleman's profession; an agreeable part-time occupation, largely defined by the nineteenth-century army's appetite for hunting, sport, mess life and ample leisure; a pleasant, undemanding way to pass the time, and best suited for those with a private income and the right kind of social connections. Air force officers who attended the inter-service staff college were astonished that riding and hunting formed an important part of the formal evaluation.

It was ridiculous, John Slessor said, to pretend that a middle-aged man with years of military experience was not suited to staff work or higher command if he did not excel at chasing foxes on a horse.

Above all, many in the army and the navy saw the new air service as a threat to their traditional control of military affairs, and tried to break up the younger force in the early post-war years. The air force had no greater critic than Field Marshal Henry Wilson, chief of the Army General Staff between 1918 and 1922. His dislike of the air force was almost pathological.

Wilson, who had the thankless task of dealing with a rash of wars and emergencies across the empire at a time when the army was being ruthlessly cut, vented a great deal of his resentment on the RAF. He denounced the air force as a movement 'for killing women and children',[23] a waste of money, and simultaneously questioned its loyalty and social standing by claiming it was a pack of left-wing mechanics. Wilson became obsessed with destroying the RAF, waging a campaign that wobbled between poisonous hyperbole and outright irrationality.

The memoirs and papers of many RAF officers from the interwar era are filled with angry recriminations over what are portrayed as the older services' merciless and unreasonable opposition to an independent air force. Supporters of the RAF, who often painted the other services as Neanderthal throwbacks, ignored the fact that the value of air power was far from proven, and that the army and navy had genuine concerns, especially about whether the air force would look after their needs rather than trying to win wars on its own.

Army officers who grumbled that the air force wanted to turn their units into airfield guards were not altogether wrong. The most strident air strategists talked about the day, supposedly not far off, when air power would have a virtual monopoly on war, and the army and navy would be mere auxiliary forces. A 1920 RAF memo said that gaining a role in colonial defence was just the first step to '... become more and more the predominating factor in all types of warfare'.[24] The authors then asked if the RAF's ultimate aim was to take over the entire defence of the empire. 'I hope so,' Trenchard wrote in the margin.

3

CRISIS OF EMPIRE

British leaders were still congratulating themselves over the empire's triumph in the recent global conflict when a wave of wars and uprisings swept the colonies, from Ireland to India. A gloomy army report described the Hydra-like threat suddenly confronting the empire, 'National feeling, the spirit of self-determination, tribal turbulence, pan-Islamism, anti-Westernism, Bolshevism and general antagonism – all these are ours to wrestle with.'[1] Underlining the seriousness of the challenges, Arthur Balfour, the foreign secretary, told Parliament, 'We are only at the beginning of our troubles.'[2] Henry Wilson, the army chief, said British land forces were 'strong nowhere, weak everywhere and with no reserve'.[3] The new RAF would play a major role in dealing with the crisis, and its successes would boost the case for an independent air force with a strong colonial role.

★★★

The crisis began in the 'backward' kingdom of Afghanistan, which Britain largely controlled despite its supposed independence. Habbibullah, the Afghan amir, or king, who had studiously avoided trouble with the British during his reign, was assassinated in February 1919 while staying at a remote hunting lodge. Amanullah, the amir's ambitious third son, seized power amid rumours he was behind his father's death.

The new amir dreamed of dragging his country out of the Middle Ages and turning it into a modern, westernised state. He began his reign by donating his slain father's books to open the country's first public library. He also promised to end British domination, one of the few causes capable of uniting the fractious nobility, clergy and tribes.

Britain initially refused to take the events in Kabul seriously. Most British officials were contemptuous of the Afghans – an Indian Army handbook tartly summed up the official view, 'Afghans are treacherous and generally inclined towards double dealing. Firmness, combined with bold and vigorous action, is the proper and only safe attitude for Europeans to adopt when dealing with them.'[4] London delayed responding to the amir's letters demanding an end to British interference in Afghan affairs because protocol officials could not decide if he was entitled to be addressed as 'your majesty'. Tired of waiting, the Afghans invaded India. Bewildered officials in Delhi woke up to find themselves in what one general called the 'most meaningless, crazy and unnecessary war in history'.[5]

The ensuing Third Afghan War was mostly a story of British political and military ineptness. Many of the Indian Army's best formations were overseas or being demobilised after wartime service, and British Army units in the subcontinent were undermanned.[6] Afghan troops were disparaged by the Indian Army as almost subhuman. A 1919 army handbook claimed that they were 'distinctly below the average man of the country in both physique and intelligence. Deserters who from time to time find their way into British territory are usually intensely stupid.'[7] But the Afghans were excellent fighters, as the British knew to their cost after two nineteenth-century wars, especially the powerful Pathan tribes that lived on both sides of the frontier. It would take 340,000 British and Indian troops and camp followers to halt, although never quite defeat, a threadbare Afghan force that possessed very few modern weapons. The RAF, with just two squadrons in India at the start of the war, would play a disproportionate role in the fighting.

Afghan forces, backed by hordes of tribal fighters, streamed through the Khyber Pass on 3 May 1919, and fighting flared up and down the frontier. The war soon became an exhausting, primitive struggle for hilltops and mountain ridges in which stamina and cunning usually meant more than advanced weaponry.

Typical was a clash in the Khyber, when men of the British Army's Somerset Light Infantry and Indian Army's 1/35th Sikhs laboriously clawed their way up a mountain held by Afghan marksmen. English soldiers in shorts crawled slowly on bare hands and knees over razor-edged stones and rock almost too hot to touch as the riflemen above fired into the exposed knots of climbers. The British force eventually took the heights, leaving twenty-eight dead and 150 wounded on the slope behind them.

Conditions for the British and Indian troops were unremittingly miserable. Marching columns kicked up a fog of dust that choked men and animals while jamming engines and weapons. Daytime temperatures hovered around 120°F, with the sun radiating blindingly off the glassy rock hillsides. The reek of human and animal corpses slowly cooking in the heat seeped into the troops' skin, hair and clothing. Millions of black flies, bloated from feasting on the dead, swarmed across the faces and bare limbs of the living.

Chaotic and sporadic supply arrangements often meant there was not enough water and food. Some units survived on tinned meat which, because of the heat, squirted out in rancid liquid jets when the containers were punctured. Cholera, dysentery and other diseases killed many more men than Afghan bullets.

Planes from 31 Squadron were the first to be sent to the frontier, where they scouted for army units and acted as flying artillery. Afghan and tribal forces were unnerved by this new weapon that appeared overhead without warning, decimating opponents with bombs and machine-gun fire. The stunned tribesmen sought help from heaven to counter the aerial predators. A tribal mullah, who claimed his prayers could knock the unholy machines out of the sky, was acclaimed by his followers when an aeroplane crashed taking off from a local airstrip. The RAF, hearing of the cleric's boasting, bombed the tribe to discredit his claims.

Other mullahs said aeroplanes could be brought down by flashing mirrors at them and pilots became accustomed to seeing little glitters of light far below as tribesmen with pocket mirrors, normally used to groom their luxuriant beards, tried to knock planes out of the sky. 'Though flashes were seen none of us fell' out of the sky, one pilot recalled.[8] More pragmatic tribesmen attacked the airbase at Bannu in an unsuccessful attempt to destroy parked aircraft, only to be driven off by army guards.

Far more dangerous for the flight crews than the Afghans was the freak weather and mountainous terrain that made flying on the frontier difficult at the best of times. Two aircraft flying through the Khyber Pass were flipped upside down by freak turbulence. The elderly BE2 and Farman F27 planes that formed the front line of the RAF squadrons in the subcontinent were too weak to fly over the mountains, so pilots had to wind their way through the valleys, dodging the sheer rock sides and the fusillades of Afghan riflemen perched above them on the heights.

Pilots could not always spot Afghan forces, whose brown and khaki clothing blended with the barren landscape. 'One seldom saw the enemy for the tribesmen are artists at taking cover, and know their country inside out,' said 31 Squadron's Lt C.M. Eastley, who had transferred from the infantry to the RAF.[9] British units learned not to place too much reliance on air reconnaissance after walking into ambushes in areas the air force had just announced were empty.

Friendly fire, always a hazard of war, took on a new meaning with the advent of aviation, and there were reports of planes mistakenly attacking Indian troops. A dozen Indian soldiers were killed or wounded when they poked curiously at an unexploded British bomb.

Afghan soldiers and tribesmen fought back with some success once the initial shock of being attacked from the air wore off. Planes began to be damaged or shot out of the sky by increasingly accurate ground fire. Three planes were downed in a single day, although all the crews survived. Lieutenant F.E.E. Villiers was forced down in Afghan territory. His mind was filled with images of the tortures the Afghans supposedly inflicted on prisoners when a gang of gunmen surrounded him, but one of the men enquired in a thick West Country accent, 'I hope you ain't 'urt Zur?' and it turned out that they were men of a Cornish infantry regiment.[10]

Commanders of the tiny RAF contingent complained that their planes were being wasted supporting the ground forces and would be better employed in a strategic bombing campaign. Bombing Afghan cities and towns, they argued, would create panic, cripple supply systems and, above all, break the backward populace's morale. Army leaders begrudgingly agreed to a limited bombing campaign against Afghan forces on the border.

The first major raid with sixteen planes, virtually everything that could be got into the air, was launched at dawn on 9 May against a large Afghan camp and supply centre at Loe Dakka near the border. Sleepy Afghan troops were still huddled in frayed blankets or hunched around smoky cooking fires, boiling tea in blackened kettles, when the air attack began without warning. Terrified soldiers, horses and mules stampeded in every direction as planes roared over the camp at less than 100ft. Men and animals were flung into the air by bomb blasts or cut down by machine-gun fire that stitched across the camp like the steel needle of a sewing machine. Thundering over the tents and piles of supplies, the pilots spotted two massive shapes amid the terrified mob below.

Later the flyers would recall their confusion, and then astonishment, as they realised the shambling shapes were pack elephants. Several planes dived on the animals and within moments left two massive, bleeding carcasses slumped on the ground. What seemed like a prank to the pilots was treated by the RAF as a pioneering moment in aerial warfare. 'The destruction of two elephants during the raid on the camp at Loe Dakka,' the official history intoned, 'constitutes an unique record in the annals of Aeroplane [*sic*] bombing history.'[11] It was claimed the raid also inflicted some 600 human casualties, although subsequent army reports put the figure at twenty-five dead. Pathan villages on the British side of the frontier were bombed next as a reprisal for aiding the Afghan forces.

The air contingent, boosted by two squadrons from the British occupation forces in Germany, shifted next to raids on the main towns in southern Afghanistan. Jalalabad, the country's second largest city, was singled out as the main target. British bombers arrived over its medieval streets for the first time on 20 May as some 2,000 Afghan troops were parading at the main barracks. Bombs killed scores as they exploded in the packed ranks of men. More than 100 bombs fell on the base and the surrounding civilian areas. Black plumes of smoke spiralled over the city as explosions and incendiaries shattered and ignited the densely packed wooden and plaster homes. Terrified people jammed the narrow alleys, frantically pushing and shoving as they tried to escape the fires that enveloped the tinder-dry homes and other buildings.[12]

Jalalabad, like other Afghan towns, had virtually no way to cope with fires and casualties, and was completely defenceless against air attack. The situation was made even more chaotic when tribesmen, who had come to the city to be issued with supplies to fight the British, began looting the bazaars and houses. A second raid on 24 May further damaged the city centre. Fires started by the raids were said to be visible up to 50 miles away.[13]

British air commanders followed up the attacks with a propaganda war to demoralise the Afghan population. Leaflets luridly describing the bombing of Jalalabad were scattered on towns and villages across the south of the country. The leaflets written in courtly Persian chided the mostly illiterate peasants for letting the amir, who was described as an inexperienced and impious youth, lead them into a disastrous war they could never hope to win.[14]

Kabul, the capital and heart of the Afghan kingdom with 300,000 inhabitants, was the next target. The small aircraft of the Indian squadrons lacked the range and bomb load for such a mission. A twin-engined Handley Page 0/400 heavy bomber that was in India for military trials was pressed into service. Captain Robert 'Jock' Halley, who flew the plane to the North-West Frontier, had volunteered to be a pilot during the First World War following a spell in an army bicycle unit that never saw action. He was one of the first night bomber pilots, and had taken part in some of the most daring raids of the war with a thrill-seeking American millionaire as his observer. Halley landed the bomber at Risalpur airbase, 60 miles south of the Khyber Pass, just as a dust storm was approaching the airbase. Ground crew lashed the plane down with ropes and ringed it with trucks as an improvised defence against the approaching black wall of wind-whipped sand and grit. The crew returned during a lull an hour later to find that the storm had flipped the hulking plane on to its back and wrecked it.

A four engine bomber, the Handley Page V/1500, had been built in the closing stages of the First World War to bomb Berlin but the conflict ended before it could be used. This colossal biplane was the wonder weapon of its day with 126ft wings and weighing 30,000lb fully loaded. It had a flying time of seventeen hours, and a range of 1,300 miles at a top speed of 99mph. Even more formidable was its armament of thirty 250lb bombs and four machine guns. Halley had flown this giant to India in January on a prestige tour, and it was greeted by the viceroy and an ecstatic crowd of 30,000 people on its arrival in Delhi. Such a mighty weapon deserved a name just like a battleship, and it was christened *Old Carthusian* – the name given to old boys of Charterhouse public school. A Maltese terrier, said to be mad about flying, was an unofficial member of the crew.

This formidable symbol of imperial might was touring India, giving joyrides to rajahs and other dignitaries, when the Afghan War broke out. Halley, a chain-smoking Scot who played up to the national reputation for penny pinching, was told to ready the plane for a raid on Kabul. It had been stripped of its war gear before leaving Britain so bomb racks taken from other warplanes had to be fitted hurriedly to the wings and 20lb bombs were heaped in one of the open cockpits to be tossed out by hand.

The raid was set symbolically for 24 May, or Empire Day. Halley, an observer and three mechanics resembled giant brown penguin chicks as they waddled out to the plane in the padded leather helmets and flying suits needed to protect them against the bitter cold while flying over the mountains in open cockpits. The plane roared down a runway lit by oil drums filled with burning cotton and rose into the night sky at 3 a.m. It took more than an hour for the lumbering machine to gain the 3,000ft needed to begin its crossing of the mountainous Afghan frontier.

Ice and snow glinted on the peaks towering above the plane as it threaded its way through the mountains. Dawn revealed water spurting from one of the engines. Halley and the crew decided, after a shouted exchange over the roar of the engines, to go on even though an emergency landing would have been virtually impossible in the mountains. Halley only just managed to get the plane over the final hurdle of the Jagdalek Pass, hauling back on the controls for every last foot of altitude. A camel caravan in the pass stampeded as the bomber thundered over it, and the bomber crew watched in silent fascination as some of the terrified animals bolted over the ledge, slowly revolving as they tumbled into the depths below.

Old Carthusian's crew got their first sight of Kabul as the rising sun illuminated the amir's palace and the handful of other large buildings jutting above the packed one and two-storey houses of the ancient city. Halley dropped to a few hundred feet and roared over the heart of the capital, the plane's engines shaking the slumbering streets. The main armament of 112lb bombs was dropped on the palace, as one of the crew haphazardly tossed out 20lb bombs in the plane's wake. Terrified women from the royal harem reputedly ran into the street as explosions rocked the palace. One bomb supposedly exploded near the grave of Amanullah's golf-mad uncle, who had been buried under the first tee on Kabul's only golf course – the amir later complained that the British had deliberately desecrated the tomb of his ancestor.

Halley described the raid with the kind of nonchalance RAF crews would use after bombing raids in the Second World War:

> Still nursing our leaking engine, we made the bomb run and our missiles achieved good results, and if that didn't frighten the inhabitants, many of whom could never have seen an aeroplane before, the sound of the 'Old Carthusian' just a few hundred feet up with four engines roaring certainly did![15]

With the plane now much lighter, the return flight was easier, although the crew had to shut down the leaking engine. Halley and his crew landed after a six-hour flight to be greeted as heroes.

An almost symbolic attack by a single plane had disproportionate consequences, staggering Afghan leaders with the revelation that no part of their country was safe from air attack. The RAF stepped up the bombing in the south, and by the end of May its squadrons were dropping a ton of bombs every day, mostly on Jalalabad. Amanullah asked for peace a few days after the raid on Kabul. He accused Britain of hypocrisy for bombing civilians and holy sites despite having denounced the Germans for doing the same to London. British officials and military chiefs agreed that the Kabul raid played a major role in ending the war. General Sir Charles Monro, the commander of the land forces, wrote in his official report '... there is little doubt that this raid was an important factor in producing a desire for peace at the headquarters of the Afghan Government'.[16] Trenchard, furious at what he saw as army understatement, insisted Halley had won the war single-handed.

Victory could not conceal that British forces had performed miserably in a conflict against an insignificant and backward native power that should have been a walkover. Only the RAF emerged with an enhanced reputation. Conservative Indian Army commanders grudgingly conceded that air power had transformed frontier warfare, and no field commander wanted to be without it in any future fight. A conflict at the heart of the empire, meanwhile, revealed the political and racial limits of Britain's willingness to use air power against its own subjects.

***

Nowhere was the British Empire shaken more by the post-war crisis than in Ireland. A nationalist uprising swept much of the island after 1918, and British military commanders struggling to maintain control clamoured to employ the air force against the rebels. Government ministers, who unflinchingly sanctioned the bombing of black people, were appalled at the idea of using warplanes against a white population and refused. Trenchard strongly opposed the use of his squadrons in Ireland because he knew that air attacks were blunt weapons, and the inevitable, if inadvertent, white civilian casualties would damage the RAF's reputation.

There were only two squadrons in Ireland during most of the conflict, and many of their planes could not fly because of a lack of spare parts due to spending cuts. Most of the time was taken up with routine pilot training along with occasional patrolling of roads and railway lines for signs of ambushes or sabotage. Leaflets with pictures of wanted insurgents were occasionally scattered on towns and villages, and messages were dropped to remote British military posts. Security had to be stepped up at RAF bases after raids by nationalists for weapons and explosives. Police dogs were flown in from Britain to patrol the bases. Pilot George Carmichael recalled that the frightened dogs travelled in the second cockpit, whining and licking the pilots' necks.[17]

Airmen ended up regarding the fighting outside their bases as something that did not really involve them, although RAF supply columns were sometimes shot up by nationalist gunmen. Carmichael[18] recalled that his time as a young officer in Ireland was dominated by the frustration of trying to form a rugby team from men obsessed with football. Another officer, Ernest Haire, who had been a teacher before the world war, was oblivious of the conflict until a man accosted him in Dublin one evening and warned that strolling about in a British uniform could get him killed; a policeman who saw the encounter told the young airman that the kindly stranger was a notorious nationalist gunman.[19]

The nearest the RAF came to action were a few half-hearted experiments at breaking up anti-British demonstrations with mock air attacks. Haire said pilots were supposed to cut their engines at high altitude and then drop silently to about 2,000ft before turning the power back on and roaring over a crowd to scare the people and make them scatter.[20] Results were mixed. Carmichael was once ordered to fly over Mountjoy Prison in Dublin during a demonstration, and dive and fire flares if the police could not handle the crowd, but nothing happened.[21] With the situation deteriorating, the military was given permission to use air attacks in remote rural areas if troops were in direct clashes with rebel forces, but the government imposed so many conditions as to be unworkable.[22]

★★★

Politicians, who baulked at using air power in Ireland, were appalled when civil servants drawing up post-war contingency plans for dealing with possible unrest in Britain asked if aircraft would be used to maintain order. Radicals and conservatives were competing with dire predictions of an imminent left-wing revolution, and an army report fretted that the days when only gentlemen and their gamekeepers knew how to use guns had passed.[23]

Military aircraft had been used once or twice in Britain to help deal with labour unrest: planes had dropped leaflets on strikers at a Coventry aircraft factory in 1917 appealing to them to go back to work, and the RAF had ferried government dispatches and copies of *The Times* to provincial towns during a 1919 railway strike. The idea of the RAF bombing British cities and towns, even in a revolution, was too much for ministers and officials. Trenchard deliberately deepened the apprehension by saying that innocent bystanders would be killed if warplanes were used to put down civil disturbances. Nobody pointed out that this undermined the RAF's usual claim that its bombers were so accurate that they never harmed innocents in colonial operations.

Government ministers quickly ruled out any aggressive use of aircraft in Britain, although John Slessor, who routed the horsemen of Darfur, recalled his squadron flew over working-class districts in northern England during the 1926 general strike in what was supposed to be a show of strength. It was a distasteful role, he said, for airmen who thought that their duty was fighting Britain's enemies and not intimidating their own countrymen.[24]

Ironically, it was left to South Africa, the empire's foremost bastion of racial supremacy, to use aircraft against white citizens when striking miners seized parts of Johannesburg in March 1922. South Africa's fledgling air force flew reconnaissance missions and dropped warnings on armed miners, who fired at the planes. Aircraft bombed and strafed the miners at least once before the rising was crushed by troops and tanks.[25]

★★★

British leaders who would not use military aircraft against white protesters or even rebels had far fewer reservations when it came to putting down unrest in non-white colonies. Some of the most serious post-war disturbances erupted in Egypt in early 1919 after demands for independence were rejected and police arrested nationalist leaders. British personnel and property were attacked by mobs as anti-colonial fury spread from Cairo to the provinces. A large RAF contingent was stationed in Egypt because of the Suez Canal, a vital imperial artery, and the air force supported army units putting down the unrest. There was uproar in London when some MPs claimed that British pilots had behaved like the Germans and committed atrocities against civilians.

Colonial officials decided that recently arrived RAF officers and men must be educated on their duties as imperial guardians, and political pep talks were arranged. One speaker, an army officer, mocked the idea that Egyptians were capable of understanding or wanting freedom, and blamed the unrest on 'low class foreigners, chiefly anarchists or Levantines, who were in touch with Continental Bolshevism'.[26]

Like most young RAF officers, F.R. Wynne had no interest in the local people or the causes of the unrest. Officers and men barely saw natives as human beings, let alone equals, and would have been bewildered if anyone suggested they learn about the views or feelings of the local people. Such indifference would be typical of many air force and other military personnel in the interwar era.

Wynne and other pilots from the flight school at Heliopolis outside Cairo were formed into two scratch squadrons with Avro 504 biplane trainers, to patrol railway lines and other facilities at the height of the unrest. It was fairly monotonous, until an order arrived for every available aircraft to break up a protest in a nearby village by buzzing the crowd. Wynne recalled:

> When we arrived, the spectacle was both diverting and terrifying. The operation being quite unorganized, was highly dangerous and 'near misses' were frequent. A number of airplanes were gaining what height they could, diving towards the village to collect more speed than they were capable of and whizzing across it at roof top height from all directions. Some, having reached what they considered to be the prudent limit of their fuel, performed an acrobatic or two over the centre of the party before leaving for home. The row in the village must have been infernal. People were running out of it in all directions, but I did observe a number … who were not running. They, I imagine, knew that no harm was intended or were enjoying the display. A strange operation. Not certainly, an operation of war but one might, I suppose, call it an operation of politics.[27]

★★★

Anti-British riots and demonstrations also erupted in India in the spring of 1919 as protesters demanding independence attacked police stations, courts and other government buildings. A handful of British and Indian officials and businessmen were killed and their bodies tossed on bonfires of documents and furniture in the streets as crowds cheered. Shaken British administrators talked ominously of a second Indian mutiny.

In one of the most norious incidents in British colonial history, some 380 people were killed when Brigadier General R.E.H. Dyer ordered troops to fire on unarmed protesters on 13 April in Amritsar. Now virtually forgotten was the RAF's bombing and strafing of unarmed civilians on 15 April in Gujranwala in the Punjab. Police had lost control of the town, and British officials and their families were trapped in a compound. With the army unable to get troops to the town, it was decided to send three planes of 31 Squadron under Captain D.H.M. Carberry, a highly decorated officer, on a reconnaissance flight. Arriving over the town, and seeing burning buildings and what they took to be mobs of rioters, the pilots strafed groups of Indians and bombed a school and two nearby villages. At least twelve people were killed, most, if not all of them, apparently innocent bystanders.

A subsequent inquiry concluded that while the use of machine guns was necessary, the bombing of villages and a school could not be justified. It absolved Carberry of any blame, however, because of what it said were the pilots' imprecise orders. A dissenting report by an Indian member of the committee said that Carberry was at fault because he had used excessive force. Overall, the inquiry applauded the RAF's actions, saying they were 'not only justified but, in their view, invaluable, and the fact that the disorders were ended long before the troops arrived is in large measure attributable to this act'.[28]

Colonial administrators in India, who could never forget that the British were a mere handful among many millions of Indians, were not going to rule out using such a versatile weapon as the aeroplane to bolster their control. A committee tried to draw up guidelines on using aircraft to put down demonstrations when the police lost control.[29] Most of the regulations were wildly impractical, including a stipulation that civilian officials on the ground would authorise air attacks beforehand in writing, preferably specifying how many bombs and bullets could be used. While the guidelines were adopted, planes were never used against civil unrest in India because of the likely human cost and resulting political backlash.

★★★

The use of aircraft to put down unrest in Ireland, India and elsewhere raised daunting questions: could a weapon as terrifying as the bomber be employed against local populations in an empire that claimed to rule solely for the good of the ruled? British leaders could not imagine bombing Cairo, Calcutta and the other great cities of the empire with their vast populations, ancient histories, monuments, markets, universities, temples and churches. Such an idea genuinely appalled them, and they knew that the inevitable carnage would shatter every justification for British rule. There was also a desire to avoid any precedents that might justify the bombing of British cities in a future war. Growing numbers of people in Britain were starting to fear the bomber in the same way as later generations would dread nuclear weapons. And yet air power, with all of its potential, could not be discarded by an empire that had neither the men nor the money to fend off the rising threats to its control.

The politicians tacitly left it to Trenchard, as with so much else in these early years, to spell out where and how his squadrons should be used for imperial policing. Echoing traditional British military thinking, the RAF chief said that repressive measures could only be employed against uncivilised tribes in sparsely populated areas. Bombing was too destructive and indiscriminate to use in 'settled countries' like Britain, or the 'settled portions' of colonies like India where most people lived in cities or towns.[30] Attacking urban areas would mean wholesale slaughter, he said, and drive hordes of civilians into the countryside where they would have no way to survive. 'The aircraft at present is an inaccurate weapon and the dropping of bombs or direction of machine-gun fire from the air cannot be carried out with such a degree of nicety as to ensure that the innocent and unoffending people should not suffer with the guilty,' he wrote.[31]

The post-war crisis had shown the value and versatility of air power in dealing with various threats in the empire. But Trenchard knew that even the service's spectacular success in Afghanistan had not vindicated his claim that air power alone could control the wild parts of the empire. Even the most Luddite army officers saw the value of aircraft in colonial operations; if anything, it made them even more determined to break up the RAF and put its men and machines back under their control. It would be left to a small RAF detachment in the Horn of Africa to score the first major victory in the campaign for an independent imperial air force.

4

THE CHEAPEST WAR IN HISTORY

British Somaliland was seen by generations of colonial officials as the most forsaken and backward of the empire's far-flung territories. A textbook for army officers described it as 'the most useless possession in the whole of the British Empire'.[1] It seemed to most British visitors that this wilderness on the Horn of Africa had been designed by a malign intelligence to torture any living thing foolish or mad enough to blunder into its embrace. Searing daytime heat gave way to bitterly cold nights; droughts lasting years were punctuated by flash floods that drowned men and animals, and the Somalis were as hard and deadly as the parched landscape. Churchill, as a young minister, described the country after a 1907 visit as a dusty pit of poverty peopled by murderous fanatics that cost millions and would never serve any purpose. Abandonment, he said, was the only sensible solution.

Britain's unhappy involvement with Somaliland began after Egypt gave up its nominal control in 1884. London felt compelled to fill the ensuing vacuum to protect sea routes to India in the Gulf of Aden, but colonial officials then did their best to ignore the unwanted orphan. Government handbooks on the protectorate were notable mainly for their lack of information – a 1920s Foreign Office guide said it was thought there were three or four schools in the territory, although one might have closed in 1909.[2]

Unfortunate administrators sent to turn the Somalis into model imperial subjects had little success. One official said, as he left after thirty years, that there was no point building roads or schools for a people who could not be civilised. Policing this violent, unruly land was almost impossible, and British control was confined mostly to the coastal fringe. A governor told London, in the 1930s, that he was reluctant to send troops to a remote region because an attempt to occupy it in the 1890s had been defeated, and the local tribe 'have lived on the recollection of their success ever since'.[3]

Not every Englishman was repelled by this luckless land. Adventurous army officers, ascetics and misfits were drawn by its savage hardships. Few were as exotic as Adrian Carton de Wiart, an army officer, future general and a connoisseur of killing. He left India in disgust after the authorities fined him for ungentlemanly conduct for shooting a coolie who had disturbed his afternoon nap.

Somaliland was a haven for those who could not afford the lavish lifestyle an army officer was expected to fund from his own pocket in Britain or India. The Horn of Africa was one of the few places on earth where cash was said to be useless, so a few years of service reputedly could rescue the most depleted bank account. Somaliland was garrisoned by a small force of native soldiers and police led by British officers. Somali troops were valued as brave, strong and dashing.[4] Carton de Wiart, who would lose an eye in the Somali wars, recounted the story of a Somali soldier who, having run out of bullets in a battle, smilingly marched into the ranks of screaming tribesmen to be hacked apart by their flashing spears and knives. 'These are the gestures that sound so useless on paper,' he wrote, 'but are so gripping in fact and give to war the touch of the sublime.'[5]

Life for those who served in Somaliland, willingly or otherwise, tended to be dull and uncomfortable. Stupefying heat, deadening routine and the lack of any diversion besides the lure of a whisky bottle could turn each day into a purgatory. Veterans sardonically joked of contracting the 'Somali clap' in desert outposts where there were no women. This curious affliction was caused by the fine specks of mica and gypsum in desert water that built up in the urethra and made urinating so painful that old army sweats compared it to the agony of gonorrhoea.

Many thought that nothing was as bad as the annual fly season when millions of the swarming black insects covered everything. Men woke to find their naked bodies covered with a black, living blanket of flies gorging on the congealed sweat that had coated the sleeper in the night. Sickness was endemic, particularly malaria, gastric illnesses and fever. And yet there was also beauty and majesty in the bleak Somali wilderness. Stretches of the desert and the hills came alive after the rains with a carpet of deep green grass dotted by vivid yellow and red flowers; wild figs and the aromatic gum trees from which the ancients had extracted myrrh and frankincense flourished in the mountain groves and nomadic tribes tended to their flocks in an ageless cycle of wandering from one waterhole to the next.

Out of this wilderness came a man who was to humiliate the world's great-est empire for twenty years. Mystery and contradiction surround the Somali mystic and warlord, Mohammad Abdille Hassan. Contemporary reports do not even agree on his exact name; to the British he was simply 'the Mad Mullah'. No accounts survive of what this remarkable man looked like, although most chroniclers agree he was tall and imposing. Some accounts claim he became monstrously fat from luxurious living, others that he suf-fered from elephantiasis. Some Somalis, then and now, saw him as the first fighter for the country's independence. To British officials and soldiers he was a maniacal fiend at the head of an army of zealots and criminals, and they spread stories of his supposed depravity and cruelty. A typical tale claimed the mullah had 300 women mutilated and executed after dreaming that they had neglected their prayers.

The mullah was born some time in the 1860s in a desert tribe, to par-ents who were desperately poor even by Somaliland's barebones standards. He should have been just another nameless goatherd, but the boy showed remarkable religious passions from the earliest age – he was said to crave the sacred in the same way that a man dying of thirst longed for water. Somehow he found his way to Mecca while still a teenager to learn in the schools of the strict Wahabi creed. He returned to Somaliland after years of study and won a reputation as a holy man and poet.

It was not enough for a man who believed he was destined by heaven to rule, however, and in 1896 he and a few followers began to conquer and unite the desert tribes, achieving remarkable victories against far larger forces. The former religious scholar soon ruled vast tracts of the interior with an army of 5,000 warriors, or Dervishes. He next challenged the British, denouncing them as infidel intruders. The mullah, like his contemporary, the Sultan of Darfur, delighted in writing letters mocking the courage and competence of British officials.

A missive in 1899 ordering the British to leave the territory instead goaded them into moving against the backwater prophet. The series of ineffectual campaigns that followed count among the most dismal and clumsy in British colonial history. Thousands of British, Indian and African troops failed to crush the mullah and suffered several humiliating defeats. A British force was ambushed and nearly wiped out in thick bush at Gumburu in 1903, and a column was decimated in 1913 at Dul Madoba, where a band of survivors made a final stand behind the heaped carcasses of dead camels and ponies. 'Horrible Disaster to Our Troops in Somaliland' ran a newspaper headline when the news reached London,[6] while another newspaper said it was time to quit 'this waste corner of the earth'.[7]

Military operations in Somaliland were halted at the start of the First World War, although the mullah was not forgotten. British officials worried that he might inspire resistance in other colonies. 'The continued immunity of the Mullah, who now stands alone as an unsubdued native potentate in Africa, is a source of constant anxiety,' a War Office report said.[8] Ending this embarrassment was a major British priority and work on a new expedition began even before the end of the war.

Major General A.R. Hoskins of the army said in December 1918 after visiting Somaliland that modern weapons were the key to victory, above all the aeroplane. He drew up a plan to defeat the mullah with three RAF squadrons, a large ground force that would use Ford motor vans rather than baggage animals, and six warships for coastal bombardment.[9] It would be the most modern, technological force Britain had ever sent to fight a colonial war in Africa, and very expensive.

The RAF, looking for a new role to justify its survival, was also eyeing the Somali imbroglio. Major Wyndham Birch, an air force staff officer, arrived in the Somali capital of Berbera in December 1918 on a rival reconnaissance mission. Birch said the RAF alone could defeat the mullah with three squadrons and a small ground force. He asserted that 'intensive bombing of forts and machine-gunning of ground targets' along with 'machine-gunning and bombing of water holes' would destroy the mullah's forces.[10] Friendly natives would be given red headbands, he said, to ensure that they were not bombed or machine-gunned.

Henry Wilson, the head of the British Army, thought that both plans were far too modest. He insisted it would take at least 30,000 men, including eighteen infantry battalions, up to a year to do the job at a cost of £6 million. Wilson wanted to avoid another failed Somali campaign, but government ministers were appalled at what they saw as an insane scheme to transpose the Western Front to the African desert. Lord Milner, the colonial secretary, turned to Trenchard, who airily said his men could do the job for mere pennies.[11]

Air force staff officers promptly produced a plan for twelve DH9A bombers and 229 men to rout the mullah in three months. There would be no need for army reinforcements, they said; any survivors could be mopped up by the existing garrison after the bombers had crushed the mullah's forces. Wilson ridiculed the RAF's claims, and planning for the Somali expedition bogged down amid inter-service bickering. A meeting was held in June 1919 under

Churchill, as secretary of state for war, to end the impasse. Spluttering with sarcasm, Wilson said relying on a handful of aeroplanes and grubby mechanics to tame the Somalis would lead to disaster and the RAF would have to be rescued by the army. Government leaders, tired of Wilson's histrionics and army extravagance, backed the air force plan.

Group Captain Robert Gordon, a cheerful and humorous man who knew desert conditions from wartime service in Mesopotamia, was assigned to lead the RAF expedition that would be a crucial test in using air power for colonial control. Aircraft had never been seen in the territory and elaborate efforts were made to keep the expedition secret to maximise the psychological impact of flying machines on the Somalis. An advance party led by Gordon posed as oil prospectors and the expedition was designated, with the British military's usual penchant for schoolboy drama, as Force Z to confuse any Dervish spies. The disguised RAF men were accosted as soon as they arrived by Somalis amiably asking when the flying machines would arrive.

In the best tradition of Victorian explorers, the main party of pilots and ground crew left London by train at dawn on 13 November, while the planes were transported in wooden crates stencilled with a large 'Z'. The men travelled across France, took a boat to Egypt and there, along with some local RAF personnel, embarked with 800 tons of stores, including 1,235 bombs, on the seaplane carrier HMS *Ark Royal*.

The RAF had learned much about colonial conditions since the Darfur expedition three years earlier, and Force Z had far fewer problems getting ready for the Somali operation. Somaliland's Public Works Department provided labourers to hack landing strips out of the scrub with crude wooden scrapers and twig brooms. Walls of thorn brush and sandbagged machine gun posts ringed the dirt runways in case of Dervish attacks. There was no material for hangars, so shelters of matted rushes and wire were put up to protect the planes against the sun, wind and dust. Detailed drawings of the improvised shelters were sent to London to be used by future desert expeditions.

The RAF, with its scientific ethos, was determined to revolutionise, or at least update, colonial campaigning. Elaborate arrangements were made to keep the air contingent healthy and avoid the staggering sick lists that usually afflicted colonial operations. To protect them from the sun, the airmen were issued sunglasses and pith helmets that sat on their heads like huge mushroom caps. They were inoculated against every imaginable ailment and their teeth had been inspected by military dentists before leaving England. Fresh vegetables and fruit to combat disease and keep the men healthy were sent from the coast by camel, or even runner. Fresh drinking water was laboriously carted by camels in metal containers over 100 miles to the airstrips – officers received a daily ration of 10 gallons while the men, who were presumably no less thirsty or dirty, got just 5 gallons. Stomach ailments would be the main medical problem, with the entire contingent suffering diarrhoea of 'varying degrees'.[12] In a fit of puritanical mistrust or extreme optimism, a doctor lectured the contingent on the horrors of venereal disease just before it left for the empty interior.

Force Z's main contingent had arrived at Berbera on 30 December. Navy carpenters helped the RAF fit a wooden deck on a lighter because the port could not handle large ships, and the crated aircraft were ferried to the beach and manhandled ashore. Work on assembling the DH9As began on New Year's Day 1920, with the first air tests a week later. Some of the planes had been damaged on the long voyage and problems increased as heat, sand and dust took a growing toll on the fragile wooden and canvas structures. Fitters and mechanics battled throughout the campaign to keep the planes flying, and never got more than six machines at a time into the air.

After being assembled the planes were tested off the coast to keep their presence secret, a ruse that, as Gordon noted, not only failed, but gave the mullah a small propaganda coup. 'I make all the machines flying go along the coast away from Berbera out of sight, and this has started a rumour among the Somalis that they cannot go inland as the Mullah blows them back when they try,' he ruefully wrote.[13]

The DH9A was the unsung hero of the RAF's early post-war colonial campaigns. This wooden and canvas two-man biplane was perhaps the most potent weapon in the imperial arsenal, massively multiplying colonial fire-power for a pittance and giving British forces a one-sided advantage against native opponents from Africa to Asia. It was a versatile and rugged plane that stood up well to harsh colonial conditions. Each plane could carry up to 460lb of bombs and two Lewis machine guns, and had a flying range of four and a half hours with a top speed of 111mph.

Two of Force Z's planes were modified for use as experimental air ambulances. One patient was carried on a sloping seat in the rear cockpit while a stretcher bolted to the top of the fuselage carried a second invalid. Wits promptly called the ambulance planes 'flying hearses'. Eight men were to be evacuated during the campaign, flown in just hours to medical help instead of facing debilitating and potentially fatal trips by cart or camel that could take days or weeks. It was one of the first uses of aircraft in the medical evacuation role that has become a hallmark of modern war.

Force Z's bombers were ready at the advance airstrip of Eil Dur Elan by 20 January 1920. Gordon and his men were sure the coming campaign would be an easy triumph. Among the treasures at Britain's National Archives at Kew in south London is a battered old address book filled with neat handwriting in fading black ink. It is the combat diary of Force Z, a daily record compiled in the desert of its missions against the mullah. Why so important a moment in the early history of the RAF is recorded in such a curious manner is not clear. Perhaps the address book was hurriedly purchased at a railway kiosk at the last moment to keep a record, or maybe the pinched air force was using up old stationery to save money. Its neat rows of figures resemble a merchant's ledger except that the entries meticulously record every bomb and bullet expended rather than cash transactions.[14]

Six of Gordon's bombers set out early on 21 January to start the war. The target was the mullah's massive stone fortress at Medishi, located some 25 miles from the northern coast. Things started to go wrong as soon as the little formation climbed unevenly into the thin desert air. One plane developed engine trouble within minutes and broke away to make an emergency landing. Four of the planes then lost their way over the featureless stretch of rock and sand and ended up attacking a smaller fortress at Jid Ali further inland.

Only the DH9A flown by Pilot Officer E.R.C. Hobson found Medishi with its warren of walls, towers and dwellings. Warriors, servants, women and children rushed out to gape as the machine sailed over the fortress, more amazed than frightened as they saw a plane for the first time in their lives. The mullah and his personal retinue stood in a courtyard below watching the heavenly apparition – Hobson and his observer, their faces obscured by goggles and leather flying helmets, must have seemed like creatures from another realm as they stared back.

Legend claims the mullah thought the plane was a chariot sent to carry him to paradise. Such thoughts, if true, vanished as a 20lb bomb hurtled into the knot of gawking attendants and advisers ringing the Somali leader. Its blast killed several people, including the man the mullah was standing next to, or even leaning on, and singed the cleric's billowing white robes. Hobson flew back unaware that he had almost ended the campaign in its opening moment.

Force Z methodically bombed Medishi, Jid Ali and other Dervish settlements over the next few days. Jubilant pilots returned with claims of killing and wounding hordes of Dervishes. No distinction was made between warriors and the large numbers of civilians, including many women and children, in the settlements. Excited crews recounted how their bombs had shattered the homes, storehouses and other structures within the walls. Incendiary devices were dropped on subsequent passes into the gaping holes that the bombs had torn in the buildings, and black smoke soon leaked from the rubble followed by fierce yellow flames.

Pilots swooped to 300ft to machine-gun the swarms of frantic people below, some of whom tried to flee while others battled to put out the fires and rescue possessions from burning homes. 'When last seen village was still burning,' one entry in the force diary noted crisply. The vast herds of camels, sheep and goats that were the Dervishes' principal source of food and wealth were singled out as prime targets. The animals were easy targets, which the planes first bombed and then strafed at low level. Force Z's diary entry for 22 January recorded the use that day of two 112lb bombs, sixty-four 20lb bombs, 300 incendiary devices and 2,500 machine gun rounds on such targets.

Enemy losses were 'severe', it noted, although there were never specific numbers or independent corroboration. Colonial officials later claimed that leaflets were dropped before the first air attacks to warn the Dervishes about the bombing and give them a chance to surrender. The RAF history of the campaign makes it clear, however, that there were never any warnings because surprise was considered essential to achieve the maximum effect.[15]

There was no resistance from the ground apart from the occasional rifle shot. A growing list of the aircrafts' mechanical problems caused by dirt, heat and other factors was a far bigger menace; three of the six bombers that set out on a bombing raid on 23 January turned back with engine trouble.

The RAF declared the war virtually won after just five days when air patrols returned on 24 January from Medishi to say that the fortress had been abandoned. Gordon announced the end of the RAF's 'semi-independent action' the following day, and nonchalantly said the army could round up any Dervishes who had not been killed or fled over the border. Local ground commanders, whose units had been kept waiting in the rear for weeks, fretting that the mullah would slip away, were not impressed by this declaration that it was safe for them to join the war.

Admittedly the grandly named Somaliland Field Force, led by Colonel Hastings Ismay, who would be Churchill's chief military assistant during the Second World War, did not look that impressive in its sun-bleached, ragged khaki uniforms. It was a makeshift little legion composed of the Somali Camel Corps, a few African and Indian regular troops, and 1,500 tribal auxiliaries who were regarded even by their British officers as a dangerous rabble. Still, most of the men were tough, excellent soldiers who knew how to fight the Dervishes.

The army's doubts about the effectiveness of the air campaign seemed justified when Camel Corps units arrived at Jid Ali on 28 January as RAF planes were attacking the fortress. Most of the bombs appeared to miss or bounce off the stone walls, and it seemed to many of the watching soldiers that the air attack was as lethal as the flies buzzing around their heads. Dervish gunmen blazed away from the tops of the stone walls at the newly arrived troops, and taunted the white officers with vividly obscene insults about their mothers. The army's mortars seemed much more effective than the air attacks, the plump little bombs blasting away slabs of masonry and shaking the walls and towers; what was left of the garrison fled the next day. Similar scenes were played out at the fortress at Daran, about 100 miles to the east of Jid Ali, which only fell after men of the King's African Rifles blasted an opening in the wall.

A Dervish leader, who came in to surrender on 30 January, said the mullah had fled to his fort at Thale almost 200 miles to the south in the Somali interior. RAF commanders later accused the Camel Corps of letting the Somali leader get away.[16] Long, exhausting treks followed as Ismay's men chased the Dervishes into the desert. Hunger haunted the column after supplies ran out, and the men and their animals survived by drinking the thick green slime that filled the filthy desert pools. Ismay and his adjutant bolted down a piece of rancid fat they found in the corner of an empty haversack one evening, savouring every bit as if it were a feast. Many of the British officers collapsed from constant vomiting and diarrhoea.

RAF patrols swept the desert, meanwhile, for signs of the Dervishes. Any natives spotted from the air were judged to be hostile and attacked, even though there were many friendly and neutral tribesmen in the vast wastes. Planes bombed a pony caravan spotted on 31 January near Daringahuje. Dervish deserters later said it was transporting the mullah's wives and sons, but he was sheltering several miles away at the time.

An air patrol flew over Thale for the first time on 1 February. It bombed a large convoy of at least 1,500 camels that was spotted near the fort. Gordon ordered a major raid on Thale two days later. Exhausted ground crews at Eil Dur Elan could only make three planes airworthy, including one with a faltering engine. The little formation bombed the fort and then swooped low so that the inhabitants could be 'heavily and effectively engaged with machine gun fire'.[17] Much of the settlement was ablaze, with the wind spreading darting flames as the aircraft headed back to base.

It turned out to be Force Z's last bombing mission; the RAF declared the mullah had been defeated and the little air detachment packed up and returned to the coast. Thale fell a few days later, virtually without a fight, to Somali auxiliaries fighting for the British, but the elusive Dervish leader once again had vanished. It was left to the ragged troopers of the Somali Camel Corps to catch up with the mullah and the remnants of his army. A detachment surprised the Dervish encampment at night, and six of the mullah's sons died in the fighting as the Dervishes frantically tried to hold off the attackers. Four of the mullah's wives and nine sons and daughters were among the prisoners, but the Somali leader escaped with some of his bodyguards. The British column, exhausted and hungry, its supply packs empty, and now hobbled with scores of prisoners, was forced to turn back. There was no way to contact the air force at a critical moment when its planes could have helped locate and finish off the fleeing remnants of the Dervish army.

Most accounts of the campaign end at this point, saying only that the mullah limped away and died a few months later, but British officials knew the holy man would be a threat as long as he was free. A deputation of Somali notables was sent to find the mullah with a promise of living out his days in a religious community if he surrendered. It was difficult to find suitable emissaries – one man retched with terror when he was asked to go.

Eventually the delegation met the mullah at his camp. He silently stared at the terrified visitors for several hours before they were allowed to dismount, and then further unnerved them by carving their names with a thorn on the flesh of one of his attendants. Predictably, little came of the talks, although the mullah made a point of boasting he had destroyed six British planes, suggesting the RAF had shaken the Dervishes: 'The British brought twelve birds against me, but they could not hurt me. Their droppings fell on the top of my white canopy but did me no harm,' he told the delegation.[18]

A force of some 3,000 troops and irregulars chased the mullah and what was left of his followers into Ethiopian territory in July and attacked their camp. Most of the 800 weak and famished Dervish defenders were killed, wounded or taken prisoner, but their leader escaped. Reports soon reached the British that the mullah was building fortresses and trying to raise a new army. And then, after so many years of defiance, came word that this strange mix of prophet, nationalist and tyrant had died of illness somewhere in the wilderness at the end of 1920. His reign had been costly even by Somaliland's standards; one modern historian estimated that two decades of war, disruption and famine claimed the lives of some 200,000 Somalis.[19]

News of the Dervish defeat had already been hailed by the British Government as the cheapest war in history. It had cost the imperial treasury a mere £77,000 to crush a threat that had haunted the empire for so long. British losses were negligible, with only four dead and eleven wounded in the fighting, while hundreds of Dervishes had been slaughtered, wounded or captured. The RAF, which suffered no combat deaths and lost just three planes in accidents, seemed to have performed a miracle. It was lionised by government leaders, revelling in their own wisdom at letting the young service finish off the Mad Mullah instead of yielding to army demands for a bloated land campaign. The colonial secretary told the House of Commons it marked the dawn of a new age in warfare. 'For the first time, in fact, the aeroplane has been deliberately employed as the primary striking instrument, and not merely as an ancillary weapon,' he pronounced.[20]

Air force leaders, with a flair for public relations they were to demonstrate repeatedly in coming years, held up the campaign as proof of how air power could transform colonial policing and defence. The official RAF history of the campaign pronounced that the empire now possessed ' ... a form of attack against which no counter measures could avail'.[21] Ismay and other army men were far less impressed, claiming that air attacks had scattered the Dervish forces rather than wiped them out; Dervish morale was never broken; and inspections of Dervish forts showed bombing achieved few hits and even less damage. Government officials replied that the Dervishes had been crushed and insisted a handful of aircraft had achieved in days what half a dozen army expeditions had failed to do in twenty years – and all at a fraction of the cost. Force Z's little triumph was the first major victory in Trenchard's campaign to make the RAF the indispensable guardian of the empire.

5

THE AIR SERVICE OF THE FUTURE

While Force Z was pursuing the Mad Mullah in Somaliland in the summer of 1920, Hugh Trenchard was intently studying the seemingly insignificant exploits of a tiny RAF force in the southern Sudan. Three planes and twenty-seven airmen had subdued a ferocious tribe at a cost that was trifling even by the bargain rates of the Somali campaign. The RAF chief saw the Sudanese operation as a model of how small, locally based air detachments could control the largest and most hostile territories. Trenchard, who rarely gave praise, scribbled on the report of the Sudan operation, 'This is one of the reports that I hope are being extracted and printed and kept in [airbase] reference libraries for the use of the Air Service of the Future.'[1]

Sudan was administered by a handful of British officials and a small force of native troops and police led by seconded white officers from the British Army. It was 'a mad dogs and Englishmen' sort of place with a reputation for attracting eccentrics. 'When God made the Sudan he laughed' was an old Arab proverb, and one veteran said that anyone posted there needed 'a sense of humour, better still a sense of the ridiculous'.[2]

Sammy Butler, an officer in the defence force for many years, was said to be the best-dressed man in the British Army, reputedly sending his dress shirts to England to be starched. The small defence force was scattered across the vast, anarchic country, with detachments of a few hundred men guarding districts the size of France. There were very few roads, and it took days or weeks for help to reach isolated outposts. Nowhere seemed better suited for the RAF's claims that air power, with its speed and reach, could police the wild fringes of the empire.

The defence force had been trying for years to pacify the tribes that lived in the vast swamps of the Sudd in the south and were always fighting and raiding each other. Punitive columns struggled to find tribal settlements hidden deep in the maze of elephant grass, streams and bogs. British officers complained about having to fight elusive 'web-footed savages'. Fresh trouble erupted in 1919 when the Garjak Nuer, one of the largest tribal groups, ignored British orders to stop raiding other tribes. The colonial administration, remembering what aircraft had done in Darfur in 1916, asked the RAF for help when a punishment expedition was sent against the Nuer.

An air detachment with two DH9A aircraft, four officers and twenty-three airmen was assembled in December 1919 from the RAF contingent in neighbouring Egypt. For once there was none of the inter-service bickering which had delayed preparations for the expedition against the Mad Mullah for months, and the little force, named H Unit, was ready in days. There were no airstrips in southern Sudan, so the planes had to be crated and shipped by sea and river with enough spare parts and supplies for four months.

Most of the airmen were new recruits who had been in Egypt for just a few weeks. H Unit established a base with a crude airstrip at Nasser on the edge of the swamps and not far from the Ethiopian border. It struggled to find enough dry land to set up the tents and repair facilities. Venomous snakes and insects were a constant hazard, and inquisitive crocodiles wandered into the little base. Mechanics and fitters unpacked and assembled the planes, and, despite the difficulties of working in a swamp, got both machines into the air by the end of January 1920.

Operations began a week later as two small columns of soldiers and police advanced into the Nuer domains. The first air patrols revealed that the campaign was not going to be the walkover the RAF had imagined. Flying over the swamps, the flight crews were astonished at how difficult it was to see anything because of mist and the dense green vegetation. Even at low altitude, pilots and observers often could only make out things right below the planes; it was impossible to spot humans hiding in the thick reeds. A war band of some 2,000 warriors easily eluded the aerial patrols, and mauled one of the columns at the start of the operation.

Puzzled pilots returned from patrol to report that these natives were not terrified by the sight of aircraft, and even thought they might be friends and potential allies. Colonel C.R.K. Bacon, the army ground commander and a veteran of this type of fighting, realised that the Nuer did not understand that the planes were war machines. He later wrote:

At first it was thought that the very appearance of aeroplanes would cause the enemy to vanish, but as a matter of fact they had no such effect so long as they took no offensive action and the Nuers commonly thought the machines carried no one on board and, as objects from the 'unknown', were to be placated by sacrifices and enlisted on their side.[3]

Nor did things improve when the British airmen made the first attacks with machine guns. Instead of fleeing when planes strafed people and villages, pilots said, the Nuer 'seldom panicked even when attacked from as low as 100ft'.[4] The results of the first bombing attacks were more encouraging. The planes, each carrying eight 20lb bombs, finally caught hundreds of Nuer in two areas, and bombed and strafed them 'with good effect'.[5] The crews said 80 per cent of the bombs hit targets and many Nuer had been killed or wounded. Subsequent ground inspections tended to show actual losses were fairly light, and that the tall vegetation and smoke from burning grass interfered with the pilots' aim. Nuer forces quickly learned not to assemble in large groups, and fled from villages and hid in the bush when aircraft flew over.

H Unit tried to develop tactics to counter the Nuer's elusiveness, the dense vegetation and other obstacles. In an early form of carpet bombing, pilots were told to bomb everything in the map square where a target was thought to be located. Most bombing was done at low level, often below 100ft, to ensure the best chance of hitting running people. Small bombs were said to be most effective against humans and cattle. Heavy bombs simply flattened the Nuer's flimsy grass and animal hide huts before they exploded; pilots said it was like dropping an anvil on a haystack. Flight crews complained that their 8½oz incendiary devices – officially called Baby Incendiary Bombs – were too small to set reed huts on fire. A subsequent report called for a more robust, heavier incendiary that could be dropped in neat rows to incinerate villages systematically.[6]

The unit soon had other problems. One plane crashed because of mechanical trouble, and a fire at the airstrip on 18 February destroyed the workshops and most of the spare parts. A plan to fly in replacements was abandoned because the dirt landing strip was too small to handle a cargo plane. It took weeks to transport spares from Khartoum by boat and camel. The surviving plane was kept in the air by cannibalising its disabled companion. It shadowed the British columns, providing intelligence and watching for lurking Nuer to forestall ambushes.

There was jubilation in the RAF camp on 25 February when the surviving plane caught several groups of Nuer in the open and attacked them. Troops methodically destroyed the deserted villages, meanwhile, setting fire to huts and storehouses, and the RAF helpfully dropped 2,000 boxes of matches when the army's supply was ruined by the incessant damp.

The surviving aircraft crashed taking off on 3 March and could not be repaired until the spare parts from Khartoum finally arrived two weeks later. Faced with this new setback, the RAF decided to risk flying in a plane from Egypt despite the vast distance and the lack of intermediate landing strips. A replacement DH9A landed at the camp on 1 April, after an epic 1,800-mile flight from Cairo that took twenty hours and ten minutes. H Unit soon had two planes in action, a feat held up by air strategists as proof of how swiftly air units could be replaced, in contrast to the months it normally took to move ground reinforcements.

It was becoming clear that the expedition, despite some successes, had not broken the bands of young warriors who were the backbone of Nuer resistance. Bacon, the ground commander, decided to stop the aimless marching through the swamps to try to force a battle with the elusive war bands and to instead assault the entire Nuer nation with the old colonial tactic of destroying food stocks. He acknowledged it meant the 'punishment' of elderly, women and children who had no influence over the fighting men who were the source of the trouble, but it was the best way to break the Nuer resistance.[7]

The change in tactics made the air detachment even more valuable. Nuer efforts to hide their cattle on remote outcrops of dry land deep in the swamps could not conceal them from the air patrols. Pilots reported that the herds, unable to flee, were 'ideal bombing targets' and that the results of the ensuing bombing attacks on the herds were 'tremendous'.[8] A two-plane raid on 3 May found and attacked several large herds. Dozens of carcasses were left strewn on the ground after the planes riddled the cornered herds with bombs and machine-gun fire. Soon the Nuer, staring at slow death from hunger, began to submit, paid fines and promised to stop the raiding that had prompted the police action. Air operations ended on 23 May after one of the planes roared over several of the now cowed villages in a victory flight.

Mechanics and fitters dismantled the planes, packed up the remaining supplies and loaded everything on to boats for the long trip back to Egypt. Satisfaction and congratulations rippled up and down the RAF chain of command in the wake of H Unit's return. An internal assessment claimed the little air detachment had ensured 'the complete success of the operation'.[9]

Victory, the RAF said, had required just 165 bombs, 50 incendiary bombs and 7,000 machine gun bullets. There had been no RAF casualties despite the two crashes, and Nuer losses were said to be severe. Even the army agreed that air power had made a decisive contribution.

Bacon's only quibble, which made the RAF look even better, was that more planes should be assigned to future expeditions to ensure there would be no gaps in air cover because of accidents or other mishaps. And even though some of the Nuer had not been unnerved by air attacks, H Unit's exploits reinforced the RAF belief that aircraft crushed the will of 'primitive' races even without bombing. The force's final report confidently concluded:

> The moral effect was tremendous and although this was probably enhanced by the accuracy of the attacks – information gleaned showing the casualties inflicted on people and stock to have been severe – there is no doubt that this type of warfare will produce excellent results even if carried out when less favourable conditions render accurate bombing more difficult.[10]

Trenchard saw the scuffle in the Sudan as a model for the future of colonial policing. The Afghan War had been a conventional campaign, and the army had played a significant role in the Somali expedition, even if the RAF got the credit for the victory. Sudan, on the other hand, was held up as proof by the young air force that it could hold down a backward colony or region. Air strategists pressed their argument with the homely analogy that, just as one or two fire engines protected every English town, so a few aeroplanes based at key points could safeguard the empire. Events in the Middle East, meanwhile, were about to give Trenchard and his followers the strongest justification yet for their claims.

6

THE MESSPOT MESS

Mesopotamia was revered by the Victorians as an ancient cradle of civilisation and the site of the Garden of Eden. The general in command of British forces in the region in 1920 said that the Old Testament was one of the best guides to understanding the country, but his men did not see anything alluring in the barren, baking landscape, and derisively called it 'Messpot'. An RAF officer wrote home, 'It all may be very historical and the scene of ancient civilisations, but how can one enthuse over miles of sweet F.A. [sweet Fanny Adams, or nothing at all] as Tommy song [*sic*] suitably describes.'¹ Whatever the ribald mutterings of the rank and file, this land that was soon to be renamed Iraq would play a crucial role in ensuring the survival of the RAF and Air Control.

Critics could not comprehend why anyone would want this wasteland. British forces had conquered the Ottoman vilyets (provinces) of Baghdad, Basra and Mosul during the First World War. The provinces had never been regarded by the Turks as a single entity, and the disparate races, religious groups and tribes who inhabited them were united mostly by mutual loathing. Poverty and centuries of neglect and deprivation blighted the land. British visitors compared conditions in the towns to the ravages of the Black Death in medieval Europe.

A great deal of blood and treasure had been expended in conquering Mesopotamia, however, and the ingrained habits of empire made it difficult for the British to walk away. Imperial strategists argued that Mesopotamia was the key to British domination of the entire Middle East and its retention was vital to the security of India. It was decided to form a new country called Iraq, a name derived from the ridge that separated the land from Syria, and rule it under the auspices of a League of Nations mandate.

Iraq's post-war administration was turned over to white colonial officials who knew very little about local conditions and tried to set up a government modelled on British India, with the assistance of thousands of imported Indian clerks and coolies. The new rulers made many of the political and cultural blunders their American and British successors would repeat blithely some eighty years later – few British administrators could speak Arabic or knew anything about the country; officials and army officers of the old regime were dismissed summarily, depriving the new administration of their expert knowledge, and turning men who might have been useful into implacable opponents; while the serene British belief that they were bestowing a superior system on a backward race only made the Iraqis more resentful. In words that ring uncomfortably across the years, a chastened official, looking back, said that the British, inspired by a 'guileless confidence. Strong in goodwill ...',[2] never had a chance:

> ... what measure of success is likely ever to attend the effort of any Western power, with its strong prepossessions grown from its own evolutions, character and environment, to mould an Eastern and Islamic population into something resembling itself.[3]

Most of Mesopotamia's people did not want to exchange the yoke of a Muslim empire for the rule of a Western Christian power, and had resisted British rule even before the end of the war. British forces had started using aircraft during the war to put down opposition to their administration. An uprising in the Shia holy city of Najaf was put down with aerial attacks in March 1918, and a tribe in the Middle Euphrates area was bombed two months later for refusing to pay taxes.

Rapid cuts in British forces after the war, the vast size of the country and the lack of roads encouraged the continuing use of bombers in roles that would normally have been handled by armed police. Bombing was frequently indiscriminate and haphazard. The DH9As flown by Victor Groom's squadron lacked aiming sights, and pilots used a rough calculation of speed and height to drop their bombs. Groom said the crude maps issued to crews were useless, and planes often bombed the wrong targets.[4] A local British civilian official sometimes flew in the leading plane to point out targets.

A few British officers worried that bombing was being used to settle the most trivial issues. John Glubb, an RAF intelligence officer who would become a giant figure in the region, complained that civilian officials found it easier to pick up a phone and order a bombing raid rather than face an uncomfortable trek into the desert to deal with a truculent Arab tribe. 'It could be carried out without it being necessary for the civil officials concerned to leave their office chairs, above which large electric fans were coolly revolving,' he observed.[5] Even the Air Staff in London expressed concern in 1920 that fairly junior officials could order bombing raids by initialling a chit in the same way as they signed for drinks at the club or officers' mess.[6]

Flight crews were rarely told the reasons for attacking villages, and few, if any, questioned why they were bombing civilians. 'One lived in a little circle of one's own within the squadron and did what one was told and never questioned anything. You just did it and got on with it, whatever you were told to do,' said Groom, who enlisted in the army as a private in 1916 before volunteering for pilot training. He later rose to the rank of air marshal and played a key role in the planning of D-Day.[7]

Most RAF men, infused with the British military's sense of racial and imperial superiority, despised the local people, seeing their extreme poverty and filthy, disease-ridden villages as proof of abject inferiority. In their eyes, the natives only had themselves to blame if they refused to submit to British authority. D.H. Allen, who served as a bomber pilot, said bombing operations actually raised morale because they were an exciting diversion for homesick men fed up with living in decaying tents, exposed to extremes of heat and cold, and with nothing to eat but rancid tinned meat and tasteless biscuits.[8]

G.V. Howard wrote home that after just a month in the country he wanted to shoot the entire population. 'Why the devil we spend so much money on them I can't think, I am sure we can't get it all back in oil,' he wrote.[9]

While there was rarely any resistance from the ground, the bombing missions could be hazardous. Flying conditions were difficult, especially over the featureless desert, which crews called 'the blue' because the immense emptiness mirrored the vastness of the sky. Planes could be slammed into the ground by freak turbulence, while sand devils or whirlwinds that rose thousands of feet into the sky and raced across the landscape were a regular menace. Aeroplanes built for European conditions crumbled and fell apart as the heat and dust rapidly withered the wooden frames and canvas coverings. Poorly ventilated engines frequently seized up while climbing or in mid-flight.

Flight crews dreaded locust swarms, when millions, even billions, of the insects blotted out the horizon. Pilots were blinded and plane engines spewed hot, green jets of mashed insect from the exhaust pipes. Howard said:

They are the most hideous things I have ever seen, measuring about 2" in length and coloured yellow with black stripes – something like a wasp. They have long legs shaped like a grass hopper and a head one sometimes sees in a nightmare – a sort of Klu Klux Klan [*sic*] affair. They are perfectly filthy things, they seem to live on each other, three or four attacking one and sucking his body until nothing remains but the husk of the body … one just simply has to get used to them as they are so numerous that they are continually on your bare knees, neck and head – even face if you allow them to get as far.[10]

Funerals for aircrews killed in flying accidents were a mundane part of life in the early post-war years, along with auctions of the dead men's effects. 'We became expert at the slow march and resting on arms reversed, and the station band's rendering of the "Dead March" from *Saul* could hold its own with the best,' wrote pilot S.J. Carr.[11] The heedless young flyers rarely worried about dying, always thinking it would happen to somebody else, never to them. Most accidents were not fatal and could be treated as a joke; the common reaction was to rush to a crash site with a camera to record a friend's mishap.

And yet, for all the dangers and hardships, most airmen were fascinated as they flew over the ancient landscape. One pilot wrote after one of his first flights:

To the right the Tigris, to the left the Euphrates, threaded the sandy waste, the former with innumerable bends and twists, the latter flowing sedately. The bright green of palm groves, vivid as the cube in a paint-box denoted settlements of the living, while what looked like geometrical patterns traced on a giant scale, or the architectural sand drawings of a child at the sea, enormously magnified, marked the sites of long-forgotten cities of the dead.[12]

A semblance of stability was imposed on Iraq in the months after the war. Many at home still saw it all as a monstrous waste of money at a time when Britain was caught in a post-war recession. Opposition politicians and the press dubbed it the 'Messpot mess', and demanded withdrawal. A headline in *The Times* in September 1919 spoke of 'An Orgy of Waste'.[13] Churchill, as war secretary, said that Britain could stay only if the cost of the garrison of 25,000 British and 80,000 Indian troops was cut. Wing Commander C. Edmond, an early Air Control theorist and advocate, neatly summed up the problem by telling a London audience, 'First, we are all of us imperialists, and wish to see the empire defended as securely as possible. Second, we are all taxpayers, so we want the defence to be as economical as possible.'[14]

Looking for a solution, Churchill decided Mesopotamia was the best chance to test the schemes he and others had been discussing since 1918 of revolutionising the policing of the empire with aircraft. On 19 February 1920, Trenchard received a brief note from Churchill's aide that would help decide the future of the RAF. It said the army wanted to abandon Mesopotamia, after its request for £21.5 million a year to garrison the territory was rejected by the government as 'more than the country is worth'.[15] 'He [Churchill] wishes to know whether you are prepared to take on Mesopotamia,' continued the aide with typical British understatement, as if assuming responsibility for one of the most lawless and violent places in the world was like sitting on a committee or doing some extra paper work.[16]

'Taking on' Mesopotamia meant that for the first time the RAF would be in charge of a country's defences, with the responsibility of holding it against external and internal threats with a handful of squadrons and a small ground force – a task the army said could only be done in Mesopotamia by tens of thousands of troops, a large air contingent and a huge support system. It was the chance Trenchard had been seeking since the end of the war, to find a major role for the RAF that would justify its preservation as a separate service. Churchill sweetened his offer by saying the RAF commander in Iraq would be in charge of all British forces, something that would enrage the older services.

Within days Trenchard and his aides had produced the first systematic plan for Air Control. They began by listing the traditional problems of colonial warfare: land forces were slow, vulnerable and expensive; they could take months to organise and reach remote areas; the effect often was temporary, and trouble soon flared again. Aircraft would transform the policing of the empire by constantly patrolling even the most desolate regions; any sign of unrest would be detected and checked at the very beginning.

For the first time in its history, every part of the empire would be under direct oversight. Air patrols would make 'backward' races think they lived under an all-seeing, all-knowing eye that never slept. RAF analysts calculated a plane at normal cruising height could be seen by every native within 400 square miles. Later reports said that extensive experience proved any native who saw a plane anywhere in the sky believed it was 'looking directly at him'.[17] If air patrols failed to prevent unrest, the paper continued, bombers could strike within hours and squash any trouble at minimal risk and cost before it spread. There might be a need for massive bombing 'day after day and week after week, without intermission'[18] to break the will of some of the most fierce tribes at the outset, the theorists said, but after that they would never again dare challenge British authority. It stated:

> The Air Staff are convinced that strong and continuous action of this kind must in time inevitably compel the submission of the most recalcitrant tribes ... With certain stubborn races time is essential to prove to them the futility of resistance to aerial attack ... but it is held that the dislocation of living conditions and the material destruction caused by heavy and persistent aerial action must infallibly achieve the desired result.[19]

Best of all, the tribes would be defenceless with no way to hit back against aircraft, ending the heavy casualties British forces suffered in colonial campaigns.

Trenchard's plan to hold Mesopotamia called for a force of ten squadrons or about 100 planes operating from bases at Baghdad in the centre of the country, Mosul in the north and Basra in the south. They would be linked by a network of auxiliary landing strips dotted all around the country. There would be just 350 RAF officers and 3,100 other ranks, plus a small land force of native troops. Churchill bombarded his Cabinet colleagues with memos praising the plan and urging its acceptance. He unleashed all of his rhetorical powers in a May note, attacking the extravagance of the army administration in Mesopotamia:

> The result of this vicious system is that a score of mud villages, sandwiched in between a swampy river and a blistering desert, inhabited by a few hundred half naked native families, usually starving, are now occupied [by] garrisons on a scale which in India would maintain order in wealthy provinces of millions of people. To hold these worthless villages, sums are being spent varying from £200,000 to £1,000,000 a year.[20]

Mesopotamia would never be able to pay its way, Churchill said, and putting the cost on British taxpayers would expose the government to public anger. Only air power could halt this insane waste of money and control the country. Equally important, he told a fellow minister, was that it would 'give the Air Force that share of real work in time of peace which is so essential to its well-being'.[21]

But Churchill's enthusiasm failed to move most of his Cabinet colleagues. Many ministers thought the idea of replacing 100,000 troops with a few aeroplanes was mad and dangerous. There were mutterings about Winston's latest madcap scheme. Officials in Mesopotamia chimed in with warnings against betting everything on the RAF, and the unproven capacity of aircraft to control an entire country. Wilson and the army high command mocked what they portrayed as a scheme for a few mechanics and native troops to hold down a whole country. 'I do not believe in Winston's ardent hope of being able to govern Mesopotamia with hot air, aeroplanes and Arabs,' Wilson wrote.[22]

Churchill's plan seemed to have stalled when Mesopotamia exploded in a massive anti-British revolt. Complacent British officials believed they had established peace and order across Mesopotamia by the spring of 1920. 'The first impression one gains on a visit to Mesopotamia is that the countryside is remarkably quiet,' wrote a visiting official on the eve of the uprising.[23] What the British viewed as their own benevolent administration was seen by Arab nationalists, Shia religious leaders, Kurdish chiefs and others as foreign oppression. 'The Pax Britannica and level justice made no appeal,' said a bewildered British functionary, as large parts of the country rose up that summer to drive the British out.[24]

British forces almost collapsed despite fielding thirty infantry battalions, five cavalry regiments, eighteen artillery batteries and two RAF squadrons. Most units were short of men or filled with half-trained young recruits; many formations were scattered around Iraq in tiny detachments, and some of the best units were fighting Bolshevik forces in Persia and southern Russia as part of the Russian Civil War. Life for the soldiers was unremittingly bleak, and morale was low; there were endless complaints about the food. 'Lads whose idea of dinner heretofore had been of roast beef, Yorkshire pudding and potatoes had to learn to eat and like curry and rice. There were no potatoes at all,' said one RAF officer.[25]

A disastrous string of British defeats and disasters marked the start of the uprising. The army's habitual haughtiness was replaced by nervous talk of abandoning the territory and a fighting retreat to the sea. The revolt began when a British official arrested a sheikh at Rumaithah in June for failing to repay an agricultural loan. He was forcibly freed from the town jail by his tribesmen. Two Indian infantry companies, sent to punish this assault on British authority, were routed by thousands of well-armed Arabs, and forty-eight soldiers were killed and more than 160 wounded. What was left of the force barricaded itself in several buildings. A rescue column of two infantry battalions was chased off by the insurgents, with the loss of another fifty dead and close to 200 wounded.

Air power was vital in helping the British forces hold on in the first chaotic weeks of the uprising. Planes aided the trapped army force at Rumaithah with low-level attacks against the encircling insurgents. Flight crews dropped provisions to the detachment as its supplies ran low. Wooden boxes crammed with food, cigarettes and medicine were tossed out as the planes swooped at 50ft over the army perimeter. Many of the loads fell short, and one box killed an Indian NCO (non-commissioned officer) and injured another man.[26] Eventually, a second relief force battered its way past the insurgents to extract the besieged survivors and hurriedly retire.

The small RAF contingent paid little attention to the revolt at first. Squadron Leader E. Brewerton was more worried about where he could get his tennis racket repaired, but thought it might be a chance for some shooting. 'Arabs in state of unrest. Trouble expected, so shall do lots of flying,' he noted with satisfaction in his diary.[27] The air force bombed dozens of towns, villages and other targets in the coming weeks. Squadron Leader G.C. Pirie said that there were few restrictions on the bombing as isolated British units and bases around the country faced being overwhelmed. A Bristol Fighter pilot of 6 Squadron said in a letter home:

> We have been going in for massed raids lately and it is the thing to do. We, No 6, have had on two occasions 11 B.Fs [out of 12] out in formation on bombing, with excellent results, and G.H.Q. realise how futile it is sending the odd machine out to bomb a tribe.[28]

Bombing techniques were adapted and honed as pilots learned to pursue groups of mounted insurgents or how to winkle out gunmen hiding in palm groves. Planes generally carried 20lb bombs, the smallest in their arsenal, because they proved the most effective against people and light shelters or huts. Incendiary bombs were used to attack villages. Tins of petrol were dropped to accelerate blazes started by incendiaries.[29]

Crews flew missions from before dawn and until well past dusk as the situation worsened. A pilot of 6 Squadron wrote home of exhausting sixteen hour days filled with dodging the dual dangers of enemy fire and sandstorms. To increase their operational range, pilots flew out each morning from the main airbases to unmanned desert airstrips, where they had to single-handedly fuel their planes and fill the wing racks with bombs from supply dumps, a routine repeated several times a day:

I think the first ten days were the most arduous days I've ever spent in my life. We were up on eight of them before dawn, off to Diwaniyah where we had to fill up [with fuel] ourselves – no joke on a B.F. [Bristol fighter] – then bombing of the Diwaniyah-Samawah area, landed at Samawah, again filled up by ourselves, bombed by ourselves, left again, bombed the same area again and landed Diwaniyah to fill up and back to Baghdad. You can just imagine doing that with machines that boiled except the greatest attention was continuously paid to speed and climb, with shaded temperature 115 degrees, usually a sand storm blowing, and then filling up in the wind, spitting petrol all over one and that did burn, and no food all day.[30]

Pilots used scraps of chamois leather to strain dirt, rust and water from contaminated fuel that had been sitting in metal drums at the desert airstrips sometimes for many months. An abiding memory was of being stung by the fuel as it splattered on their bare skin.

An attempt to contain the unrest by sending out ground columns to overawe key districts led to a new disaster. A force that set out on 23 July from Hillah was made up of an English infantry unit, the 2nd Manchester Regiment, Indian cavalry of the 35th Scinde Horse, and artillery. The mostly inexperienced and not very fit English infantry were shattered by heat and thirst as the column blundered into a region swarming with insurgents. The commander ordered the column to camp, only to decide a few hours later to retreat despite the onset of night. Nervous transport animals pulling heavy wagons and carts stampeded and plunged into the shambling ranks of exhausted troops. Hundreds of local tribesmen, who had been lingering in the dark, took advantage of the confusion to rush in and slash at the soldiers with daggers and knives, slitting open torsos and severing throats. Only charges by the cavalry and point-blank artillery fire avoided the column's annihilation. At least 338 men, mostly of the Manchesters, were dead or missing by dawn.

British control collapsed in many regions as tens of thousands of Arabs, heartened by the insurgency's successes, joined the uprising; the insurgents would field 130,000 fighters at the height of the rising. Indian and British units were cut off in some of the larger towns or abandoned them to avoid being overwhelmed. A retreating force of seven infantry battalions, hobbled by a train crammed with civilians, was only able to move a few miles a day as it battled its way through insurgent-held territory from Diwaniyah to Hillah.

It had to stop every few miles to repair the railway track that had been ripped up by insurgents. RAF formations bombed and burned villages near the rail line to hold back enemy gunmen.

The British even suffered setbacks on the rivers, despite their monopoly on gunboats. One vessel, the *Firefly*, was sunk by insurgent fire at Kufah on the Euphrates and two planes were shot down trying to drop supplies to the crew. One of the most celebrated episodes of the campaign involved its sister ship, *Greenfly*, which held out for almost eight weeks after running aground on 10 August at Khidr on the Euphrates. Crewmen surrounded by Arab gunmen were cooped up inside the iron hulk in blistering heat with only muddy river water to drink. Food was dropped by the RAF until a plane was shot down; the two crewmen survived the crash only to be killed as they climbed from the wreckage. The supply flights were ended to prevent further losses of valuable aircraft. A relief force that finally reached the gunboat found only a filth-smeared hulk, and the bullet-riddled corpse of one of the officers.

It was a miserable war for the troops even by the grim standards of colonial conflicts. Most of the fighting was at the height of summer when temperatures could reach 130°F in the military's canvas tents. 'When God created hell he thought it was not bad enough,' an old Arab proverb said, 'so he made Mesopotamia and added flies.' Each soldier and airman felt he was followed by his own swarm of the buzzing insects that covered any exposed bit of skin, and crawled into nostrils, mouths and eyes. Worst of all were the voracious sandflies that covered men's bodies with the red swellings of their maddening bites, and made it almost impossible to sleep. Exhausted men doused themselves with kerosene, which alone repelled the hungry insects, so that they could sleep. Kerosene became priceless to exhausted soldiers desperate for a few hours of rest. Thousands of men were stricken by sandfly fever that inflamed the liver and caused ferocious temperatures and pain. More than 100 men of 6 Squadron were hospitalised with sandfly fever within days of the unit's arrival in the country.

General Aylmer Haldane, head of the Mesopotamian Army, feared that Baghdad, with its vast supply dumps and hundreds of British women and children, would be overrun by the insurgents. Army units were pulled back from outlying regions to protect the capital and forestall an uprising by the city's 200,000 inhabitants. A 16-mile perimeter, studded with forty double-storey brick blockhouses, was hastily built around the main British base and airfield. Indian coolies were given rifles and turned into temporary soldiers. Haldane, haunted by the fear that he might go down as the general who suffered the worst defeat at the hands of a native army in British history, pleaded for reinforcements. Two divisions of Indian and British troops were dispatched as London and Delhi glumly watched the floundering situation in Iraq.

Haldane was so worried that on 18 August he asked the War Office for permission to use chemical weapons. Ensuing events have led to a sort of historical urban legend that Britain employed poison gas in Iraq decades before Saddam Hussein's use of chemical weapons against the Kurds. A year before the revolt, RAF commanders in Mesopotamia had proposed using gas 'against recalcitrant Arabs as an experiment',[31] only to be told that the Air Ministry had yet to develop a chemical aerial bomb. Trenchard said, after Haldane's request arrived in London, that the RAF had since experimented with porcelain gas bombs, but no operational versions were available.

Unperturbed by such mere details, Churchill gave Haldane permission to use gas: the secretary of war had derided what he saw as the public's illogical squeamishness over chemical weapons. It then turned out that the British forces in Mesopotamia did not possess any of the gas-filled artillery shells that were the only chemical weapon then available. Haldane asked for 15,000 shells from the army's stocks in Egypt, but these were filled with non-lethal tear gas. Some historians assert the shells were used against the insurgents, while others say there is no conclusive evidence.[32] The legend that British forces used chemical weapons has persisted ever since, despite the lack of any proof that lethal gas or other agents were employed.

British fortunes reached their nadir in the second week of August. It was, a petulant Haldane thought, '... almost [enough] to make one feel that the gods were not fighting on our side'.[33] The tattered British garrisons held on, however, and a quickening flow of reinforcements, including RAF units from the occupation force in Germany, enabled the British to take the offensive in September. The insurgents' lack of unity and failure to form a single force allowed the British to gain the initiative over the next few weeks and months by attacking the rebel bands one by one.

Aircraft, which had been pivotal in staving off disaster in the early days of the revolt, now spearheaded the British counter-offensive. Insurgent forces were chased and broken up by sustained low-level air attacks. Kufah, where 800 encircled British troops had held out for ninety days, was relieved in late October. Bombers swooped in above the relief force to strafe and scatter 2,000 Arab riflemen concealed in dense palm thickets around the city. Karbala, a key centre of the rising, was taken next. An Indian Army garrison at Samawah was relieved in mid-October, after a column of five battalions of infantry with air cover took fourteen days to fight its way across country to the city. Hounded by British ground and air attacks and bereft of supplies, the last bands of insurgents were crushed.

Pilots now had plenty of easy targets as the demoralised Arab formations fell apart. Brewerton, who occasionally filled in as an air gunner when his own plane was unavailable, laconically wrote in his diary, 'I got in some good shooting from 1,500ft. Arab bullet struck our air speed indicator and the glass cut Culley's wrist and arm.'[34] It was a cruel war with little mercy on either side; the skulls of seventeen Gurkha soldiers were found displayed in a row in one insurgent village.

Despite its domination of the battlefield, the RAF suffered significant losses from enemy fire. A single rifle shot could disable an engine or some other vital component, and crews were especially vulnerable to ground fire when they made low-level bombing and strafing runs. Ten pilots and observers were killed and seven wounded, mostly by ground fire. Almost every plane that saw action was hit; eleven planes were shot down and fifty-seven others were so badly damaged they had to be scrapped.

Every effort was made to rescue flyers who went down in enemy territory. Groom was picked up by another plane that landed when his DH9A was forced down by engine problems. He sat on top of the observer in the second cockpit while his pilot clung to the wing as Arab horsemen tried to overtake the overloaded plane as it lumbered across the sand and clawed its way into the sky. It was only when they got back to base that they realised the plane was still carrying sixteen bombs, and it was a miracle it had not crashed.[35]

Lurid tales of the castration that supposedly awaited captured airmen at the hands of Arab women were a staple of gossip in RAF messes and canteens. The anthem of 55 Squadron included the chorus:

No balls at all, no balls at all,
If your engine cuts out,
You'll have no balls at all.[36]

There are no indications that any flyers suffered such a fate, despite plenty of squadron legends to the contrary, and several captured airmen were returned safely by tribal leaders. Flying Officers Gardiner and Herbert, forced down after a 14 July bombing raid, said they were attacked by Arab women who tried to throttle them. A sheikh rescued the pair and sent them to a British unit with their weapons and belongings.

Crews carried cards with Arabic script that promised large rewards for their safe return – flyers called them 'blood chits' or, in a macabre joke about castration, 'gooly chits'. Flying Officers G.R. Gowler and H.G.W. Locke, forced down in October, showed their captors a card promising the huge sum of £500 for their safe return, but it did little good. They were tied to a horse, dragged through camel thorn and then taken to a village where men hit them with rifles and prodded them with knives as women and children spat in their faces. A sheikh later got them to safety. No one pointed out that the chits were likely to be of limited value in territories where virtually everyone was illiterate.[37]

The revolt shook the British Empire's aura of invincibility across the Middle East; the mighty British Army had been routed by poorly armed Arabs, and captured British soldiers marched naked through insurgent areas in front of jeering crowds. The British administration, shocked at how close the rebellion came to driving it out of Iraq, unleashed brutal reprisals. Collective punishments and fines were imposed on the tribes and towns that backed the uprising. British columns demolished and burned villages, water supplies and irrigation channels were blocked up and food, livestock and other possessions confiscated.

Troops ordered to demolish mud homes were told to remove the wooden frames so the structures could not be rebuilt because timber was almost priceless in the mostly treeless regions. Column commanders were instructed to leave the people with nothing. 'Villages will be razed to the ground … efforts to carry out cultivation will be interfered with … the area being cleared of the necessaries of life,' read orders to one column.[38] Aircraft bombed and strafed villages as part of the reprisals. Troops would surround insurgent villages at night so nobody could escape, and aircraft would bomb the houses at dawn. Brewerton wrote in his diary, 'Clearing up after the war. Lot of villages being burned for reprisals. The Army have taken a firm hand with the Arabs. Killing them off and burning their villages.'[39]

With the revolt crushed, London was again confronted with the question of what to do with this hostile land. Haldane said it would take thirty-three infantry battalions and six cavalry regiments to control Iraq. It was an unthinkable commitment, financially and politically, even to those who believed that Britain had to stay. Air power seemed the only feasible solution and leading civilian and military officials in the territory agreed that aircraft had broken the revolt. Arnold Wilson, the chief British representative in Baghdad, wrote, 'Aeroplanes have been the saving of us. Without them

I really believe we should have been out of Baghdad by now.'[40] The army was outraged, but the generals had made too many empty promises, and the government was coming round to Churchill's and Trenchard's claim that air power was the solution to the empire's military problems.

7

'EVERYBODY MIDDLE EAST IS HERE'

Throngs of protesters, police and the merely curious crowded Cairo's main railway station in March 1921 to greet Winston Churchill as the new secretary of state for the colonies arrived in the Egyptian capital. Worried about anti-British protests, officials had ringed the building with police. Local newspaper accounts claimed later that RAF bombers had circled high over the station in case the authorities lost control. Churchill and his party alighted at a stop on the city outskirts to forestall any disagreeable scenes. The jostling crowds at the station only got a glimpse of the minister's hat boxes and luggage being unloaded when the train pulled in.

Virtually every senior British diplomat, administrator and general in the Middle East had been summoned to Cairo for a conference on the future of the Ottoman territories now held by Britain. T.E. Lawrence was among the entourage of advisers who accompanied Churchill from London. 'Everybody Middle East is here,' he quipped.[1] Lawrence's admiration for the RAF bordered on hero worship. He was enthralled by the power and romance of aircraft, and likened the conquest of the sky to the challenge of mastering the desert. Also in Churchill's delegation was Trenchard, as awkward and truculent as ever, to help make the case for Air Control.

In moving to the Colonial Office from the War Office at the start of the year, Churchill told the prime minister that his biggest challenge would be 'the burden & the odium of the Mesopotamia entanglement'.[2] He was determined to find a way for Britain to keep the territory on at an acceptable price. The Arab revolt had provoked a backlash in Britain, where opposition politicians and large sections of the press were denouncing the enormous costs of holding on to what they saw as a patch of waste ground.

Churchill's first impulse had been to tour Mesopotamia to see the situation first hand, and he asked for advice on suitable clothing for the trip. Officials were horrified at the idea of the notoriously energetic Churchill roaming around the country, talking to whomever he liked and stirring up pandemonium. They were not much happier when he changed his mind and called for a grand conference in Cairo. The meeting would also try to resolve the future of Palestine, where British promises of a Jewish homeland had angered the Arabs, and consider what to do with neighbouring Transjordan. Churchill hoped there would be time to do some painting in between the political manoeuvring – he had packed plenty of yellow, purple and crimson paint to capture desert scenes.

Churchill had come to the conclusion that Britain's ascendancy in the Middle East could only be maintained by setting up closely controlled client states backed by a force of British aircraft and locally recruited levies or troops. Now he had to wring backing for the plan from the largely conservative officials and generals who ran British interests in the region. Churchill's febrile imagination was bursting with schemes to police the Middle East. His more pragmatic notions included creating an Arab army with white officers to replace regular British and Indian units in Mesopotamia. Less promising was a plan for a force of 2,000 white police officers who, like the famed Mounties of Canada, would roam the desert keeping order. Colonial officials were aghast at this idea of non-Arabic speaking whites with no experience of the region blundering around the wastes alone or in small patrols. A committee buried the plan by concluding that it would only attract criminals and drunks, 'This would tend to depreciate the general prestige of the white man, and the loss of such prestige would have consequences of the gravest situation.'[3]

Churchill and the other conferees gathered at the Semiramis Hotel in Cairo, a flamboyant outcrop of marble and gleaming metal work that was a favourite spot for wealthy Westerners. Lawrence, ever the rebel, said its garish opulence made him feel like a Bolshevik. Work started on 12 March, with Churchill stating that two-thirds of the existing British military forces in Mesopotamia would be withdrawn within a year, and that a pragmatic, inexpensive alternative must be found if Britain was to remain in the country. Committees were set up to consider the political and military future of Mesopotamia, and Churchill, who had already decided on the outcome, alternately wooed and harried the mostly bemused or hostile conferees.

It was accepted that an Arab regime of some kind must be set up if Mesopotamia was ever going to be stable. London had agreed to guide the future Iraq to independence under the League of Nations' mandate, but it wanted a government that would be tied to British interests even when formal controls ended, and it wanted it at minimal expense to the British taxpayers. Churchill favoured something modelled on the lines of the princely states of India – ostensibly independent native entities run from behind the scenes by British officials.

The general consensus in Cairo was for an Arab monarchy with British officials in charge behind the throne. As to who should sit on this new throne, Feisal, eldest son of the Sharif of Mecca, was the most acceptable candidate. The sharif and his sons had led the pro-British Arab Revolt against the Turks during the First World War, but their hopes of ruling Syria were dashed after London let France take the country. Britain now proposed making Feisal King of Mesopotamia, and putting his brother Abdullah on the throne of a separate kingdom in Transjordan. It was seen as a way to stabilise the region under dependent and conservative governments, as well as going some way to making up for broken British commitments to its wartime Arab allies.

An agreement on the military question, especially replacing the large army garrison with air units, proved more difficult to reach. Everyone accepted that the new Iraqi monarchy would be weak for some time, and that British forces of some kind would be needed to prop it up and protect London's interests. Trenchard said it could all be done with six of his squadrons, a few RAF armoured car companies and a force of local levies or troops – the original plan for ten squadrons had been trimmed to save money.

He presented an almost idyllic picture of how the air force would control the country. As well as regular patrols to demonstrate the government's power and forestall trouble, flight crews would fly into remote areas, sometimes with a local political officer, to meet the chiefs and gauge their mood for any signs of discontent. Errant chiefs might be flown down to Baghdad for a fatherly talk or a dressing down. If there was unrest, the patrols would pick up early signs long before it became serious. If the levies could not handle the situation, air patrols would stage demonstrations over villages and attack if the inhabitants did not submit. Trenchard explained:

> The air scheme is based on the principle that if the Arabs have nothing to fight against on the ground and no loot or rifles to be obtained and nobody to kill, but would have to deal only with aeroplanes which are out of their reach, they

are certain to come in and there will be no risk of disasters or heavy casualties such as are always suffered by small infantry patrols in uncivilised countries.[4]

He insisted an RAF force of just 1,400 men could handle any foreseeable threat. Even if the levies mutinied, always a risk with native troops, Trenchard said that the RAF would be able to defend the airfields and hold out until reinforcements were flown in.

Trenchard's confident assertion that a handful of aeroplanes and a few hundred pilots and mechanics could do what the army had failed to achieve with 100,000 soldiers received a glacial response from the generals. Nor did it go down well with the political officials when he summoned up visions of fresh-faced young pilots hopping out of their planes and deftly defusing tensions with a few cheerful words to grizzled tribal chiefs. Others, who suspected the RAF would do more bombing than talking, were not happy with the idea of incinerating villages the British were ostensibly shepherding to civilisation.

Some of the generals argued it was madness to denude Mesopotamia of white troops, although their case was not helped when one senior officer argued there would be health risks if Indians or Arabs replaced European personnel in military kitchens. Churchill brushed aside the soldiers' opposition by saying the only choice was abandoning Mesopotamia or handing it to the air force. He knew his audience would see leaving the territory as a shameful retreat and loss of British prestige which they could never stomach.

A turning point came when some of the army men conceded the Air Control plan might have benefits for the entire empire if it allowed the RAF to develop tactics for future wars. It was also decided, in a concession to the sceptics, that a brigade of British or Indian infantry would be retained as insurance. And with that, a grudging acceptance of Air Control was prised from the conference. Churchill asked Trenchard if the RAF would take over Mesopotamia's defence at once. It was now Trenchard's turn to protest, saying the RAF would need a year to prepare for the task.

★★★

There were more victories for the airmen when it was decided Palestine and the neighbouring Arab kingdom of Transjordan would also fall under the RAF's command. Lawrence left with an RAF flight on a visit to Amman soon after the conference to show backing for the newly anointed King Abdullah, who had been clamouring for British air support. 'Abdulla[h] had been long-ing for aeroplanes, and gave us a great reception and a large lunch,' Lawrence reported back.[5]

There was time in Cairo to make a trip by camel out to the pyramids, where press photographers were waiting, followed by a last-minute panic over the hotel bill. Churchill sent a telegram to the Treasury, which appar-ently had raised questions about the cost, to defend the choice of a luxury hotel for the conference as necessary for security reasons. He denied a report that the hotel had hiked its rates, and defended his use of a suite at a cost of £11 a day on the grounds he worked Sundays. Attendees, he said, would pay for their own wine, spirits and cigars. With that, he asked if money could be wired immediately to settle the bill and allow the guests to depart.[6]

Churchill still needed the approval of the Cabinet to transform Britain's control of the Middle Eastern territories and implement Air Control. The army, alarmed at how things had gone in Cairo, renewed its campaign to break up the air force. Wilson venomously denounced Churchill, predicting the whole scheme would fall apart, and the hapless politician would only be able to '... hop into an aeroplane and fly away, shouting Ta-ta to any poor bloody native who is stupid enough to back us'.[7]

A note by the army General Staff warned that the RAF bases in Mesopotamia would be surrounded and cut off as soon as the army was with-drawn, and Britain would face another disaster like Gordon at Khartoum.[8] The army campaign to block the RAF was led by the secretary of state for war, Laming Worthington-Evans, an earnest man who was quietly derided with the nickname of 'Worthy'. He said RAF plans for armoured cars and gunboats were a cover to construct a private army and navy. Worthy also tried to blacken the RAF as immoral killers, accusing the airmen of murdering women and children:

> The only weapons which can be used by the Air Force are bombs and machine guns. I have no doubt that in case of attack the Air Force could defend themselves by these means; but the forces in Mesopotamia are intended to keep order and gradually to reconcile hostile tribes to civilized rule. Punitive measures may have to be taken against disturbances of the peace; the only means at the disposal of the Air Force, and means now in fact used, are the bombing of women and children in the villages. If the Arab population realize that the peaceful control of Mesopotamia ultimately depends on our inten-tion of bombing women and children, I am very doubtful if we shall gain

that acquiescence of the fathers and husbands of Mesopotamia as a whole to which the Secretary of State for the Colonies looks forward.[9]

It was the start of one of the more ugly phases of the feud between the army and the RAF. Infuriated RAF commanders responded that the army was never troubled about blowing helpless civilians to pieces with high power artillery each time it shelled a frontier village. The Foreign Office insisted British dominance in the Middle East must not be given up, however, and generally backed Churchill. Still, Lord Curzon, now foreign secretary, was unhappy about the idea of youthful pilots holding talks with tribal chiefs. 'An aviator must necessarily be a young man and it did not follow that he would necessarily be the best person to conciliate tribesmen,' he said.[10]

Army and navy efforts to break up the RAF, meanwhile, led the Cabinet to authorise a review in the summer of 1921 by former prime minister, Arthur Balfour, on the whole issue of air power and military co-operation. For two months he listened to presentations from the three services before deciding there was a strong case for an independent air force. He even said the RAF would be the dominant wing in some campaigns, such as defending Britain against air attack, with the older services taking a subordinate role. Trenchard handled such challenges adroitly, always trying to work with investigating bodies; he answered their questions methodically and patiently, working his small staff overtime to provide facts and figures to back the RAF's case and undermine the claims of the other services, who were often far less well prepared.

Trenchard was equally successful when a committee was set up under Sir Eric Geddes in the autumn of 1921 to prune government expenditure. The country was caught in recession and there were widespread demands for cuts in government spending. The committee, popularly dubbed the 'Geddes axe', made the three armed services one of its first targets. A despairing Wilson said the reductions would be the kiss of death for the British Empire, and the army fought the committee at every turn.

Trenchard was more subtle and pragmatic. He spent many hours explaining the value and versatility of air power to the committee, backing up his arguments with detailed figures that were the language many civil servants understood best. Wilson, as vituperative as usual, made little effort to hide his contempt for the committee and what he saw as ignorant civilians prying into military affairs. He demanded the RAF be scrapped and its planes divided between the army and the navy.

Arguing every point and backing up his case with meticulous details and figures, Trenchard persuaded the Geddes committee that returning the air role to the army and the navy would create two air services with massive and expensive duplication. He did his job so well that Geddes ended up championing the air force, stating, 'It can no longer be denied that by the intelligent application of air power it is possible to utilise machinery in substitution for, and not as a mere addition to, man power.'[11] The RAF had to accept cuts, but its share of the reductions was less painful than the army's, which lost twenty-two infantry battalions and eight cavalry regiments.[12]

Churchill, meanwhile, had brought the case for Air Control before the full Cabinet in August for a final decision. He said the existing Mesopotamia garrison would be reduced to eight or nine British and Indian infantry battalions by the end of the year, with the RAF taking over full control in October 1922. Worthington-Evans made a final, half-hearted effort to scuttle the scheme, repeating the old arguments that aircraft alone could never hold a country. Political and financial reality, however, were against the army and its allies – the government did not have the money or the men to hold down half of the Middle East. The Cabinet agreed that if Britain wanted to control the region it would have to be through client Arab regimes and British air power. Churchill subsequently told Parliament in March 1922 that Britain would hold the Middle East by 'control from the air'.[13]

Churchill and Trenchard had won; now the RAF had to prove that it could do all they had promised.

8

A NEW PLANET

Gertrude Bell wrote home in the autumn of 1922 about the newest member of Baghdad's little British community. It took a great deal to impress this extraordinary diplomat, explorer and archaeologist, who spent her days shaping the future of the Middle East over tea with Arab princes and British statesmen, but Bell was almost breathless as she scribbled her first impressions of the man she was convinced would transform Iraq:

> A new planet has arisen in the shape of Sir John Salmond, Air Marshal, who takes over command of all British forces on October 1st ... He is alert, forcible, amazingly quick in the uptake, a man who means to understand the Iraq and our dealings with its people.[1]

Trenchard knew that proving Air Control would work in Iraq was vital to his force's future. The army and the navy and their civilian supporters were determined to break up the RAF, whatever the rulings of Geddes and other mere politicians. A worried Trenchard wrote on the eve of Salmond's arrival in Iraq that the RAF must keep its promise of holding down the country effectively, and above all, cheaply, 'The future of the Royal Air Force itself is bound to be affected, either favourably or otherwise, by the success or failure achieved in Mesopotamia ... the keynote of the scheme is economy.'[2]

Trenchard needed the RAF's best commander for this first, crucial test of employing air power to police a country, and there was wide agreement within the service that Salmond was the obvious candidate. Salmond was, in many ways, the opposite of his superior and mentor. He was lithe, cheery and charismatic where Trenchard was gangling, aloof and dour, and yet their experiences and thinking uncannily mirrored and complemented each other. The two men were determined to save a force that they both loved and saw as essential for the security of Britain and the empire. Many RAF pioneers later agreed that Salmond was almost as vital as Trenchard in ensuring the force's survival in those early years.

There were striking similarities in the two men's early lives. Born in 1881, Salmond, like Trenchard, had been an indifferent student as a boy and struggled to pass the army entrance exam, getting into Sandhurst on the second try in 1900; both came from families that were not well off; they forgot their troubles as young subalterns by playing polo and supplemented their meagre pay with a little horse trading; and both served in the Boer War, and then the West African Frontier Force. But where Trenchard spent years as an obscure and awkward junior officer, Salmond was liked and admired, and his early career was much smoother with rapid promotion.

Salmond loved West Africa, where he arrived in 1903, although the 22-year-old was shocked by the harsher aspects of British rule, including punitive missions against hostile tribes when he helped burn villages and watched a superior officer flog Africans. Alone at the head of a small detachment of black troops, he depended on his much older African sergeant major for advice and support. Salmond noted one day that the NCO had more than the two wives permitted under British regulations, only to be told the other women were the man's 'sisters'. Wisely, the probably virginal Salmond let the matter drop. Recurrent fevers forced Salmond to leave Nigeria after just a few months.

Flying caught Salmond's imagination several years later while he was serving as an infantry officer in England. He earned a pilot's licence in 1912, making his first solo flight after a single lesson on the ground when an instructor merely pointed out the controls and their functions. Salmond enlisted in the RFC and soon set a British record for high-altitude flying.

His career soared with the coming of the First World War. A major at the start of the conflict, he was a brigadier general by 1916, rising to major general the following year when he replaced Trenchard as chief of the RFC on the Western Front. Salmond showed a bravery and selflessness that won the hearts of those he commanded. In one telling incident, a bomb being loaded onto a stationary plane fell off and exploded, killing the pilot and eleven other men. Salmond sent everyone away except for a single sergeant, and together they cleaned up the mangled body parts, washed away the blood and defused several unexploded bombs.

Salmond was just 41 when he was named air officer commanding (AOC), in charge of all British forces in Iraq – the first ever such appointment for an airman. The new commander inspired and impressed many with his enthusiasm, confidence and charisma. Sir Henry Dobbs, the head of the British administration, said Salmond helped restore calm after the Arab insurrection. Critics sneered that Salmond was a boy wonder, not overly bright and out of his depth, but he had keen political and diplomatic skills that helped him win friends and allies and best opponents. Salmond was immensely popular with the RAF units in his new command, not least because he had the reputation of leading from the front. The AOC's maroon-coloured DH9A became a familiar sight in the skies above Iraq, and he often accompanied bombing raids. Salmond once rescued a pilot who had to make an emergency landing during a raid, landing on rough terrain and taking off with the retrieved aviator jammed into the second cockpit with the observer. Philip Game, a future air vice marshal, wrote of him, 'He is a real commander and is exempt from petty faults.'[3]

When he took command in Baghdad in the autumn of 1922, Salmond faced the double threats of a looming confrontation with Turkey and widespread internal unrest. Iraq might have a new king and a new name, but it lacked unity and any sense of national identity. Many Iraqis wanted the British to leave and did not support the new monarchy. A resurgent Turkey, meanwhile, was not reconciled to the loss of its former Mesopotamian possessions, especially the northern province of Mosul, and it was sending irregular forces across the border to destabilise the British-backed government.

In Turkey itself, a British force that had been holding Constantinople and the Bosphorus since the end of the First World War came close to clashing with Turkish troops. A ship carrying 1,000 RAF officers and airmen to Iraq was diverted to the city at the height of the 1922 crisis. The young RAF was still little known. After the crisis was defused, the air force contingent marched through the city on the eve of resuming its journey to Iraq. An English woman watching from a balcony was heard to drawl, 'Smart, aren't they? But how in God's name did the Portuguese in those adorable blue uniforms get mixed up in this mess?'[4]

British attempts to stave off the infiltration of Turkish forces in northern Iraq had not gone well before Salmond's arrival. A detachment of Iraqi troops had been trounced in August 1922 by Turkish irregulars and local tribesmen, and an Indian Army relief column was chased off with the humiliating loss of two field guns. Villages and towns fell to the insurgents as Turkish agents spread anti-British propaganda and handed out arms and ammunition to the tribes. Irredentist forces got to within 40 miles of Kirkuk, and British officials had to be evacuated hastily by air from Sulaimaniya. Salmond wrote later, 'Prestige had naturally suffered greatly … our hold over the greater part of Kurdistan … was, to say the least, more than precarious.'[5]

Southern Kurdistan was threatened at the same time by Sheikh Mahmoud, a charismatic leader who wanted to create an independent Kurdistan. Mahmoud was to become an inveterate opponent of the RAF. Pilots ironically referred to the Kurdish chief as the 'RAF Director of Operational Training' because so many of them learned their trade in the campaigns against him. With only limited forces under his command and little support in London, Salmond decided he must first counter the Turkish threat if Iraq was to be held.

The situation in Iraq appeared bleak when its defences were turned over to a tiny air force still less than five years old. The huge army garrison had been run down precipitously after the Cairo conference, and twenty British and Indian army battalions were sent home before Salmond took command. It had been decided eventually to give Salmond eight squadrons to hold Iraq – four equipped with DH9A bombers, two with Vickers Vernon heavy transports, and single squadrons of Snipe and Bristol fighters. He also had a British-officered ground force of 7,000 Arab, Kurdish and Assyrian levies of varying quality and reliability.

An independent Iraqi Army with about 4,000 men was being formed. There would be a residual contingent of nine British and Indian infantry battalions, along with artillery, armoured cars and engineers. Salmond was confident about the ability of his squadrons, but the British-led levies, who would be his main ground force, were of dubious value.

The RAF's first task was to change the way air power was used in Iraq. Aircraft had been frittered away in knee-jerk fashion under the army, with dozens of small, random raids by one or two planes that usually achieved little or nothing. The RAF insisted that air operations had to be part of an overarching air and land strategy; success would come only by hitting targets repeatedly with well-planned and massive bombing raids.

Within days of taking command, Salmond had drawn up plans to counter the threat in the north, and on 30 September the RAF began sustained attacks on the Turkish irregular forces and their tribal allies. Waves of bombers attacked the mountain settlements, smashing homes and driving inhabitants and insurgents into the countryside. The attacks halted the Turkish advance, and there was no resistance when a British political officer and a police detachment occupied the area a short time later. The onset of winter soon brought virtually all fighting to a standstill, and Salmond used the resulting lull to build up the levies and, above all, get them used to working with aircraft for the new type of fighting methods he intended to employ.

Arthur Harris, the future head of RAF Bomber Command who would preside over the destruction of so many German cities in the Second World War, was one of Salmond's young squadron commanders who led the bombing campaign. Harris played a major role in the RAF's interwar colonial campaigns, and his experiences in Iraq and elsewhere did much to inspire his belief that mass bombing could win wars.

A difficult youth, Harris had been sent to Rhodesia in 1908 at the age of 16 by his despairing family, where he tried everything from gold mining to farming. Enlisting in a Rhodesian infantry regiment in 1914 as a bugler, he fought the Germans in Africa before later joining the air force and becoming a pilot. It seemed for a while that the acerbic young airman did not have a future in the peacetime air force; he had been hustled out of India after publicly mocking an army general.

In Iraq he commanded 45 Squadron, which flew unarmed Vickers Vernon biplane troop transports. The Vernons resembled giant, horizontal ice cream cones with the pilot perched in an open cockpit atop the dome-like nose. The engines struggled with Iraq's thin atmosphere, and had to be run at full pitch, turning the cabins into ovens. 'The heat was insufferable and no relief came by opening the windows. The air itself was red hot and the engines were coughing out enough extra heat to scorch the hide off a brass monkey,' said C.H. Keith, an expert on flying in desert regions who never forgot the 'great wicked tongues of vivid blue flame' streaming from exhaust pipes that glowed 'bright cherry red'.[6]

Harris, who thought flying 'flat-footed infantry' around was a waste of time, turned the transports into heavy bombers by fitting improvised bomb racks under the wings and sawing holes in the floor so the crews could aim the projectiles.[7] The planes, capable of carrying much larger bomb loads than the DH9As, were used against the Turkish and Kurdish forces with devastating effect, and Harris boasted in his autobiography that he had devised the first prototype of the heavy bombers the RAF would use in the Second World War.[8]

Turkish guerrillas began crossing into northern Iraq again in the spring of 1923. British Intelligence reported that large contingents of regular Turkish troops were massing near the border to intervene if the British showed any sign of buckling. Salmond decided to put nearly all of his forces into holding the Mosul region, even though it meant leaving virtually nothing to hold the rest of Iraq. A force of 10,000 infantry and cavalry with armoured cars and artillery was centred on Mosul by March, with six RAF squadrons. Salmond insisted that air power was the key to victory – and he later justified his risky strategy by saying it gave him greater firepower and manoeuvrability 'than any Command in small war has hitherto possessed'.[9]

Salmond said the Turk's Kurdish allies would not be able to stand up to air attacks because of 'the weakness of their individual psychology',[10] while the Turks would be hampered by their 'well-known slow habit of mind and movement'.[11] Salmond knew he could not face a full-scale Turkish invasion, however, and contingency plans for a retreat to Baghdad, 'and if necessary straight to Basrah' and the sea,[12] were quietly prepared along with provisions to evacuate 6,000 British civilian personnel by air, something which had never been attempted. The British Government, desperate to avoid full-scale war with Turkey, gloomily read the reports from Iraq and gave Salmond little encouragement or support.

Salmond was certain he could inflict crippling losses on the Turks and their allies with air attacks, but he also had to occupy and hold the land if the authority of the new government was to mean anything. The ensuing campaign, the first time a British colonial force had operated under a large air umbrella, was the start of what would come to be called 'combined operations'; it was also the harbinger of the kind of wars against irregular forces that the West has been waging ever since.

Two ground columns were sent out to take the key town of Rowanduz and pacify the north-east of the country. The first column, named Koicol under Colonel Berkeley Vincent, had three British and Indian infantry battalions while the second column, dubbed Frontiercol under Colonel H.T. Dobbin, consisted of three levy battalions. Each column had an RAF liaison officer and massive radio transmitters that took eight mules to carry when broken down. The columns set out from Mosul in March.

Yet another one of those ironic Arabic proverbs about the most forbidding parts of the Middle East says that Kurdistan is the land forgotten by God. Indian Army officers who had served in the subcontinent's mountain and jungle regions said that it combined the worst aspects of both. Kurdistan's mountains soar to 8,000ft, their sheer slopes made even more treacherous by rain and snow that falls for days at a time. Forests, thick scrub and countless boulders hindered movement and provided perfect cover for snipers and ambushes. Virtually everything the columns needed to live and fight had to be carried by camels and mules or on the soldiers' backs through the narrow valleys, where progress was made even more difficult by rocks and boulders blocking the valley floors, and rapid streams and rivers.

British troops had never entered the region before and the columns lacked maps and guides. The Kurds were natural guerrillas, experts at ambush and lightning attacks: they knew the land intimately and their ability to blend into the landscape helped hide them from air patrols and the ground columns. Incredulous British soldiers said that the enemy were like mountain goats who seemed to run up sheer rock faces. Infantry detachments had to scale every peak to set up pickets to forestall ambushes on the columns, a demand which cut progress to a few miles a day and exhausted the troops. Enemy marksmen shot into the camps at night so that men weary from marching and climbing all day did not get much sleep. Uncertainty and brooding isolation dogged the columns as they advanced into the mountains. The commanders worried about being surrounded, knowing that there was almost no hope of rescue if they were trapped.

Flying in the mountains was difficult and the squadrons providing air cover for the columns had to fly low through the valleys to spot ambushes and protect the ground forces. A little too much pressure on the controls or an error in calculating distances could slam a plane into a sheer wall of rock in the blink of an eye. A pilot flying over this wilderness remembered:

> ... row after row of misty white peaks, looking like sleeping giants; dark deep valleys, whose sides are so sheer that one wonders that even light cares to penetrate into their depths; angry little silver streams, working themselves into white fury as they twist and turn in their relentless quest for the freedom of the sea. [13]

Pilots had no maps or charts and the weather could turn treacherous at any moment with rain, hail or snow blocking out the surrounding heights. Flight crews were shot at by Kurdish riflemen perched on rocks alongside or above them as they flew up the valleys. Spencer Viles, an air gunner, said the roar of the engines meant crews sometimes only knew their plane had been hit when they returned to base and saw the bullet holes in the fuselage. [14] There were rarely any safe places to land if ground fire or mechanical problems forced an aircraft down. Nineteen planes were lost because of weather, enemy fire or mechanical defects, but remarkably none of the crewmen were killed. [15]

Planes wove in and out of the valleys and peaks, bombing enemy posts and keeping watch for insurgent attacks. Bombing and strafing were difficult in the narrow valleys, where the enemy hid amid the rocks, protected by trees, overhanging cliffs and the peaks. Pilots often had to make one or more preliminary runs to determine the best approach before attacking; few planes had aiming devices, and it was all done with swift mental calculations. 'You relied on judgement of speed, angle of descent and drift. It was rather like trying to spear fish in a barrel,' said pilot S.J. Carr.[16]

Two hundred tons of bombs were dropped, mostly old First World War stock that ground crews had to inspect for faults that might cause premature detonations and blow planes to bits. The air cover raised the spirits of the tired British troops as well as providing a decisive advantage over the Kurds. An army report acknowledged:

> When weary infantry are doing a 2,000ft climb it is a blessed relief to them to see an aeroplane fly over the top and over the neighbouring heights and gorges. Though the enemy may be there all the same, invisible from the air, still the presence of planes is a great help.[17]

Pilots' claims that the bombing attacks obliterated targets sometimes turned out to be overly optimistic; inspections of bombed villages showed that the Kurds' rugged stone houses stood up remarkably well to the blasts of the mostly small bombs. 'It must be confessed that though shooting was good the actual damage by the bombs was disappointing,' an RAF report admitted.[18]

The bombing clearly shook the Turkish and Kurdish fighters, nonetheless, and the insurgents began to flee rather than face air attacks. The Kurds' flocks of sheep and goats could not hide from the bombing, and these were attacked to deny food to the villagers and the fighters. One pilot turned this tactic on its head by using bombs and machine gun fire to drive a flock of sheep to a British unit low on food; it was said that it took him an hour of patient shepherding to get his flock home.

The campaign saw some of the first air supply operations in the history of warfare. Generally, items were tossed over the sides of planes without parachutes; many loads were either broken by the fall or strewn across rugged country, forcing troops to spend hours hunting for whatever could be retrieved. More fragile supplies were packed in straw to protect them against the fall, but most items were smashed. A few rudimentary experiments of attaching small parachutes to cargo were more successful. The troops were grateful for the supplies, especially 1,000 pairs of boots, 7,500 pairs of socks and 190 sets of horse and mule shoes.

In another major development, wounded and sick soldiers were evacuated by air on a much more ambitious scale than during the campaign against the Mad Mullah in Somaliland. Scores of wounded and sick men from the two columns were flown out whenever suitable landing spaces could be found. Dysentery was a major problem – 270 British soldiers from Koicol were stricken after drinking from a contaminated stream. The RAF rose to the peculiar challenge of evacuating men who could not control their bowels with a simple improvisation that was primly described in a later report, 'It was found that by covering the body of the machine with a thick layer of grass the patients were made comfortable and the risk of soiling the body of the machine was greatly diminished.'[19]

The campaign saw another first when loudspeakers were fitted to a Vernon transport plane in one of the first attempts at modern psychological warfare.[20] It flew over villages, booming out warnings of imminent bombing and other punishments if the inhabitants did not surrender. A prototype had been tested beforehand at Farnham in southern England to the astonishment of the local rustics.

There was less progress in other areas. Communication with air patrols was spasmodic despite the giant radios accompanying each column. Atmospheric conditions and the mountains often blocked radio signals, and the machines frequently broke down. It was more reliable to dangle messages on a wire stretched between two poles or trees so that planes could swoop down and pluck them with a hook.

Protected by the air shield, the two columns forced their way through the mountains. Koicol took Kok Sanjak and cleared the surrounding area of a large force of Turkish irregulars. A strong tribal force tried to block Frontiercol at the Spillak Pass. Levy infantry, showing new confidence from the knowledge that they could depend on air support, caught the enemy in a pincer attack and cleared the pass. Both columns reached Rowanduz by 22 April, after which most of the Turkish irregulars withdrew across the border.

The success brought by Salmond's determined defence and air power helped convince the Turks that Britain was determined to hold on to Iraq, and Ankara later accepted a League of Nations ruling that Mosul Province belonged to Iraq. Salmond and the RAF had achieved an impressive first victory in Iraq with a fairly small force at a very low cost.

Salmond moved next against Sheikh Mahmoud, after the Kurdish leader ignored an order to come to Baghdad and submit to the new government. A force of British bombers attacked his de facto capital at Sulaimaniya when an ultimatum to surrender went unanswered, destroying a number of public buildings and homes. Koicol took the town in the second half of May and chased the insurgent leader and what was left of his forces into Persia. A chastened Mahmoud was later allowed to return to Iraq on the condition that he stayed out of politics and lived the life of a retired country gentleman. Salmond said the Kurdish leader was a 'man of a most unstable character, and of inordinate vanities and ambitions',[21] and doubted that he was ready to spend the rest of his days gardening.

Mahmoud used a clash between Christian soldiers of the British Levies and Muslim townsfolk in Kirkuk to engineer another uprising. Salmond, employing his now well-honed methods of concentrated air attacks, unleashed a major offensive. Planes from five squadrons dropped 28 tons of bombs in forty-eight hours on Sulaimaniya in July in one of the first saturation bombings of a town.[22] Subsequent reports say nothing about the casualties and damage inflicted by the raid, but British forces faced little or no resistance when they moved in to occupy the town. The Colonial Office, alarmed at reports of the bombing of a large town, asked the RAF for assurances it was 'absolutely necessary for [the] preservation of peace'.[23] The airmen blithely responded that it was quite necessary.

Mahmoud rose again in 1925, 1927 and 1930, despite the growing hopelessness of the Kurdish cause. Air power was instrumental each time in putting down the revolts, although the charismatic Kurdish leader always got away. An RAF report said that Mahmoud's followers pleaded with him at one stage to end the bombing, 'He answered that unfortunately the aircraft had cut his communications with Allah and he could do nothing.'[24]

Finally an RAF formation caught the remnant of the Kurds' mounted forces in the open in the spring of 1931 and attacked it in relays for several hours causing serious losses. It was the end for the old tribal chief. He sent word that he wished to give up, and the Iraqi Government agreed his life would be spared. At a surrender ceremony in the Kurdish hills, Mahmoud, with his usual dramatic flair, won the hearts of the RAF by pointing to the pilot's wings on an air force officer's uniform and declaring, 'You are the people who have destroyed me.'[25]

The campaigns against Mahmoud also saw key developments in aerial operations. Salmond claimed credit for mounting the first major airlift of troops in history when Mahmoud's forces attacked Kirkuk in the autumn of 1922. Some 500 men of the Indian Army's 14th Sikhs were airlifted to the town in the Vernon transports of 45 and 70 Squadrons. The Sikhs, most of whom had never seen a plane, acted as if it was an everyday event. 'This is the first time in history as far as I know that formed bodies of troops have been transferred by air on operations,' Salmond boasted.[26]

A detachment of the Northamptonshire Regiment was airlifted in from Egypt in 1924 to help deal with more unrest in Kirkuk. The regimental band played solemnly as the men filed onto the aircraft. B.G. Amos, one of the soldiers, remembered that the troops were wary, and there was a stunned silence in the cabin when they saw clouds beneath the plane for the first time. He recalled:

> I, personally, shall never forget that tensely dramatic moment, and it is further beyond my power of expression to describe the faces around me, which looked incongruous in a variety of fear, consternation and surprise. However, the procedure was not nearly as horrible as we had expected and the men took it extremely well.[27]

It was a new kind of warfare, and the RAF experimented with everything from the best ways to load troops to providing small disposable cardboard boxes like those carried on ships for seasick passengers. Drawing up the first set of rules on airlifting troops, the RAF made a point of telling the army that it could not bring its beloved horses. 'The movement of troops by aeroplanes will be confined to dismounted personnel,' it stated.[28]

★★★

The RAF's achievements in Iraq were not rewarded with any increase in its funding. Air commanders, alarmed by the loss of nineteen planes in the 1923 operations in Kurdistan, said equipment, especially aeroplane engines, had to be salvaged, even in the middle of a campaign. Staff officers in their London offices drew up strict tables on how long it supposedly took to dismantle an engine from a crashed plane and how many animals were needed to transport it. It was stipulated that an engine from the largest plane, a Vernon, required ten hours to break down and five camels or ten mules to carry; at the other end of the scale it was supposed to take four hours to dismantle the engine of a Snipe fighter and a single camel or three mules to transport the parts.[29]

The men who had to do these tasks, often in the most difficult terrain and weather, and at time under enemy fire, were not impressed.

The RAF's satisfaction in the wake of the Iraq triumph was marred only by Turkish claims that civilians had been murdered and raped. A Turkish statement claimed:

> In southern Kurdistan English ... troops and aerial guns are committing frightful atrocities. It has been noticed in particular that Armenians and Nestorians in British service are violating the honour of all Kurdish women and girls, and are massacring the Kurds and that English aeroplanes are destroying Kurdish crops and villages.[30]

Britain was not used to being criticised by a nation it had long used as a metaphor for sadistic cruelty; the RAF complained that the claims had caused a 'bad impression'.[31]

9

DEATH AND TAXES

H.A. Goldsmith was a British political officer in northern Iraq in the early 1920s who believed that bombing was the only way to impose civilisation on the tribes in the region he administered. 'We are committed to the risk of maintaining law and order among people who understand no other policy than that of the whip',[1] he told his superiors.

Goldsmith's gusto for bombing was marred only by frosty comments from the RAF about his wasteful use of their aircraft. He was enraged after receiving an air force note saying, '… I had bombed Baitwata five times and asking how much longer I intended bombing an empty village'.[2] The RAF agreed that bombing was the best way to civilise 'backward' people, but it insisted air power could not be entrusted to army officers and civilian officials, who used it as a mere adjunct of the ground forces to haphazardly bomb random targets. Air officers denounced such methods as, 'the continuous and promiscuous use of aircraft with no definite policy'[3] that did little damage and just inured the tribesmen to air attacks. Unruly tribes could only be broken by the professional airmen of an independent air force, it was argued. A June 1920 RAF memo stated, 'When air operations are resorted to, they should be carried out in a strength sufficient to inflict severe punishment, and in numbers [of planes] adequate to sustain the attack for as long a period as may be necessary.'[4]

★★★

With the Turkish threat in the north checked, Salmond set out to pacify the vast areas where the government had no control. A spiderweb of airbases, secondary landing strips and aerial patrol routes was set up to cover the entire country. Five of Salmond's eight squadrons were based in and around Baghdad, two at Mosul in the north and one in the south at Shaibah outside Basra. Aircraft criss-crossed the country on routine patrols to awe the population and show that, for the first time ever, the reach of the government extended anywhere and everywhere.

This was the vast flying eye which air strategists claimed would detect any unrest and crush it at birth. Sir Walter Raleigh, the official historian of the RAF, flew in a patrol over the holy Shiite cities of Nejef and Karbala in the south to see how the system worked. He was delighted at the intimidating effect, writing to his wife that people had run in terror as the plane circled over a mosque. 'We would not drop [bombs] on a mosque, but they don't quite know that,' he chortled.[5]

With only a small force to control all of Iraq, Salmond decided to force rebellious districts to their knees one by one with meticulously planned and overpowering attacks. An operation at the end of 1923 in the Samawah area on the Euphrates, some 170 miles south-east of Baghdad, was the testing ground for Air Control methods. The local Beni Huchaim tribes had refused to obey government orders or pay tax since the 1920 insurrection, and the heavily armed tribesmen had easily repulsed the attempts of the Iraqi Army and police to enter their territory.

Baghdad asked the RAF to arrange a 'punitive action'[6] but Salmond wanted the tribes to be given a final warning before authorising air attacks. The tribes were ordered to pay huge sureties or face military action. They refused, as the British had anticipated, and a major air operation, which had been planned weeks before, smoothly unfolded. Three freight trains packed with bombs, incendiary devices, petrol, mechanics and stores arrived at Samawah on 28 November.

Little was known about the tribes' territory so two RAF intelligence officers had toured it weeks earlier to scout the villages and draw up lists of targets. Local chiefs, who seemingly knew what the visitors were doing, entertained and protected them because of strict tribal laws of hospitality. A force of five squadrons began a massive attack on selected villages at dawn on 30 November. Homes, food stores and animal shelters were obliterated with heavy bombs. Incendiary devices tumbled from the sky in the wake of the bombs to start fires in the gutted wooden and straw homes and storehouses.

Low-flying planes chased fleeing people and animals, bowling them over with machine-gun fire.

One of the intelligence officers who had toured the villages was in a plane that dropped a 500lb bomb on the home of one of his recent hosts. There was no let-up in the bombing for two days. The planes were refuelled and rearmed in relays at Samawah to allow continuous bombing, and every weapon in the RAF armoury from 500lb bombs to pocket-size Baby Incendiary Bombs was employed. Night raids ensured the people could not rest or return to their homes to collect food or possessions.

There was virtually no resistance from the stunned population, although the British crews had some unnerving moments. A DH9A of 8 Squadron, flown by Pilot Officer Neville Vincent with Flight Lieutenant J.I.T. Jones as his observer, was forced to make an emergency landing because of a leaking fuel pipe. Two planes landed alongside to extricate them, but Vincent and Jones decided to stay with their aircraft to try to repair the leak. Arab riflemen began shooting at the downed crew as soon as the other planes took off. With remarkable strength, Vincent lifted the tail end of the plane and swung it back and forth for almost an hour as Jones used the machine gun to hold off the tribesmen. Four planes eventually landed and rescued them.[7]

The scale and intensity of the bombing swiftly crushed the terrified and defenceless Arabs. All of the tribes had surrendered by 2 December, with their chiefs coming to the British lines to submit. A subdued gathering of some seventy sheikhs were lectured like errant schoolboys by a British official, who warned them to behave or face more bombing. Mounted police covered by RAF fighters occupied the tribal territory and tore down the village towers and other fortifications.

An official statement on the operation gave few details, saying only that civilian casualties were light, but the RAF estimated at least 144 people had been killed and many more injured,[8] while local press reports hinted at even higher numbers. Salmond's official report claimed the bombing did not cause much damage because most of the targets were 'small and indifferent' hovels.[9] British forces suffered no casualties.

Samawah was hailed as a breakthrough. To the Air Ministry it was a model 'of how air action should be used against uncivilised tribes'.[10] Salmond said it would have taken a division of troops and months of fighting if the operation had been left to the army. A 1924 RAF pamphlet *Iraq*, which was circulated to members of Parliament, included an enthusiastic description by Harris of the new pacification methods:

Whereas a year ago we largely relied on noisy inaccuracy and moral effect, we now cause real casualties, and material damage that produce a real, as opposed to purely moral effect ... Where the Arab and Kurd had just begun to realise that if they could stand a little noise, they could stand bombing, and still argue; they now know what real bombing means, in casualties and damage; they now know that within 45 minutes a full size village ... can be practically wiped out and a third of its inhabitants killed or injured by four or five machines.[11]

British officials in Baghdad were equally ebullient, although the Colonial Office in London worried that press reports on civilian casualties might upset British public opinion and it asked if insurgent areas could be pacified without bombing. Baghdad retorted that such places were islands 'of anarchy' that could only be subdued by the 'terror of the air'.[12]

With his usual keen political sense, Trenchard agreed with worried government officials that public reports on air raids should be purged of details of civilian deaths and other unpleasantness to avoid criticism. He instructed Salmond not to report that tons of bombs were being dropped 'on some little village daily', in case it gave 'a wrong sense of proportion at home'.[13]

Details on casualties and damage inflicted by bombing raids would be omitted or played down in RAF reports throughout the interwar era to deflect criticism and bolster the contention that Air Control was humane because it worked by breaking a tribe's morale rather than their bodies. Civil servants in London were especially keen to remove details on the killing of animals to avoid upsetting a British public that could show more concern for dumb beasts than tribesmen.[14]

The only real restraint on Salmond's squadrons was Trenchard's regular demands to keep costs to a minimum so that the British Government would see what a bargain it was getting with Air Control. Salmond's crews tended to agree: they said there was little point using 500lb bombs because they simply flattened the flimsy native mud and wood homes before exploding; 250lb bombs detonated on contact, doing more damage at half the price.[15] Inexpensive innovation was encouraged. Long before napalm had been thought of, squadrons hurled cans of petrol into villages to stoke fires started by bombs. Four hundred gallons of petrol were dropped during a raid on a Kurdish settlement by nineteen planes in July 1922; a report said the raid had a 'stabilising effect' on the inhabitants.[16]

Most of the rebellious areas had been pacified by 1924, but air raids were used routinely until the early 1930s to suppress challenges to government control. One of the RAF's main roles was forcing tribes to pay tax. Taxation was as much a symbol of submission as a source of revenue; Iraqis, whether rich or poor, traditionally resisted tax because it was seen as yielding to the heavy boot of the state. This prompted British officials and their Iraqi protégés to chase taxes with an energy and efficiency the Turks had never attempted. Haldane, the general in charge during the 1920 insurrection, said colonial officials imported from India had 'a fetish' about meeting tax targets.[17]

Churchill thought it ignoble that British forces were being used to collect taxes for an Arab regime. The *Daily Mail*, a strong critic of the British presence in Iraq, claimed in a 1922 editorial that 'rule by bomb in Mesopotamia has as one of its underlying motives the collection of taxes from turbulent Arabs'.[18] After the RAF took over Iraq, Churchill said using aircraft to make Iraqi peasants pay tax was an outrage. 'Aerial action is a legitimate means of quelling disturbances or enforcing maintenance of order, but it should in no circumstances be employed in support of purely administrative measures such as collection of revenue,' he wrote.[19]

British officials retreated behind a veil of denial and secrecy, insisting throughout the 1920s that the RAF was not being used to force Iraqis to pay tax. 'No bombs have been dropped for any such purpose,'[20] the House of Commons was told in February 1924 in one of several such statements. And yet even a cursory look at RAF records, memoirs and other sources show tribes or regions that refused to pay tax were bombed. S.F. Vincent, the veteran pilot, described taking part in regular tax bombing flights:

> Then we dropped high explosive bombs on the village to break up the roofs and expose the timber underneath the mud covering, and then showered small incendiaries into them to catch afire the rafters and the wood inside the huts. Village after village was destroyed like this until they gave up. I took part in exactly fifty of these bombing raids, and others in the Squadron built the total up to many more.[21]

Richard Brooks, who served with 84 Squadron in Iraq, said his unit was bombing tribes that failed to pay taxes until the end of the 1920s.[22] Some British crews thought the raids were unfair because the people were clearly poor, and bombing grain stocks and destroying homes only made their plight worse and reduced the ability to pay tax.

Even in areas that accepted the government's authority, the RAF gave the people occasional reminders of the penalty for disobedience. A mock village would be constructed on wasteland and then obliterated by bombers as an audience of tribal leaders and other dignitaries watched. A thrilled Gertrude Bell attended one such demonstration:

> They had made an imaginary village about a quarter of a mile from where we sat on the Diala dyke and the first two bombs dropped from 3,000 feet, went straight into the middle of it and set it alight. It was wonderful and horrible. Then they dropped bombs all around it, as if to catch fugitives, and finally fire bombs which even in the brightest sunshine made flares of bright flame in the desert. They burn through metal and water won't extinguish them.[23]

Protests from some government officials and British opposition politicians over the killing of women and children in air policing operations forced the RAF, in the early 1920s, to start dropping warnings before raids. Leaflets in the local language printed on red or white strips of paper were scattered on villages to give the inhabitants a chance to flee. The timing of warnings varied – forty-eight hours became standard, but in the early years it could be as little as thirty minutes.

Air Ministry guidelines stipulated that warnings must explain the reasons for an attack, the time of the raid and sometimes the location of safe areas where people could shelter. The warning system, for all its good intentions, had flaws, not least the fact that very few tribesmen could read, and leaflets tossed out of a speeding aeroplane from 10,000ft could be scattered far from the intended target. Warnings were sometimes ignored by the people on the ground for reasons the RAF could never explain. A squadron sent to bomb an Iraqi village in 1924 said the inhabitants ignored the leaflets, and still did not leave their homes when a patch of nearby waste ground was bombed twice as a further warning before the settlement finally was attacked.[24]

While warnings might have saved lives, they did nothing to lessen the damage to homes and food stores that often meant suffering and death from starvation and exposure. Nor did warnings prevent planes attacking the wrong target, as frequently happened because there were no reliable maps and villages of mud and stone houses nestled on a brown landscape looked much alike from thousands of feet above. The commander of 30 Squadron apologised to his superiors after a mistaken 1925 attack on a village left one person dead and three others wounded. 'The error is deeply regretted as every care is always taken to endeavour to avoid a possible mistake,' he wrote, adding that the 'right' village was bombed later, and all the pilots were struck by how much it resembled the settlement that had been mistakenly attacked.[25]

Flight crews fervently believed that the warnings avoided civilian casualties but put their own lives at risk by alerting the local fighting men of an impending attack. T.C. Traill spoke for most when he said villages were never bombed 'till they had been given enough warning to evacuate women, children and goats and for the men to station themselves on the heights around from which they could get the best shooting at the low-flying aeroplanes'.[26] Planes became increasingly likely to return from raids with bullet holes in their fuselages as some tribesmen and villagers lost their initial dread of raids and tried to fight back. S.J. Carr counted seventy-five holes, including one in the parachute he had sat on, after a single day of operations in Iraq.[27] Still, casualties among aircrew from ground fire were rare, and deaths even rarer.

One way to avoid warning inhabitants of an attack was to classify it as a punishment raid, which were intended to inflict casualties, usually as a reprisal for killing British personnel, and were explicitly exempted from the requirement to drop warnings.

★★★

There were constant efforts to develop and refine Air Control in Iraq. Air force scientists came up with a range of devices for colonial policing, ranging from the visionary to the bizarre. A December 1922 report by the RAF's Operations Branch included some of the first outlines of rockets, napalm and guided weapons; there was also a list of non-lethal devices to cow the natives, such as giant stink bombs. A cover note jokingly referred to the new contraptions as instruments of 'frightfulness', the term used at the time for inhuman forms of warfare and something that the British had always claimed to shun. The report's only reservation was that some of the devices might be too heavy or unstable for aircraft to carry safely, thereby endangering the crews.

One proposal was metal darts – it was calculated that a single plane could drop 10,000 of the razor-sharp projectiles. Another idea was to use crow's feet, the four-pointed metal spikes used since ancient times to maim men and horses. It was calculated that a single plane could drop 25,000 of the devices, and they would cripple livestock and barefooted natives. 'Lying down on the approach of aircraft (to take cover from aircraft) will also be discouraged' in areas that had been littered with the devices, it added.

Noting concern in Britain about growing coastal pollution, it was suggested that oil could be spewed from aerial tankers on ponds and rivers to make the water undrinkable. The Research Department, which actually built new weapons, was not impressed. There was no point in making stink bombs, it said, when planes could drop poison gas; rockets and liquid fire were rejected as too heavy for aircraft to carry; and crow's feet hardly required new research. Poisoning water supplies, stun bombs and gliding bombs received half-hearted nods of approval, but the Research Department was emphatic that bombs, of which the RAF already had an abundance, were the best method. 'To sum up, I am of the opinion that ... high explosive bombs or shrapnel bombs are superior to any other form of frightfulness, except gas,' the research chief wrote.[28]

Undeterred, air strategists continued to advocate the use of chemical weapons. The RAF and the army looked at using poison gas during the interwar era as an agent of imperial control. Churchill was supportive, ridiculing as illogical claims that gas was inhuman. He said in a memo:

> I do not understand this squeamishness about the use of gas ... It is sheer affectation to lacerate a man with the poisonous fragment of a bursting shell and to boggle at making his eyes water by means of lachrymatory gas. I am strongly in favour of using poisoned gas against uncivilized tribes.[29]

The army and the RAF agreed that gas should be used in frontier wars because it was cheap and more humane than conventional weapons like artillery. 'It is essential that we should be able to use gas bombs against savages, etc. if we want to,' an RAF memo argued.[30] Air force researchers favoured highly toxic mustard gas because it was heavy and would saturate the ground, infecting natives with bare feet or open sandals for up to six months. 'I also understand that natives of India or Africa would be liable to be killed off by Mustard Gas more than Europeans would be', because they were physically weaker, the research director told Trenchard.[31] The government was horrified at the idea of employing such a controversial weapon against Britain's colonial subjects and blocked its use.

★★★

Revelations that British planes were bombing villages and tribes in parts of the empire shocked some people in Britain and led to the first questioning and criticism of the RAF's colonial operations. Even the most ardent civilian supporters of air policing were disturbed by some of the reports.

Churchill had been furious when a report crossed his desk in 1921 describing an attack on the encampment of an Iraqi nomadic tribe. Many of the people had run into a lake in a pathetic attempt to hide, only to be trapped, making, as the squadron's subsequent report cheerfully explained, 'a good target for the machine guns'.[32] Churchill told Trenchard he could not believe that British airmen had committed such acts. 'To fire wilfully on women and children taking refuge in a lake is a disgraceful action and I am surprised you do not order the officers responsible for it to be tried by Court Martial,' he said.[33] His complaint appears to have been ignored, and no action was taken.

Questions were raised in Parliament about RAF operations by a handful of opposition Liberal and Labour Party radicals. George Lansbury, an ardent pacifist and future leader of the Labour Party, would be the House of Commons' most persistent critic of air policing. Lansbury denounced the Air Ministry as 'baby killers' long before the term became a cliché. In March 1923 he said:

> I know there is a sort of feeling that a coloured person is of less value than a white person, but I do not think so. I think you are baby killers, and inhuman baby killers, whether you kill a black baby or a white baby, I do not see any difference. I think that one is a crime and the other is a crime.[34]

Lansbury also questioned RAF claims that air policing caused few casualties, shrewdly pointing out that the attacks took place out of sight in mostly inaccessible areas and 'no one but the airmen concerned is ever present to know whether any of the inhabitants have been killed!'[35]

Trenchard and other senior RAF commanders were incensed by the criticism. An RAF riposte, ponderously entitled 'Memorandum by the Air Staff on the Psychological Effects of Air Bombardment on Semi-Civilised Peoples', insisted that the effect of bombing was mainly psychological and casualties were minimal. It claimed it was not immoral to bomb black women and children because native communities saw it 'as a legitimate and proper form of warfare which they dislike for reasons unconnected with its alleged illegality or otherwise'.[36]

Critics of Air Control denounced the annual RAF air shows for the general public at Hendon in north London for staging the bombing of mock native villages, along with the usual fare of acrobatic stunts and fly pasts. Planes would drop bombs and incendiary devices on replicas of native huts, mosques and palaces as thousands of spectators looked on, in what was one of the most popular parts of the shows. The finale of the 1922 show was the destruction of a desert fort defended by airmen masquerading as the

'Wottnott tribe' in native robes with their faces smeared with black boot polish. The would-be tribesmen were withdrawn before the wooden edifice was engulfed by incendiary bombs as the spectators applauded.

Opposition members in Parliament asked if the government was aware that posters advertising the 1927 pageant depicted the bombing of a Muslim village. Sir Philip Sassoon, the undersecretary of state for air, replied that the questioners were taking 'the designer's fanciful efforts altogether too seriously'.[37] He assured a female MP that the bombing of villages was suitable entertainment for families and young children. When Air Secretary Samuel Hoare said the 1928 show would not feature the bombing of a native village, critical lawmakers sardonically asked if a civilised village would be bombed or, failing that, a replica of the House of Commons.

Lansbury and his handful of allies had as much hope of halting the bombing as the victims did. Most MPs, with their visceral support for the empire, backed the use of what government ministers said were humane and effective methods, especially when they were told that it also saved taxpayers' money and the lives of British soldiers. A government spokesman in the House of Lords claimed that bombings had tamed the wildest regions and ushered in idyllic peace, saying, 'Army officers move about the country; picnicking troops are welcome on all sides.'[38]

The Labour Party made a half-hearted attempt to review the use of police bombing when it formed a government in 1924 for the first time. Arguments by Trenchard and others that their methods saved lives were accepted by an administration eager to show it could be trusted with the guardianship of the empire. A steady stream of official assurances in the interwar years that Air Control was humane soothed most misgivings, not that a nation suffused with a sense of imperial and racial superiority really required them: the crowds that enjoyed the bombing of fake native villages at air shows in Britain knew that real villages were being destroyed on the fringes of the empire.

★★★

Air Control faced a completely unexpected challenge when the deputy RAF commander in Iraq protested that the air force was murdering defenceless women and children. Air Commodore Leonard Charlton was among the young service's most able administrators; Trenchard selected him as Salmond's deputy at a time when the success or failure of Air Control in Iraq was vital to the RAF's future.

At first glance, Charlton came from the same social and military template that stamped out Trenchard, Salmond and other early RAF leaders: a penny-pinching childhood of shabby gentility; indifferent performance at school and laboured efforts to pass entry exams for the army; service in the Boer War, and then the West African Frontier Force. In reality, he was quite different from most RAF officers of the time. Photographs suggest a slightly plump, thoughtful man with the distant gaze of a dreamer rather than the wiry angularity and suavity of most senior officers.

A long, difficult voyage of personal discovery turned Charlton from a slightly silly, if exceptionally courageous, young officer into a complex, contradictory man who defied the conventions of his class, contemporary morality and the ethos of the military profession. He preferred books and art to the usual military passion for hunting and sport; he became a socialist in a service where most officers were conservative; and left heavy hints about homosexuality in his later writings. In one revealing scene in his autobiography, written in the third person, Charlton recounted how he had once watched almost naked African tribeswomen fetching water, and wished he could be one of them because of what he saw as their carefree ignorance of civilisation.

Still, Charlton for many years was a model officer. He won more than one medal for bravery, played a key role in early aerial reconnaissance missions and rose to the rank of brigadier during the First World War. The only discordant note in the war had been when he tried to stop half-trained pilots being sent to the front, insisting that it was monstrous to throw men who could barely fly into combat against hardened enemy veterans. He once blocked three postings, only to be immediately overruled by Trenchard – an incident that left Charlton, as he later wrote, with 'hate in his heart'.[39]

This unusual officer's world was turned upside down early in 1923 when he accompanied Salmond and an RAF entourage on a goodwill visit to Diwaniyah, south of Baghdad, where they inspected various facilities, including the local hospital. Amid the usual broken bone and childbirth cases, Charlton was astonished to find several beds filled with women and children badly injured in a recent British punishment bombing of some nearby villages. The smashed torsos and shattered limbs, the moans of the pain-racked patients and the stench of suppurating wounds shocked him. It brought home to Charlton the bloody reality of Air Control, and how people were killed and maimed for fairly mundane offences – or as he put it, '... an air bomb in Iraq was, more or less, the equivalent of a police truncheon at home'.[40]

The analogy of the bomber as the equivalent of a friendly, protective bobby on the beat was regularly employed by the RAF to portray Air Control as benign, but Charlton said that it really meant terrible deaths and maiming, and fell mainly on the innocent and the helpless. He protested to Salmond that while bombing armed men was acceptable, Air Control was no different from a medieval horde butchering every inhabitant in a fallen city, '… the indiscriminate bombing of a populace without the power of selecting the real culprits, and with the liability of killing women and children, was the nearest thing to wanton slaughter.'[41]

Charlton was caught between growing disgust at what he saw as the barbarous nature of Air Control and his strong sense of duty. There was also a gnawing fear of losing his livelihood if he was thrown out of the service. Relations between Charlton and Salmond, which had been cool from the start, deteriorated rapidly. Charlton asked his chief if there was no alternative to bombing, saying that it nearly always killed and wounded the innocent while the troublemakers got away. He protested the bombing of Sulaimaniya in the north during operations against Kurdish separatists, and criticised RAF claims that only combatants were targeted. He later wrote:

> … from a height of three or four thousand feet such accuracy could not be guaranteed, so that the innocent townspeople were bound to suffer … [I] knew the crowded life of these settlements and pictured with horror the arrival of a bomb, without warning, in the midst of a market gathering or in the bazaar quarter or any other populous centre of the town. Men, women and children would suffer equally, and the agony of wounds would be as great as the agony of death.[42]

It was perhaps the most frank account ever written by a serviceman of what Air Control meant for the victims. Charlton later claimed that Salmond conceded there was some truth in what he was saying, but insisted that there was no alternative to bombing, and justified it by saying even the women were 'savages' who defiled and looted the bodies of dead British soldiers.

Charlton's relations with Salmond became increasingly strained. Charlton said he was shunted aside with no clear duties or responsibilities, a situation he did not help by shunning the rest of the British community for the solitary pleasures of his books. Salmond complained to Trenchard that he was saddled with a chief staff officer who could not loyally carry out orders. Finally, Charlton said he could no longer obey orders, and asked to be relieved of his post after he saw aerial photographs of butchered camels caught in air attacks on desert raiders. He was called to London, ostensibly for routine discussions, and reassigned.

Air Staff officials feared there would be a scandal if it leaked out that a senior officer was opposing the Iraqi operations as cruel and immoral. Trenchard acted as if nothing had happened, according to his biographer's account of what happened next. A puzzled Charlton, who had been expecting a confrontation with Trenchard, waited for several weeks and finally had to ask to see the RAF chief, according to this account. Charlton said he thought Trenchard would want to know why he had left Iraq, to which the air chief replied that it was his decision and there was nothing more to be said.

Trenchard flicked away Charlton's question on whether there would be an investigation into the bombings by saying, 'An inquiry into what? Your conscience? Certainly not.'[43] Charlton's own account of the meeting with Trenchard, who he disparagingly described as 'Head of All Things',[44] gave virtually no details except to say it was 'long and argumentative'. Charlton was immensely relieved when Trenchard said he would not be fired, but he was forcibly retired a few years later when he could no longer be an embarrassment.

Charlton's was a unique voice of protest within the air force at the time: a 'minority of one', as he wryly put it.[45] Very few airmen were troubled by the bombing of native villages or nomads' camps; it was seen as necessary, almost inevitable, because of the 'savage' nature of the people. 'It takes a long time to fathom the mentality of these people. They best understand a .303 [rifle] bullet,' wrote C.H. Keith,[46] while one squadron leader in Iraq exulted in 'the bombing of a cruel and uncivilized race'.[47]

Most airmen had an invincible faith in the rightness of the British Empire and never doubted the necessity and morality of the orders they were given. 'Well, our people in London know what it's all about and we're doing it in the interests of the British Empire ... who are we to question it?' said Wilfred Page.[48] It helped that the airmen never dreamed of comparing the Arabs and Kurds they bombed to their own families back home. Moreover, these athletic, adventurous young men, many of them reared for a military career, had joined with the explicit hope of fighting, accepting that they could be killed or badly hurt. Or as Geoffrey Tuttle put it with devastating candour, what was the point of training to be a bomber pilot if you did not get a chance to kill somebody?:

The great attraction was that we wanted to bomb people. That isn't a good idea in a modern society, but I think it is important to emphasise that we were all trained as professional assassins and we wanted to see if we could kill people. We didn't know them, we weren't fighting a crusade, we were merely exercising our professional skill.[49]

It helped that flight crews rarely, if ever, saw the human cost of bombing. Instead, they returned to the tidy comfort of their bases where lunch in the mess or a game of tennis awaited. Many airmen saw it as just a jolly game equally enjoyed by both sides. Charlton's epiphany only came after he had the very unusual experience of seeing the victims of a raid.

Air Commodore J.G. Hearson, who took Charlton's place in Iraq, admitted he preferred not to think about the effects of air attacks, 'if I were to allow myself to consider the matter in the light of sentiment I could never carry it through.'[50] He consoled himself with the thought that bombing was justified because it helped lead its victims to civilised behaviour – 'either in this world or the next'.[51]

★★★

Without Air Control's first great success in Iraq, a Britain short of men and money might well have abandoned the territory and its other wartime conquests in the Middle East. The RAF had held off the Turkish threat, put down internal unrest and bought the time needed for politicians and diplomats to build a functioning state. No one could deny that the RAF had done with a few squadrons what the army and others had insisted was impossible without a massive force, and all at minimal cost.

Diatribes in British newspapers about the 'Messpot mess' gave way to articles about intrepid young airmen besting thuggish tribesmen. The withdrawal of the remaining British and Indian Army units was stepped up, and the Treasury in London purred with pleasure as the bills plummeted. Military expenditure in Iraq in the fiscal year 1921–22 fell from a then staggering £23.36 million to £3.9 million by 1927.[52] What had been the despair of the empire as 'Messpot' was presented as a model of imperial policing.

Success in Iraq came at a critical time in the RAF's battle for survival. The election of a Conservative Government under Andrew Bonar Law in the autumn of 1922 revived calls for disbanding the air force. The new prime minister said the country could not afford an independent air service, and he was inclined to pull out of Iraq. Yet another committee was formed to study the issue. It decided in August 1923, despite furious attacks from the army and navy, that the RAF must be preserved and expanded because it alone could ensure control of the skies.

Trenchard, who had pointed to the RAF's successes in Iraq, Somaliland and elsewhere to make his case for the RAF, exulted that the political battle for the air force's future had been won. The committee, however, seems to have been moved just as much by revelations that the French Air Force was the largest in the world and four times the size of the RAF. A range of otherwise sensible politicians had irrational nightmares that one of their closest allies might bomb London. The RAF was happy to fan the apprehension, saying the French could drop more bombs on Britain in a day than the Germans had done in the whole of the last war.

The empire was still the only theatre of active operations, however, and no one in the mid-1920s expected another major war. The RAF had to keep proving its value in colonial policing if it was to grow and vindicate its claims that it would win future wars. Iraq and the Middle East were, as Colonial Secretary Leo Amery put it in 1925, 'a splendid training ground ... for the air force'.[53]

10

DESERT KINGDOMS

The RAF's triumph in Iraq was the start of a dramatic change in the fortunes of the young service. The force, which seemed to have little or no future at the end of the First World War, was transformed into the guardian of Britain's new Middle Eastern empire. It was the first and perhaps only time that a vast swath of territory was held largely by air power. It was a golden age for the RAF which, as one pilot, Thomas Traill, said, 'did a great deal for our confidence and our self-respect' and helped forge a new and confident spirit.[1]

Palestine and Transjordan had also come under RAF control in 1922. Palestine, with its cities, towns and increasingly modern society, was not suitable for air policing under Trenchard's own rules, but the RAF made no objection to taking over the Holy Land. The army, which saw no glory in mediating between bickering Jews and Arabs, departed without a fuss for once. British control was well established following scattered unrest after the First World War. Indian cavalry detachments and RAF bombers had chased bands of Arab horsemen in a series of minor clashes in 1919. Awed aircrews returned to their bases with tales of the cavalry's lavish desert camps, lordly hospitality and improvised fox hunts at dawn with bemused villagers as beaters and jackals as the quarry.

Air commanders saw their main role as guarding the Transjordan border against Arab raiders, and left control of Palestine's towns with their baffling sectarian politics to the police. By the late 1920s, RAF officers were grumbling about the monotony of nothing but endless border patrols. Traill said the only excitement on long, low-level patrols across the desert was when equally bored Arab shepherds tried to hit the plane with catapults – he occasionally took an egg from the breakfast table to toss back in these playful duels that usually ended with friendly waves.[2]

Life was not uncomfortable for the RAF in Jerusalem and the larger towns, although there were complaints about high prices and low allowances. The façade of colonial rule, which the British were experts at pulling out of a box when they took over a new territory, was erected with its usual trappings. Air force officers rubbed shoulders with British administrators in a little world of comfortable offices and cloistered residences largely cut off from the people they ruled. Senior officers and government officials met at formal dinners, each guest tended by his own Arab bearer in snowy white uniform and red fez, while their wives toured the holy sites and relaxed at the British-only clubs.

★★★

Impressed by the success of Air Control, and still looking for economies, the government in 1927 gave the RAF control of a far more demanding outpost. Generations of British servicemen regarded Aden as a foretaste of the torments awaiting sinners in hell. 'It is a dirty place. Nothing but sand and shells and a kind of pumice stone,' one soldier mournfully wrote.[3] The port on the Red Sea had been occupied in 1839 for use as a coaling station on the route to India.

It was still little more than a toehold on the south Arabian coast in the early 1920s when it was threatened by another of those messianic Islamic leaders that bedevilled the British and the RAF in the interwar years. Yahya, the imam of neighbouring Yemen and leader of the Zaidi branch of Islam, was determined to recover Aden, which once had been ruled by his predecessors. Little is known about the imam beyond the fact that he was a capable and forceful leader revered by his followers. For once, British records are curiously free of the kind of lurid tales used to vilify the imam's counterparts in Somaliland and Darfur.

Aden's tiny army garrison had done little more than control the port and its hinterland before the RAF took over, and Yemeni forces and tribal raiders sometimes got within 40 miles of the town. Field Marshal Henry Wilson, the post-war army chief, had insisted with his usual grandiose bluster that it would take 15,000 troops at a cost of £1 million to defeat the imam. Trenchard declared he could do it with a single squadron, and 8 Squadron was moved from Iraq to garrison Aden. Its DH9As were commanded by Wilfred McClaughry, a tough, cheerful Australian who had seen action in the Middle East with the mounted infantry during the war and later joined the air force; he and his brother ended their careers as air vice marshals. Group Captain William Mitchell took overall command of Aden's defences; he would later command all RAF units in the Middle East and rise to the rank of air chief marshal.

McClaughry's bombers operated from a base that, at best, could be described as ramshackle, and usually invoked far more ribald descriptions from its unhappy denizens. The runway was a strip of sand skirting the sea, and pilots who made mistakes risked ending up bobbing in the waves. Officers and airmen compared life in Aden to living in an oven. There were no hangars in the early years, and maintenance crews worked in the baking sun. Sweat streamed from every pore, running into eyes and making hands slippery. There was no relief in the wooden barracks, which seemed to have been designed with exquisite precision to trap the heat. Slowly rotating wooden ceiling fans merely stirred up the sand and dust, filling the rooms with a gritty haze. Aden itself was no better; most RAF men said it was the most repulsive town in the world with not a single redeeming quality.

The RAF takeover coincided with a new Yemeni push into the protectorate. Air commanders expected a swift victory after their planes attacked the raiders, and claimed to have killed seventy-nine men and wounded dozens more. Buoyed by religious zeal and warrior spirit, the Yemenis instead resumed the offensive, occupying more territory and taking two pro-British sheikhs prisoner in early 1928.

A major bombing campaign was unleashed, with repeated attacks on Yemeni military camps and border towns in which 8 Squadron expended more than 70 tons of bombs, 1,200 incendiaries and 33,000 machine gun rounds, killing and injuring dozens of people.[4] The invaders were finally driven out after weeks of heavy bombing and ground attacks by allied Arab tribes. The imam's forces tried to fight back despite only being armed with rifles. R.E. Penwarm was flying at 5,000ft when his engine was crippled by a shot from a marksmen on the desert floor. He landed amid the dunes, and laid out a strip of white cloth on the sand to attract search planes that soon found him. A caravan of camels arrived a few days later with mechanics, a new engine and a tripod and tackle to hoist it into place. It took several days of back-breaking labour to mount the engine, and Penwarm finally flew back to Aden after being stranded in the desert for sixteen days.[5]

The little war was hailed as another success for Air Control; at a mere £8,567 it cost a fraction of the campaign against the Mad Mullah. The RAF spent the next few years bringing the interior of the protectorate under effective British control. So many landing fields were constructed for operations in the desert that it was said Aden had more runways than any other part of the empire.

★★★

Air force armoured car units and legions of local troops played a significant, if largely unheralded, role in the RAF's success in the Middle East. Air force commanders were unperturbed by accusations from the army and other critics that this proved air power alone could not control an entire country, replying that aircraft did most of the work. Armoured car companies crewed by RAF officers and men were the elite spearhead of the ground forces, helping police vast areas of desert from Palestine to Aden. The sleek vehicles, seen by many airmen as a sort of land-bound aircraft with their speed, grace and powerful engines, were presented as a natural extension of Air Control.

Trenchard had wanted light tanks for Iraq, believing their tracks were better suited for desert conditions, but the army vehemently opposed turning over such weapons to its detested rival. The RAF settled for second-hand armoured cars with machine guns in what was intended as a stopgap measure, and ended up using them throughout the interwar era. Armoured car companies also had trucks to carry food, fuel, ammunition and other supplies so that patrols could operate for weeks at a time. The first two companies were formed in Egypt in 1922; the cars were repainted in RAF blue grey with the blue, white and red roundels sported by the aircraft.

Most of the armoured cars were dilapidated after years of hard service during the First World War. Samuel Wentworth was assigned to a vehicle built in 1912 when he was posted to one of the Middle East companies in the 1930s.[6] It was a constant battle to keep the ageing vehicles going. Grit fouled the engines, turrets jammed and there were never enough spare parts. The heavy cars often sank into the soft sand, and had to be dug out with shovels and hands by the sweating crews. New recruits were shocked to discover that the cars were not impervious to rifle fire despite their armoured plating; a well-aimed shot could disable the engine or even penetrate the cramped crew compartment. New models made by Crossley, introduced in 1929, were more powerful and agile, but could only move at a walking pace across sand, and there were never enough to replace all of the Rolls-Royce cars.

Men were attracted to the armoured car companies by the active outdoor life and the chance to get away from the routine and discipline of the airbases. Ernest Haire, who enrolled in the RAF at the age of 16 with vague intentions of becoming a mechanic, joined the 2nd Armoured Car Company in Palestine to escape the monotony of base life. There were few requirements, and he was accepted by the 1st Company in Iraq after a test consisting of a single question on how to change gears.[7] Many officers saw the companies as a dumping ground for those judged not good enough to fly, or as a punishment, and avoided them, but others were drawn by the freedom and adventure. Arthur Gould Lee, who became an air vice marshal, reckoned commanding armoured cars did not hurt anyone's career.

The desert, or 'blue' as it was known to aircraft and armoured car crews alike, was both an unrelenting adversary and an enchanting wilderness with its vast panorama of sky, hills and plains. Life in this austere amphitheatre could be surprisingly pleasant, and the challenges and excitement compensated for any lack of comforts. There were no reliable maps, at least in the early years, and crews frequently got lost in the trackless wilderness when they ventured hundreds of miles into the interior. G. V. Howard said, after he was assigned to an armoured car unit:

> I simply cannot understand how the devil one finds their way in the desert. There are no roads, trees or any landmarks whatsoever ... the map is only a rough guide as the country had not been surveyed.[8]
>
> It is necessary to know the desert pretty well before you can go 200 [miles] or 300 [miles] out into the blue. There are of course no land marks to guide you and a novice would not know whether he was in enemy or friendly territory, to say nothing of getting lost and not being able to find his way back to civilisation.[9]

Armoured car units patrolled remote areas for weeks at a time with little or no contact with their base. Wentworth spent three happy years in Iraq and Palestine, patrolling dirt tracks and the giant pipelines that were being erected to export oil. His unit visited remote villages, exchanging greetings and news with the local people in a guttural mix of English, Arabic and Urdu. Sometimes there were training exercises with local RAF levies playing the role of desert raiders.

Every inch in the armoured cars' cramped compartments was crammed with tools, ammunition and food, while water bags, fuel and tents were slung on the exterior, making the vehicles resemble overloaded camels. Beer was often stashed in the water bags to keep the bottles cool even though the glue from the labels dissolved and gave the water a rubbery taste. Temperatures in summer could reach 130°F in the cars' airless interiors, and men frequently passed out, while the rate of evaporation from the radiators was reckoned at a gallon an hour.

Water was always scarce and Howard said crews on a month-long patrol were lucky if they got to wash once. Patrols sometimes got lost in the desert or ran into bad weather or impassable terrain; water would run out and the men would suffer agonising thirst for days. Dress regulations were forgotten in the desert, Howard said, and 'beards are the order of the day'.[10] Crews were supposed to wear sun helmets, which resembled huge inverted mixing bowls, even inside the cars. Most men preferred the cloth headgear worn by Arabs, staining them with coffee to match their khaki uniforms.

Men with no experience of cooking had to prepare their own food, and the result was often an unappetising sludge. Attempts to bake bread were said to produce a gritty substance that even the birds refused to eat. Patrols formed diamond-shaped laagers at night in the desert, linking the vehicles with trenches to form a perimeter. Men slept in the open and hyenas and jackals sometimes crept into the camps and attacked the sleepers. More common were scorpions and snakes that frequently slithered into the bedding to share the sleeper's warmth, although surprisingly few men were bitten.

Armoured cars operated and fought in the desert like fleets of ships. A company of eight cars would form two arrow-shaped formations to encircle an enemy or advance in a single line like charging cavalry. There were no radios and commanders standing in open turrets waved coloured flags to direct the movements. The cars were extremely effective against men on horses or camels, literally driving circles around the riders and scything them down with machine gun fire.

Lee was with 5 Company in Iraq in 1925 when word came that hundreds of raiders from Syria had crossed the border. The company's eight cars, racing at 65mph, tracked down and encircled the raiders in the desert; a protracted argument followed in garbled Arabic with a lot of gesticulating as the horsemen insisted it was all a misunderstanding and they had no evil intentions. Lee felt a vague sympathy for the dejected Arabs as they were shepherded back across the border, and he was left with the guilty feeling that he had spoilt their fun.

Armoured cars were far less useful in the towns and villages of Iraq and Palestine, where they were sometimes used to help put down riots; the long vehicles could not turn around in the narrow streets, and were easily trapped if not protected by infantry.

★★★

Britain had always garrisoned large parts of the empire with native soldiers under white officers. In remoter regions, these tended to be irregular formations, lightly armed and recruited from tribes expert at fighting in the local terrain, and far cheaper than regular troops. Several exotic legions of Arabs, Assyrians and other races were raised as ground units in territories controlled by the RAF, and were a vital part of Air Control. Wits said that the auxiliaries, who wore everything from Cossack-style garb to Arab robes, resembled extras from a comic opera, but the men were tough and skilled fighters: they became adept at working with bomber and fighter squadrons.

One of these forces, the Transjordan Frontier Force, was an extraordinary mix of Arabs, Chechens, Turks, Kurds, Jews, Egyptians, Sudanese, Armenians, Russians, Yugoslavs, Javanese, Indo-Chinese, Germans, Africans and Greeks. It was run by the army, and had little time for RAF claims that horses had no role in modern warfare – for many years the regiment's only mechanised transport was a solitary Ford van. The men wore Cossack-style black wool hats, flowing robes and red cummerbunds; its badge featuring a winged horse symbolised its air force ties.

The Aden Protectorate Levies, a force of camel troops and infantry, was raised by the RAF in 1928 after the withdrawal of the army garrison from the protectorate. It was modelled on the Indian Army, and its Arab soldiers wore shorts and turbans. The Levies were good fighters, capable of taking on much larger tribal forces. British commanders said the men's only fault was their habit of firing their rifles wildly in a fight; one officer sardonically suggested this was because they had an orgasm every time they squeezed the trigger.

Foremost among the RAF's private armies was the Assyrian Levies, which served in Iraq and would be one of the most colourful and tragic formations in the empire's history. The Assyrians were an ancient Christian people who had fended off successive Muslim challenges from their mountain stronghold on what is now the Turkish–Iraqi border. Their patriarch, the Mar Shimum, disastrously decided at the start of the First World War to side with the Allies against the Ottoman Empire.

The Assyrians, who were thought to number only some 100,000 people, were driven from their mountains and suffered terrible losses. About 20,000 men, women and children fled south to meet British forces advancing from Baghdad at the end of the war. They were housed in an Iraqi camp with other refugees. Some of the men were recruited for local units that the British had started raising during the war. The Levies were almost exclusively Assyrian by the mid-1920s when they came under RAF control. Air force officers praised the men as loyal and excellent soldiers, but were not happy over a government decision in 1925 to ban flogging as a punishment.

Assyrian leaders became increasingly worried about the future of their people in the early 1930s as Britain prepared to hand control to the Iraqi Government. The Assyrians feared that they would be persecuted by the Iraqi Government because of their loyalty to the British and their Christian faith. A plot by the Levies to quit British service and march north to seize territory for a homeland was uncovered in June 1932. British troops were flown in from Egypt to forestall the scheme, and the Assyrians eventually agreed to abandon their hopes.

There was more trouble the following year when some 800 Assyrians took their rifles and fled to Syria. French officials sent the men back across the border where waiting Iraqi troops killed many of them. A wave of atrocities followed as Iraqi units attacked Assyrian villages – in one incident, some 300 people were massacred at the settlement of Semal. British officials did nothing to stop the repression, insisting that it was an internal Iraqi matter. Some air force officers were angry and ashamed over what they saw as the betrayal of a people whose loyalty to Britain had exposed them to Iraqi retribution. 'And from Britain came not a bleat of protest at this savagery against a people whose crime was to trust us and be loyal to us,' wrote David Lee.[11]

Many Assyrians stayed in the Levies because they saw no alternative, serving until the RAF pulled out of Iraq in the 1950s. This motley trinity of aircraft, armoured cars and native levies would defeat an army of fanatical Wahabi fighters some seventy years before the world heard of Osama bin Laden.

11

BEFORE OSAMA BIN LADEN

An RAF truck bumped along the rough gravel road on the outskirts of Amman on the morning of 14 August 1924. The capital of
Transjordan was a sleepy outpost; only the weekly Cairo–Baghdad
mail flights broke the little British garrison's dreary routine. Lulled by the
heat, the driver at first barely noticed little knots of Arab men, women and
children running and stumbling through the nearby scrub. A few of the men
ran to the truck, waving for it to stop; their faces grey with terror as they
babbled in shrill Arabic, their arms pointing wildly at the desert behind them.
The puzzled British driver could not see anything as he peered over their
clamouring heads at the distant landscape.

Three air force armoured cars sent out two hours later to investigate also
saw nothing as they drove into the hinterland except for what appeared to
be a few recently slaughtered horses and camels. It was not until the patrol
approached a low range of hills that the crews spotted thousands of mounted
men lining the heights. Eight large black and green war banners adorned
with white Arabic script fluttered over the horsemen. A few miles away lay
Amman, virtually undefended and serenely unaware of this army that had
materialised from the desert without warning.

The RAF waged an almost unknown war for much of the 1920s in the
barren heart of Arabia against an army of Wahabi zealots, followers of a
puritanical strain of Islam that appeared in the eighteenth century, and later
influenced Osama bin Laden. Around 1912, a Wahabi group known as the
Ikhwan, or Brethren, set out to revive what they saw as the austere purity of
the early Wahabis, and won a following among some of the tribes in the Nejh
region of what is now Saudi Arabia.

Its followers were warriors and ascetics who denounced tobacco, fine clothing, singing, dancing and even children's games as impious distractions. They shunned Western technology, such as the telephone and radio, because it had not existed in the early days of Islam, although they made an exception for guns and other modern weapons. The *Ikhwans'* self-ordained mission was to cleanse Islam and eradicate anyone who did not share their merciless creed. Their greatest strength was an adamantine belief that they were God's anointed. *Ikhwan* war bands began raiding Iraq and Transjordan from their Arabian strongholds in the 1920s, spreading their beliefs by the sword and plundering the ungodly.

Raiding was an ageless part of Bedouin life. It was like a game, and there was often little bloodshed as the tribes snatched livestock and a few possessions from each other. Raiders taken prisoner were often treated as guests and sent home, minus only their weapons. *Ikhwan* raids were very different. An anonymous correspondent wrote in the *RAF Quarterly*:

> The object of these is to spread the Wahabi faith by terrorism and the sword; to force the infidel and Moslems of gentler creed to accept their version of Islam. They observe none of the recognized rules of raiding common among the nomad Bedouin. All males, except babes in arms, are slaughtered in cold blood; no prisoners are taken. Loot is a secondary consideration. Their raids are carefully organized, planned and executed, and are ruthless in the extreme.[1]

A few minor *Ikhwan* raids on Britain's protectorates in 1922 and 1923 were driven off by RAF patrols, but the British failed to realise these were not the usual Bedouin raiders until a Wahabi army tried to storm Amman in 1924. Some 5,000 raiders from the Nejh travelled undetected for a month across more than 500 miles of desert to take the town by surprise. The slaughter started when the raiders attacked several Arab villages outside Amman, killing at least 130 men; the fleeing people seen by the RAF driver that morning were survivors from the pillaged settlements. A wedding party carrying a bride to her new home blundered into the raiders. *Ikhwan* swordsmen, incensed by the celebrants' festive clothing and music, butchered the men and stripped and beat the women.

The armoured cars that spotted the raiders later that day did not have radios to warn Amman of the danger. An airman climbed up one of the roadside telegraph poles and was tapping out an alert on the bare wire with Morse code when three DH9As from Amman soared overhead led by Squadron Leader J.A. D'Albiac, who would serve as an air marshal during the Second World War. British civilian administrators in Amman insisted the reports of raiders must be a mistake and the supposed army threatening Amman were harmless nomads or a caravan. One of these smug officials was sitting in D'Albiac's rear cockpit to ensure that the impetuous airmen did not attack peaceful tribesmen. A glance at the throng of riders instantly persuaded both men that the force below was far from friendly.

It was almost certain that no one in the *Ikhwan* force had ever seen an aeroplane before, and the appearance of the bombers astonished the riders. The planes dived on the raiders, dropping their bombs at point-blank range into the milling mob. Riders struggled to control their terrified camels and horses as the white hot explosions, scything shrapnel and machine-gun fire tore gaps in the densely packed ranks. Within minutes, hundreds of stunned riders were streaming back towards the desert.

Their bombs gone, the DH9As were flying back to Amman when they spotted the armoured cars and dropped a message instructing the little forma-tion to attack. Flying Officer H.N. Thornton, commander of the armoured cars and another future air vice marshal who would be a bomber com-mander in the next world war, caught up with the raiders as they fled across a broad plain that was an ideal killing ground for his much faster vehicles. Thornton's force raced ahead for some distance and then halted so that his machine gunners could fire from stationary positions rather than attempting the more difficult task of shooting at moving targets while bumping along at high speed over the rocky plain.

When the chaotic mass of *Ikhwan* riders lumbered past just a few hundred feet away from the waiting British formation, each car opened fire with its Vickers and Lewis machine guns. Scores of men and animals were knocked down by the sheet of bullets while others following behind tumbled over the corpses littering the sand. 'The range was so short, and the target so large' that it was impossible to miss, Thornton later wrote. [2]

A few of the raiders fired wildly back at the armoured cars with long-barrelled muskets or rifles. The one or two slugs that hit the vehicles bounced uselessly off the steel sides. The armoured cars raced forward once the riders had passed them, took up another position and again raked the raiders as they lumbered past. Thornton performed this deadly manoeuvre six or seven times over the next two hours, stopping only when his crews were down to their last drums of ammunition.

Thornton had just ordered his cars to break off the attack when the DH9As returned with fresh bomb loads to attack the riders, who by now had fractured into chaotic little knots of men and animals. Local tribesmen, no longer afraid of the raiders, helped hunt down Wahabi stragglers and wounded survivors. A flight of Bristol fighters from Palestine and one of the DH9As caught what was left of the raiders in the desert just before dark and strafed them with machine-gun fire. A pilot and his observer were wounded by *Ikhwan* riflemen in this last clash, the RAF's only casualties of the battle.

Parties of British officials and officers went out over the next few days to survey the scenes of carnage in the desert. Hundreds of crumpled corpses littered the plain where the armoured cars and planes had caught the raiders. Some of the RAF men felt a strange sympathy as they surveyed the bodies. Pilot Gerald Gibbs recalled:

> They were gallant if misguided followers of the Prophet and we were sad to see so many of their wounded succumb. It seems that they had been marching for weeks on a handful of parched grain a day, and a comparatively small loss of blood [from a wound] was the end of them.[3]

At least 500 bodies were counted, but it was impossible to compile a final figure of the dead. Many of the *Ikhwan* perished in the desert, succumbing to wounds, hunger and thirst, and their bones were scoured clean by the wind and wild animals before being covered by the indifferent sand. It was a remarkable victory for the RAF; an entire army had been defeated with just forty bombs and 10,000 bullets and two British casualties. A captured war banner was taken back to hang in the RAF officers' mess in Amman.

★★★

Later that year a British officer gloried in the brilliant, clear winter sky as he rode across the Iraqi desert with five Arab guards to investigate vague reports of trouble on the Nejh border. It was Christmas Day, but the young officer was happy to escape the drunken celebrations of the British community in Baghdad.

John Glubb was one of that small band of Englishmen who found their destiny by turning their backs on their own land and culture and embracing the unforgiving ways of the desert and the Bedouin tribes. He loved his life as an RAF Special Service officer.

When the RAF took command in Iraq, a detachment of these officers had been formed to gather intelligence on the desert tribes. This unorthodox formation, which required men with an expert knowledge of Arabic and desert life and an ability to live alone among the tribes for long periods, attracted eccentrics and misfits. One of its more colourful members was a grandson of the Duke of Buccleuch, who had been an army colonel until he had to retire because of age. He joined the Special Service as a lowly flight lieutenant, but even senior officers tended to address him as 'sir'. Trenchard was always slightly suspicious of the Special Service officers because of what he saw as their aversion to military routine; he complained they took the side of the natives and had views 'contaminated with the theories of Bolshevism'.[4]

Glubb, who certainly took pride in supporting the Arabs, was stunned when his little patrol topped a ridge that Christmas Day and saw that the broad floor of the valley below was black with swarms of running people and animals. Frantic men screamed that an *Ikhwan* army had attacked their camps and butchered many of the inhabitants. Women sobbing and moaning with fear, many carrying babies or dragging shrieking infants, ran past Glubb. 'O God help us! O God protect us!' the throng wailed.[5]

A line of warriors on camels suddenly topped the opposite ridge, slipped from their saddles and opened a swift, deadly fire into the helpless mass below. Men and women seemed to jump as bullets smacked into them, hanging suspended in the air for a fleeting moment before collapsing. A dreadful din of screams quickly drowned out the crack of rifle fire and the bellowing of camels. Glubb had blundered into the biggest *Ikhwan* raid yet.

Glubb reached the nearest Iraqi outpost the next day to call for help, but confusion and poor weather meant a patrol of three planes of 84 Squadron were not sent out from Baghdad until 27 December. Glubb was in one of the planes' rear cockpits. Ghastly signs of the slaughter inflicted by the raiders littered the desert. Flying on, they spotted a vast throng of stolen sheep, camels and donkeys being hustled along by the raiders. Glubb later estimated the moving mob of men and animals covered an area measuring some 3 miles by 2 miles. The planes' small bombs only scattered the riders and the animals while smoke from the detonations threw up a veil of sand and dust that quickly obscured the ground.

All of 84 Squadron flew out on 28 December only to find that the raiders had crossed the border, and orders not to cross the demarcation line forced them to break off the pursuit. Hundreds of Iraqi Arabs had been slaughtered by the raiders and thousands more left destitute by the theft of their herds, tents and other belongings.

The *Ikhwan* threat worsened as war bands surged across the Iraqi border and savaged the weak pastoral tribes. Patrolling aircraft found it difficult to spot the small, fast-moving bands in the vast expanse of the desert. The raiders learned to hide in the dun landscape when planes passed overhead; pilots said that even large encampments with their brown and black tents could be missed from the air. RAF commanders complained the war parties could slip across the unguarded 600-mile frontier no matter how many air patrols were sent up.

It took days, sometimes weeks, for reports of raids to reach government posts, and the raiders had disappeared long before air or ground patrols reached the spot. The few *Ikhwan* bands that were spotted by the air patrols fought back and a growing a number of aircraft were shot down or returned to base with serious damage from ground fire. Pilots were ordered not to fly below 1,500ft and to never follow a steady course because the raiders soon learned to bring down aircraft by converging their fire. Flight crews were issued with a rifle and 100 rounds of ammunition for self-defence in case they were shot down.

Richard Brooks, a young radio operator with 84 Squadron, had only flown a few patrols when his plane was hit by *Ikhwan* rifle fire. A heavy, flat-nosed slug shattered the seat and slammed into the back of his thigh, jerking his leg up and spraying the cockpit with blood and ragged bits of flesh as it exited just above the knee. The gaping wound was filled with shreds of fabric and metal from the broken seat. Brooks leaned forward, tapped the pilot to show he was wounded, and then, working from pure habit, and despite the pain of his shattered leg, methodically pulled in the 200ft wire radio aerial that trailed behind the plane while it was flying.

The pilot landed on an open strip of desert, and two other planes touched down to see what was wrong. Brooks was pulled out of the cockpit, his flying suit cut away and the wound roughly bandaged with field dressings, before his pilot flew him back to Basrah. The wound measured 10in by 7in and was clogged with debris. Doctors wanted to amputate the leg, but one surgeon insisted that it could be saved, and Brooks endured agony as debris, pus and broken bone was picked out of the wound every day for the next two weeks. Brooks was sent back to England, where he had to change his own dressings in a military hospital until an angry doctor intervened and made sure that he was looked after properly.[6]

British officials implored the Nejh ruler, Abdul Aziz al Saud, to suppress the *Ikhwan*, but they were his allies and provided shock troops for his army. Moreover, the Saudi leader was unhappy about Britain's support for the rival monarchies in Transjordan and Iraq. Feisal al Duweesh, the main *Ikhwan* chieftain, rebuked Abdul Aziz for even talking to the British infidels. Duweesh was a bearish man with protruding teeth and black, unnerving eyes; Glubb said he resembled an ogre in a dark fairy tale. The *Ikhwan* commander was a superb leader, however, who earned a bemused respect from the RAF.

G.V. Howard wrote disbelievingly of the *Ikhwan* as 'puritans who don't smoke, drink or indulge in any form of amusement other than that provided by nature', and made wry jokes about Duweesh's 'annual sport of murder and rape'.[7] Iraq's King Faisal worried that the raids could only be stopped by building a barrier like the Great Wall of China, and fretted that his tribes would convert to the Wahabi faith to save themselves and their flocks. 'The truth is that the Bedouin and the shepherd tribesmen loves his camel or his sheep more than his soul and they are dearer to him than religion,' he observed.[8]

Air commanders insisted that the raids could only be halted by bombing the *Ikhwan* settlements. London, fearful of a war with Abdul Aziz, refused until the end of 1927 to even let air patrols pursue raiders into Nejh territory. Border defences were increased in a mostly futile attempt to halt the raids; airstrips were built closer to the frontier, Iraqi tribes were ordered to move away from the border zone and leaflets were dropped on the Nejh tribes warning they might be bombed if they did not move at least four days' ride away from the frontier.

Glubb formed an Arab unit, the Southern Desert Camel Corps, to guard the frontier. Some RAF officers feared that Glubb's half-wild recruits would sell their weapons to the *Ikhwan*, but senior officers backed him and a startled bureaucrat was sent to the Baghdad bazaar with orders to purchase Chevrolet and Ford trucks for the unit. The improved defences failed to end the attacks despite some successes, and the British Government finally agreed to hit back after 2,500 raiders of Duweesh's Mutair Tribe raided southern Iraq in February 1928. RAF planes fought running clashes for three days before the raiders crossed the border. A pilot hit by ground fire in the clashes was the only RAF man killed in the decade-long war with the zealots.

A column of British armoured cars and fuel tankers slipped across the Nejh border a few days later, and drove deep into the desert, where they built a landing strip. When it was completed, twelve DH9As flew in to be followed by three hulking Vickers Victoria troop transports converted into heavy bombers. British officials had decided to attack Duweesh's settlement at Lusafa, but it was beyond the range of the RAF's airfields in Iraq, so it had been decided to set up a temporary base deep inside Nejh territory.

The planes and their crews spent the night at the strip, which was ringed by armoured cars and troops, before taking off at dawn on 24 February to attack Lusafa. It turned out to be a walled settlement with a fort and mud houses; a large encampment of tents stood nearby. A hail of 500lb and 20lb bombs rained down on the settlement; swarms of men, women and children poured out of the houses and tents, trying to evade the shattering blasts. Airmen perched by the rear doors of the Victorias, tossing out bombs by hand each time an observer in the front cockpit tugged a string tied to their arms. Other airmen in the cabins hastily assembled bombs from boxes of casings and detonators. Little was left of the settlement when the planes flew back to Iraq.

Duweesh and the other *Ikhwan* leaders, increasingly hemmed in by the improving defences on the Iraqi border, began to raid the little sheikdom of Kuwait and the Iraqi nomadic tribes that crossed into its territory every winter to graze their flocks. *Ikhwan* bands attacked the nomadic tribes in January 1929, massacring the men and looting the herds and other property.

A Christian missionary was killed when a group of Americans touring the region in cars blundered into the raiders. Word of the attacks reached British forces in Iraq, but standing orders forbade them from entering Kuwait. Glubb pleaded for permission to cross the border. Baghdad, insisting it lacked the authority, passed the appeal on to London. For three days RAF units sat helplessly on the frontier. When London finally gave permission to intervene it was too late. Pursuit parties found only the tracks of the raiders crossing back over the Nejh border.

A band of 500 *Ikhwan* raided Kuwait again in March and attacked a nomadic Iraqi tribe. The terrified nomads tried to flee to the capital, but the inhabitants closed the gates and watched from the walls as the tribesmen were slaughtered on the ground below. Planes from 84 Squadron later bombed and machine-gunned the retreating raiders.

Relations between Abdul Aziz and the *Ikhwan*, in the meantime, were deteriorating. Abdul Aziz, his grip on his kingdom growing, had less need of the Wahabis, and their leaders were increasingly critical of the king, especially his appetite for motor cars and other Western gadgets. A breaking point came when *Ikhwan* bands started to attack and massacre Nejh tribes and caravans. The *Ikhwan* were confident of an easy victory over what they regarded as the king's army of fat and indolent townsmen, but hundreds of them were killed in a March 1929 battle by the royal force's machine gunners: Abdul Aziz's passion for Western technology had not been misplaced. Some 250 captured

Ikhwan were beheaded after a second Wahabi army was defeated in August. Duweesh and a few warriors with hundreds of women and children fled to Kuwait and surrendered to the British. The old chief insisted on handing his sword to the senior RAF officer. He was sent back after Abdul Aziz promised he would not be executed and died in prison.

★★★

The RAF's success enraged the army. In a show of petulant spite, army leaders tried to block the award of a campaign medal for RAF personnel who had fought the *Ikhwan*. Such medals were the customary recognition of success and valued by all ranks in all of the military services. Disdainful generals said it had been a mere police action. An army memo handed to the Cabinet said awards were only issued 'In commemoration of arduous campaigns and well-fought and well-sustained battles and sieges'.[9]

Trenchard denounced what he saw as the army's blood-drunk stupidity. The whole point of modern weapons, he said, was to win wars without slaughtering your own men. A bemused Cabinet formed a committee to study the issue, and the unlikely trio of the Scottish secretary, the agriculture minister and the lord privy seal were told to resolve the demeaning spat.

Army representations to the committee said a medal for the airmen who risked their lives fighting the *Ikhwan* would be a 'debasement' of military honour; the RAF said it was monstrous to tell British servicemen that victory only counted if they suffered heavy casualties.[10] Air force staff officers compiled a list of minor, mostly bloodless, army actions which had been recognised with campaign medals, including a 1906 clash against Africans armed with spears, clubs 'and a few, very indifferent bows'.[11] It came as no surprise when the government approved a campaign medal for the *Ikhwan* campaign.

12

DESERT PURGATORY

Ageneration of RAF officers and men was moulded by two decades of colonial service in the interwar years. The Middle East was the most important and the most gruelling of the overseas stations. Depression and boredom were common companions for the thousands who served in the region; some men went mad and a few killed themselves. Sardonic jokes and raucous songs helped gloss over the hardships of these desert outposts, where vigorous young men found themselves confined in the military equivalent of a monastery with none of the spiritual consolations. 'And I wish I were in my coffin underground,' was the refrain of a popular RAF song about life in Iraq. And yet many airmen came to value, even love, the hardship, adventure and camaraderie of life in the desert and looked back on it as a test of character that brought out the best in them.

Ironically, life in the desert squadrons almost always began at sea with a stomach-wrenching voyage in filthy, dilapidated and overcrowded troopships that took new drafts out to the Middle East each year. L.A. Simmons went to Iraq in 1926 as an enlisted man on the same troopship that, a quarter of a century earlier, had taken his uncle to the Boer War.[1]

Hundreds of airmen were crammed into the dark, airless lower decks for three or four weeks, lying most of the time on hammocks hanging four deep from the low ceilings. Most men never forgot the stench of unwashed bodies, vomit and the toilets overflowing with a thick stew of faeces and urine. The smell and the discomfort steadily increased as the ships slowly steamed south and the temperature below decks rose; men felt as if they were being slowly cooked in floating ovens as the vessels plodded through the Red Sea and the Persian Gulf. Few of the passengers could stomach the heavy, greasy food such as fried onions and cow's stomach lining, which was served out to the lower ranks.

Life was better for the officers, although three or four junior officers usually had to share tiny cabins designed for a single passenger. S.F. Vincent and two companions performed a contortionist ballet in their tiny cabin each night as they changed into evening dress before dinner.

Things were not much better when RAF detachments travelled on merchant ships. W.H. Lawrence, an enlisted man who left England for the first time, was part of an RAF group that shared an open deck with an elephant, three monkeys, four race horses and 100 Armenian women on a voyage from India to Iraq in the 1920s – the young Englishmen were paralysed with embarrassment the first morning when the women lined up half naked to use the two showers.[2]

Men going out to the Middle East for the first time were deluged with stories about the horrors that supposedly awaited them. Pilot C.H. Keith's troopship was greeted by a sign at the Basra docks declaring, 'You are going the wrong way!' A group of tanned RAF men waiting on the quay to go home jeered at Keith and the other pale newcomers lining the ship's railings. When Keith hopefully remarked that Iraq couldn't be too bad, judging by how fit the departing men looked, another officer replied that most of the unit was probably dead or in hospital.[3]

Conditions in the Middle Eastern stations varied enormously. Iraq and Aden were hardship posts, while Egypt was one of the best postings in the RAF with its easy-going lifestyle and the cosmopolitan amenities and pleasures of Cairo. Palestine was dull, but it had patches of irrigated green, fresh fruit was plentiful, and airmen could mingle with European and American Jews in the cafes or spend their spare time visiting Biblical sites, while Transjordan was a sleepy backwater.

Officers and men served just two years in Iraq and Aden rather than the normal five years for overseas assignments because of the harsh conditions. Officers could then apply for an assignment in Britain, but airmen had to do a further three years in a less arduous overseas station before they returned home. Iraq was regarded by many men as purgatory, especially in the early years when government austerity cuts meant there was very little money for even basic amenities. Arthur Harris never forget the half-rotten food and squalid camps of the early 1920s. Newspaper campaigns at home for government spending cuts, he said, meant that the men did not even have decent toilets.[4]

Boredom and isolation could eat away at men's minds. Even the most cheerful individuals suffered fits of what was known at the time as 'melancholia' – a sense of depression or aimlessness that numbed the mind and the body. 'I don't wonder that people go down [with depression] as this is just simply a desert post with nothing outside the camp bounds but a sea of sand and mud,' wrote G.V. Howard, a junior officer whose letters home provide endless detail about RAF life in the Middle East.[5]

Afflicted men imagined that the choking despondency which gripped them would never end, and home seemed so far away it might as well be on another planet. Harsh living conditions and monotony sometimes led to insubordination, drunkenness and violence, especially in the early years. Few gave as bleak a portrait of this time as H. Howe, an airman in Iraq soon after the First World War:

> Messpot is a hell country and part of that hell was made by the men themselves, they preferring it to the otherwise cruel monotony of lonely and pious inactivity, alone sufficient to snap a man's mind. One might ask why this excessive drunkenness and gambling was allowed, why NCOs did not stop it. For one thing the country acted on them and the officers as well as the men ... NCOs out in the cantonment shut away from the world by a vast desert stretching hundreds of miles, were on many occasions assaulted and terribly manhandled by individual men.[6]

Iraq was dreaded for its ferocious climate. 'The nights were cold as charity and the day as hot as hell, and dust blew in by day and by night,' Keith recalled.[7] Men had to sit in the dark in their tents in the summer because the heat melted the candles. Officers gave up the normal routine of smoothing their hair with brilliantine because it streamed down their faces in glistening strands of grease and sweat. Men became irritable and morose in the hot months, and the most trivial incidents could trigger arguments or fights.

Life gradually improved, even in the bleakest outposts, as better equipped bases were constructed, and new technology brought such modern blessings as electric fans, the cinema and air mail. Men talked and dreamed constantly of food, especially in the early years when there were no refrigerated facilities to store imported perishable goods, and the local economy produced very little that the average British serviceman willingly ate. Harris said that what was described as lamb on RAF menus was usually goat. Alfred Earles never forgot the local Iraqi fish, optimistically called 'Tigris Salmon', but which resembled cotton wool laced with steel needles.[8]

Rations were generous to make up for the lack of choice, but few men wanted larger helpings of what they regarded as unpalatable slop. Men constantly yearned for roast beef, Yorkshire pudding, dumplings and other traditional favourites that could not be had in the desert. Ronald Ivelaw-Chapman said some of the pilots who flew the weekly mail run from Iraq to Cairo went to smart brothels, but his idea of sinful indulgence was a feast of prawns and mayonnaise at a favourite restaurant.[9]

The Middle East airbases were tiny cocoons of British life; there was very little interaction with the local people, who were seen as barely human. Howard spoke for most when he described his first impressions of the ancient and historic city of Baghdad: 'Everything smelt of Wog [the army term for a native of this country] or perhaps I should say the atmosphere smelt of Wog and this has rather a nauseating and depressing effect after a time.'[10]

Howard had more contact with the local people than most RAF men after he was assigned to an armoured car company at a remote Iraqi desert base. His superior sent him off with instructions to treat the Iraqi officers at the post as 'dirt'. The young Englishman was surprised to find that the senior Iraqi officer was pleasant and well educated. 'It is quite easy to hold a conversation without becoming matey and I think these people will do far more for you if you treat them like human beings,' he told his wife.[11] He boasted of refusing the Iraqi's offer of tea, however, saying that a white man did not sit with natives in case they got false ideas about being equal.

Some airmen had misgivings about the way local people were treated, although they tended to voice such regrets much later in life. Bomber pilot G.A. Bolland recalled:

> The Iraqis were splendid folk ... they were amazingly tolerant and friendly ...
> It was a shame that we had no real opportunity to learn the language. Most of
> us learnt only words of command and curses, for which Arabic, being guttural,
> is so well suited. We did not appreciate how beautiful it is, nor how admirable
> much of their life is in such a harsh environment nor how fascinating Arab
> Civilization and its history can be.[12]

Ironically, there was a steady run of deaths from illness, routine flying accidents and car crashes rather than active operations. Disease was the biggest killer; a legion of unaccustomed germs and bacteria overwhelmed European immune systems and baffled military doctors. Fevers were swift killers – men who seemed fine at breakfast could be dead by lunchtime and buried before dinner.

John Buckley, who had joined the air force to escape a life in the Welsh coal mines, went down with amoebic dysentery a few weeks after arriving in Iraq. He spent six months in a Baghdad military hospital undergoing painful daily injections that seemed more likely to kill him than the germs invading his body. Buckley was put in a ward reserved for patients with the same affliction, and watched seven other men die slowly in the beds around him. The young airman was emaciated and weak when he showed signs of recovery. Doctors placed him on a diet of thickly buttered bread and fried eggs to regain weight, but it made him violently ill.[13]

The dead generally were buried within hours of letting go of life, partly because of the climate and partly to prevent the living from brooding. Rows of graves were dug in advance to save time. All ranks were given formal military funerals. The coffin was escorted by an honour guard and the station band. Officers and men lined the route and then fell in behind as the sad little cortège marched to the cemetery, where the padre, incongruously clad in a khaki sun helmet and billowing white clerical robes, waited by an open hole. The final benediction was invariably of duty faithfully done, a young life cut short and a home that would never be seen again.

Sport, hobbies and other pastimes filled the hours between work and sleep, and were vital in helping most men cope. Sport was a compulsory and popular part of the daily routine, with the enlisted men playing football and the officers devoting most afternoons to tennis. Wireless operators were popular because they could get British football scores and other sporting results from home.

Officers had much more leisure time than the men, and also the means to use it. Many officers were inveterate hunters, happy to shoot at anything in sight. The keenest enthusiasts on remote bases would go out twice a day, taking shots at birds or any other wildlife that moved. The obsession with hunting overlapped with the squadrons' military duties – flight crews interchangeably used 'potting', 'bags' and other hunting slang to describe killing people and animals.

The RAF made use of its transport squadrons to form regional sporting leagues and fly teams around the Middle East for tournaments. Pilot Frederick Richardson spent a large part of his time conveying rugby, football, cricket, boxing and tennis teams to fixtures, with any spare room in the planes crammed with fans to cheer the teams on. The advantage tended to be with the home side, Richardson recalled, because the unstable Victorias and Valencias were almost always buffeted by turbulence, making the passengers violently ill; visiting teams sometimes had to stumble out of vomit-smeared cabins and go straight onto the field.[14]

There were also brainy pursuits for officers and men with such tastes. Archaeology fascinated the Western world in the interwar years with a flood of great discoveries, and leading archaeologists were celebrities, alongside film stars and tycoons. It was one of the few aspects of Middle Eastern life and culture that interested RAF men, and articles on archaeological sites and excavations were a fixture in air force journals.

The mess was the centre of life for most officers, a cross between a boarding school dormitory and a private club. Only a few senior commanders were allowed to bring their wives out to Iraq and Aden, so nearly all officers took their meals in the mess and spent much of their leisure time there. Mess life was modelled on the standards of the British upper classes at home, regardless of how uncomfortable or absurd they might be in a hut in the middle of the Iraqi desert. Officers changed into elaborate evening dress to dine on food and drink that was mostly imported from Britain despite the high expense, which the diners themselves had to shoulder.

Vincent and other members of his mess in Basra had to don tight white tops resembling waiters' jackets, matching trousers, silk shirts, black cummerbunds and bow ties for dinner. The rib-hugging jackets were only discarded at the height of the southern Iraqi summer. To relax on weekends, Earle said, the officers wore civilian dinner jackets rather than mess uniforms. Messes were made as attractive and as comfortable as the members' purses and RAF stores allowed. The general aim was to recreate the atmosphere of a London club with leather armchairs, a bar and a dining room with a long, polished wood table decorated with the unit's silverware and trophies. 84 Squadron embellished the art deco mantlepiece of its mess with skulls pilfered from the archaeological site at Ur; lighted candles were placed in them on guest nights.[15]

Life in the mess was strictly regulated, with juniors deferring to senior officers and generally not speaking until they were spoken to. There was a strict taboo on discussing religion, politics, women and 'shop' (anything to do with work). The routine and tacit discipline was a seamless continuation for those who had been reared in boarding schools. The air force was not quite so anti-intellectual as the army was reputed to be, but most officers confined their reading to magazines and light novels. For most officers it was a comfortable communal life with a group of like-minded men, a routine with plenty of sport and relaxation, punctuated by occasional moments of exhilarating danger and destruction on active operations.

The decorum or stuffiness that normally reigned in messes was abandoned on guest nights, when the young and the young at heart were encouraged to indulge in rough games and pranks. There were impromptu rounds of rugby or chair-tossing that usually ended with smashed furniture, torn uniforms and the occasional broken bone.

A lot of thought was put into shocking or amusing military and civilian visitors on guest nights. Visitors to one squadron were ushered into the mess to be greeted by the sight of the younger officers swinging by their arms from the revolving ceiling fans. Civilian guests, including women, were encouraged to take part in the boisterous after-dinner games at some squadrons. Howard, an inexhaustible source of information on the less decorous aspects of British behaviour in Iraq, said men and women would lie under a sheet and roll over each other; the squadron chaplain was usually the most enthusiastic participant. 'It is a good thing the Bishop of London could not see him!' Howard told his wife.[16]

Humour and practical jokes were a daily part of life. Arriving in Egypt for flight training, Cadet Ernest Ford was given an ass to ride from the railway station to the RAF base. At the base, he was handed a list of trainees who had supposedly been killed or injured in flying accidents the week before and there was also a mock harangue from a senior officer, who claimed that he had been flirting with married women on the troopship. It was a day or two before the befuddled Ford realised it was all a prank.[17]

Entertainment for the lower ranks was far less plentiful, and most men spent their evenings in squadron canteens, where the only attraction was warm, watery beer, or playing cards in the dormitory huts. Some units had little reading rooms with a few books and periodicals for those who wanted to improve themselves or craved quiet and solitude. Life was better for enlisted men with a bookish bent if they got a posting to Cairo or Jerusalem, where they could meet like-minded civilians.

William Edwards, an NCO who served with armoured car and bomber units, joined an amateur dramatic society in Jerusalem and performed in productions of Shakespeare's plays in Bethlehem and other towns. Films were popular with all ranks and most bases had weekly screenings in the later years. White sheets served as screens and were hung up in the dining room or suspended from steel wires outside in the hot weather. Performances would be punctuated by members of the audience shouting for native bearers to bring beers or sandwiches.

Pets were popular with all ranks and many men had dogs, cats, birds and other local fauna that they caught or bought from the Arabs. Dogs overran some officers' messes, and the more hardy animals accompanied their masters in the air. One officer was said to be so devoted to his Alsatian that he tucked the animal up in bed each night and slept on the floor, while another knitted his bulldog a pair of pants to wear in the mess for dinner. All ranks implicitly believed that the Arabs were cruel to animals. Howard bought a fox cub from a local boy because he was convinced it would be mistreated unless he rescued it; he also overcame his fear of snakes when he saw his bearer beating a cornered serpent, pushing the man aside and killing the animal with a single blow to spare it any more pain.[18]

Military pay was miserly even by the standards of the Depression, and Iraq and Aden were at least good for saving money since there was little to spend it on. 'Life is cheap here and it is rather a useful way of saving money. But Oh! The boredom,' wrote Howard.[19] And there were still plenty of routine expenses. Officers had to pay mess bills, tailor's invoices and other costs that were not easy for younger men without private incomes. Diaries, letters and memoirs from the period are larded with daily listings of every penny spent, along with complaints about high prices and paltry allowances and salaries.

Few things were more important or eagerly awaited than the letters that brought news of family, friends and the lives that airmen had left behind. The post was the only link with home and normality in the pre-electronic age, and it was not unusual for some officers and men to write several letters every day, keeping up a steady correspondence with dozens of people. Some men wrote a form of running letter or diary, daily recording their activities and thoughts in minute detail, and posting the latest instalment home each week.

Few correspondents were as prolific as Howard, who filled ten or twelve long sheets with graceful script every day to the woman he called his 'little wife' or 'little girl'. The arrival of the weekly airmail plane in Iraq was widely known as 'Passion Day' because of the sacks of letters from wives and sweethearts. Surviving letters rarely contain any emotion, passion or lust, however, although a sense of disenchantment, loneliness and bewilderment can often be sensed beneath a crust of stilted reserve or good-natured banter. It was an age when the stiff upper lip was still an essential mark of national character and empire.

Sex, or rather the lack of it, was a weight on most officers and men, although it was not as crushing as later, less inhibited generations might expect. Sex did not exist outside marriage for most people in Britain, and many of the young RAF men in the Middle East probably were no more sex-starved than they would have been at home. Carr and several other young officers who visited a French Air Force squadron in Syria in the 1920s blushed and stammered like schoolboy virgins when the colonel summoned the unit's brothel after dinner and offered them first choice of the women. The Englishmen declined, to the amusement of their Gallic hosts. Some men had no such inhibitions, and made use of local prostitutes whenever possible.

Extraordinary efforts were made to keep RAF personnel out of brothels in Iraq and elsewhere because of the empire's prudish morality and the danger of venereal disease. Military police were posted at the entrance to Baghdad's red light district to bar servicemen. Officers who inspected the place described a hellish scene, with mostly old and diseased women, many of them almost naked, lining a narrow, filthy alleyway. Sex-hungry men showed remarkable ingenuity at skirting the military police and other restrictions, nonetheless, and many of them contracted syphilis and other diseases.

Howard complained that his men were always getting VD (venereal disease); he told his wife about an officer who was banned from the British nurses' lounge at the military hospital after being infected twice in brothels. Every VD case had to be reported to the Air Ministry and reflected badly on the man's unit. A plan to open military brothels staffed by imported Japanese women was abandoned because the Air Ministry feared a scandal if the public discovered the RAF was involved in the sex trade. Enterprising Arab pimps who tried to set up tented brothels outside RAF bases were sometimes driven off with volleys of machine-gun fire over their encampments.

Homosexuality was rare or well concealed, and is rarely mentioned in any surviving official or private documents. Enlisted man B.G. Amos said that in eight years he only heard of a single case.[20] Anyone caught in a homosexual act faced humiliation and harsh penalties, including prison.

Men yearned for a little ordinary contact with white women that had nothing to do with sex; they just wanted a reminder of wives, sweethearts, mothers and sisters at home. Arab females were usually masked in shapeless gowns and despised as natives. Cairo had a large European population, but there was only a handful of white women in Iraq and Aden, and most of the lower ranks never saw a European female, except possibly for military nurses, during their two-year tours. In Baghdad, only officers had any hope of mingling with the wives of British officials and nurses who made up the city's tiny contingent of white women. European women were often outnumbered ten to one at official receptions; men joked about dancing with 'Eileen', which meant 'I lean on the bar'. Enlisted men, who were excluded from such gatherings, partnered each other at what wits called 'bread and bread' dances for the lower ranks.

The handful of white women in Baghdad had throngs of admiring young and not so young RAF officers – some sour observers said that the constant fawning gave most of these women goddess complexes. If some men aspired to bed a married woman, few of them seem to have succeeded, although some women acquired notorious reputations. Howard, chatty as ever, said the wife of a senior official boasted of having numerous affairs with officers, and that her husband did not object. 'If this is true he is an extraordinary fellow and furthermore she must be an even more extraordinary woman to be proud of it,' he wrote to his wife.[21]

A few single senior officers had mistresses, usually Russian refugees or local Christian women. Such behaviour was frowned on and could damage a man's career if discovered. Some judged it worth the risk rather than face years of enforced celibacy. A senior commander told Howard 'the only way to keep fit and happy was to take unto oneself a mistress, otherwise it meant that one was doomed to promiscuous affairs with married and other women, some of whom might be undesirable.'[22] Taking a mistress who was a good housekeeper was said to be more economical than living in the officers' mess. Marriage or open relations with native women were tacitly forbidden because of racial and social taboos – a British officer of the Levies who married a female relative of one of his native soldiers was stripped of his position.

Officers stationed near Baghdad visited the capital's handful of European nightclubs, although most found them dull and expensive. The clubs usually featured criminally overpriced alcohol and a native band that mangled its way through out-of-date Western hit songs. The biggest lure were the European hostesses, mostly Russian refugees, who danced with the guests, ran up their bar bills and might, for a price, sleep with them. Young officers, starved of female company and trying to live up to their image of fashionable rakes, had nowhere else to go no matter how they disparaged the luckless women and tawdry décor of the clubs. Howard told his wife after his first visit to a Baghdad club:

There were only four women in the place and they were too awful for words. One had red hair and blackened eyes which gave her a most weird appearance, another chewed gum the whole time – I supposed to convey the impression that she was pretty tough and the other two were not so bad looking – comparatively speaking – but very coarse.

Nightclubs were for officers only, but cabaret dancers were flown in occasionally from Turkey or Lebanon to entertain the men at remote stations. The shows were toned down, and even the belly dancers did not follow their usual habit of dancing half naked because it 'would have excited us too much', remembered John Varley.[23]

★★★

Despite the hardships and privations, many men valued their time in places like Iraq as a pristine world of male camaraderie that allowed them to shake off the cloying constraints of modern life and find their true natures. 'I suppose it is natural for a man's lonely thoughts to turn to a woman, but I think it is a pity, for when men get together in the wilds one meets the best form of communal happiness,' Keith said.[24]

Even some happily married men shared the idea that men were at their best in the wilderness without women. 'People say you must be out in the "Blue" [desert] with a fellow to discover his real worth. Funny this, but strangely perfectly true, the desert somehow or other brings out a man's real self,' Howard told his adored wife.[25] It was a concept held by both officers and men. Sydney Sills, an enlisted man, thought that 'men are happiest when they are suffering', and only hardship could build true character and comradeship.[26] Samuel Wentworth, another ranker who served in Iraq, said quite a few men volunteered for a third year because of the close camaraderie.[27]

Alcohol was the easiest escape from the stress and miseries of Arabia, and heavy drinking was a pillar of RAF life wherever its squadrons went. Men were expected to drink, and those who did not were seen as odd or laughable. Sills had a drink for the first time when he arrived in Basra, and was knocking off eight pints of beer a day when he left two years later. Carr said drinking destroyed or sublimated the need for sex.

There was resentment that the lower ranks could only buy beer in the base canteens. Stanley Eastmead, an enlisted man in an armoured car company, said this meant that senior NCOs in their 40s with a row of campaign medals did not have the same rights as a teenage officer to buy a whisky.[28] Carr recalled times when normal duties would be suspended, and the officers would go on a drinking binge that lasted for days and from which nobody was excused.

Young officers were expected to limit their bar bills to £5 a month to conserve their slender salaries and moderate their drinking, but alcohol was duty-free and £1 would buy eight bottles of whisky or thirteen bottles of gin. Many flight crews said there were no formal bans on drinking and flying, although men who crashed because they were drunk were punished. Robert Goddard, who thought he had seen everything as a naval airship officer when he dropped agents behind German lines, had a flight commander in Iraq who sobered up before operations with a self-administered enema.[29] Goddard later became an air marshal.

Extravagant efforts were made every Christmas to ease the sense of home-sickness and isolation by recreating a little bit of England or Scotland in the middle of the desert. Rather than putting up a tree or a few ornaments, the men of each hut selected a theme reminiscent of home, and then transformed it into a London tube station complete with a man-sized train or a Yuletide grotto. Skilled carpenters, mechanics and riggers spent weeks turning the drab dormitories into something resembling the Christmas displays in the windows of the grandest London department stores.

Men saved for months to buy beer and other treats to stock little bars in each hut for the celebrations. Christmas Day lunch was the highlight of this annual bacchanalia, with the officers waiting on the men, serving them turkey, roast potatoes, plum pudding and mince pies. Normal duties were suspended for a week, with men wandering between the huts to see the displays and drink at the bars. Wentworth, one of two non-drinkers at the Mosul airbase, said everyone but a few guards was drunk for a week and pud-dles of vomit carpeted the cantonment as men drank themselves insensible.

★★★

Life in Iraq, Aden and elsewhere was tough and demanding, but most men had joined up to escape ordinary lives and many of them wanted to taste combat and danger. Officers and men generally liked, or loved, their work and took huge pride in their skills, whether it was flying an aircraft or keeping it airworthy. There was a proud sense that they were guardians of the greatest empire the world had ever seen. They had, as one of their admirers noted, a deep sense of pride and purpose that carried them through any number of hardships. 'I'm much attached to the Air Force; they have the same sort of charm that sailors have, they are so keen and busy with their job, and it's a job that they are always at, just as sailors are. And they are so amazingly gallant,' Gertrude Bell wrote.[30]

13

THE ELUSIVE PRIZE

I f Britain was the head of the empire, then India, with its hundreds of millions of people and vast expanses, was its beating heart. 'The British Empire is pre-eminently a great Naval, Indian and Colonial power,' the Committee for Imperial Defence declared in 1904.[1] Safeguarding India was second only to the protection of the British Isles in imperial strategy and Hugh Trenchard believed that winning control of its defences would make the RAF the paramount military service. While air power achieved some major successes in the subcontinent, Trenchard's dream would be foiled by the Pathan tribes of the North-West Frontier and local British officials.

The RAF struggled throughout the interwar years to win acceptance in India. The deeply conservative and snobbish Anglo–Indian establishment was mistrustful of any kind of change and for years it looked down on the air force as a rabble of upstart mechanics. Contempt for the service was reflected in the Indian Table of Precedence, the bible of official life that ruled everything from the right to give advice to the viceroy to seating at the most insignificant backwater dinner parties. Provincial army commanders were at the 14th level while the RAF commander for the subcontinent was relegated to the 23rd level, equal to the vice chairman of the agricultural council.

The Indian Army was even more mistrustful of innovation than its British counterpart and was hopelessly besotted with the horse. Major cavalry exercises with thousands of horsemen were held as late as 1925, and senior commanders diligently studied Napoleon's mounted tactics despite the stark lessons of the recent world war. The Indian Army had twenty-six cavalry regiments in 1936, very few trucks and virtually no tanks. Its chief, Field Marshal Philip Chetwode, denounced his own officers in 1934 with an outburst almost unmatched in modern British military history:

I am horrified as I travel up and down India at the number of officers I find, senior and junior alike, who have allowed themselves to sink into a state of complete brain slackness. Their narrow interests are bounded by the morning parade, the game they happen to play, and purely local and unimportant matters. I have found men all over India who evidently scarcely read the papers and are quite unaware of the larger aspects of what is going on in India around them, and still less of the stupendous events outside this country that are now in the process of forming an entirely new world.[2]

★★★

India got its first glimpse of the military potential of the aeroplane when a salesman from the British & Colonial Aeroplane Co. arrived in 1911 with two light aircraft and hopes of selling them to wealthy maharajahs for joyriding. An Indian Army officer, Sefton Brancker, who was a flying enthusiast, arranged for one of the planes to take part in a military exercise as a scout. Brancker squatted precariously behind the pilot as the frail contraption was buffeted by the heat radiating off the dusty red plains. When they found the opposing force, Brancker wrote details of its dispositions on a piece of cardboard suspended by string on the pilot's back. Brancker scribbled so furiously that the pilot wondered if he was making out his will.

Even the stuffiest Indian Army generals were impressed by the potential of aerial reconnaissance and it was decided that the Indian Army must have its own air wing. Plans for a flying school had got as far as stipulating that non-whites would not be accepted when the outbreak of war in Europe in 1914 forced the shelving of the scheme. Brancker, an inspired administrator, later joined the air force, and became an air vice marshal before perishing in 1930 in the wreck of the R101 airship.

India needed aircraft despite the collapse of plans for an Indian air wing, and a flight from the Royal Flying Corp's 31 Squadron with five crated BE2Cs arrived in Bombay on Boxing Day 1915. Aircraft were used on the North-West Frontier for the first time in October 1916 with thunderous success. The Pathans, who were used to leisurely shooting at British troops from the safety of the mountain tops, fled from these deadly machines that soared over their hiding places, cutting down the tribesmen with bombs and machine guns.

Further successes followed in 1917 when the air force bombed villages that the army had never been able to reach in parts of Waziristan on the North-West Frontier. Political officers boasted like the proud parents of a precocious schoolboy when a pilot dropped a bomb into the heart of a tribal gathering, killing twelve people and wounding many more. These early bombing raids devastated Pathan villages and did massive damage to the impoverished tribes' meagre possessions. 'They dislike intensely the burning of … [their] huts as it generally results in the destruction of their bedding and the few spare clothes they possess,' a note to aircrews said.[3]

Large stretches of the North-West Frontier had never been seen by the British until aircraft flew over them for the first time. Army commanders were astonished when aerial reconnaissance revealed that there were more than fifty villages in a valley long thought to have just half a dozen settlements – it helped to explain why so many army expeditions had come to grief in the hills. Air strategists said the empire finally had a weapon that could tame the frontier. Aircraft had '… opened up a new chapter in the history of our relations with the trans-frontier tribes and in our methods of ensuring tranquillity on the border,' the RAF declared.[4]

India's military establishment, while admitting that aircraft had their uses, insisted the air force was just a minor technical service of no great importance. The Indian Government was responsible for funding RAF units in the subcontinent, and after the First World War it began ruthlessly slashing the little contingent's spending in the name of economy.

By the early 1920s RAF squadrons in India were close to collapse for lack of maintenance and spare parts. Squadrons had to cannibalise planes for enough parts to keep one or two flying. Aircraft were fitted with homemade wooden wheels, and mechanics purchased used nuts and bolts in the local bazaars. Pilots took off in planes literally held together with crude local rope. Arthur Harris, who had applied for a posting to India because he thought the North-West Frontier might be fun, said just a few of 31 Squadron's Bristol Fighters were airworthy when he joined it. John Slessor served in a squadron whose fighters bore unrepaired German bullet holes from the European war.

By 1922 the six RAF squadrons in India had only a handful of aircraft that could fly. All but one of the twelve planes involved in frontier raids in April that year made forced landings because of engine failure or other problems, and by August just six planes could be scraped together from the entire Indian force for a bombing mission. A growing number of flight crews were killed or injured as aircraft literally fell apart in the air at a time when the British Government was selling off 10,000 aircraft and 30,000 aerial engines at home, mostly as scrap.[5] Harris said that when 31 Squadron requested supplies for the planes' reconnaissance cameras they received photo paper that was brown with age and decomposed developing chemicals that were useless.[6] Things were no better on the ground, where RAF units were given decrepit barracks with leaking roofs and rotting walls considered unfit for army troops. A senior army officer told Harris he should be honoured because the quarters assigned to his unit dated from the Indian Mutiny – Harris caustically asked why nobody had bothered to whitewash the hovels in the intervening decades. Aircraft at the Calcutta airbase were housed in straw huts that had been ruled as unfit for donkeys.

Reports on the lamentable state of the RAF in India eventually appeared in the British press, angering the public and forcing the government to order an inquiry. John Salmond was the obvious candidate for the task, and he went out to India in the summer of 1922. He had an unnerving taste of just how bad things were when the biplane assigned to fly him around the subcontinent appeared with a gaping crack in its top wing; the pilot explained that a request for canvas to patch the hole had been rejected. Salmond's subsequent report gave a scathing picture of a force that had been virtually hounded into extinction by mindless bureaucratic penny-pinching.

'I have to report that the Royal Air Force [in India] is to all intents and purposes non-existent as a fighting force at this date,' he wrote.[7] Just seven planes out of a nominal strength of seventy could get into the air, he said, and some of those were 'so old and decrepit' that they were not safe to fly. It was a force 'bordering on impotency', he continued, whose morale was near collapse because the Indian Government begrudged even a few rupees for nuts and bolts. It was a devastating indictment that shamed the Indian Government into immediate reforms.

Looking ahead, Salmond tried to use the report to secure a much bigger role for the RAF in the subcontinent. He belittled the army's failure to tame the North-West Frontier and said that with just two additional squadrons the air force could single-handedly subdue the Pathan tribes at an enormous saving in money and British lives. He predicted a future where bomber crews would be as familiar with the frontier as they were in their off-duty hours with the streets and squares of central London. Salmond rounded out his vision by suggesting aircraft could put down the growing number of demonstrations in Indian cities against British rule. Bombing would only be necessary in 10 per cent of cases, he added reassuringly, because most urban Indians were cowards who would run at the mere sight of an aircraft.[8]

★★★

For more than half a century the British had tried and failed to subdue the Pathan tribes of the North-West Frontier. Inhabiting a vast natural fortress formed by the jagged peaks and hidden valleys of the mountains along the Afghan border, the ferocious tribes regularly attacked government posts and raided the rich lowlands. Holding the Pathans back was the pre-eminent task of the Indian Army, with its British officers and native troops, and the British Army units based in the subcontinent.

Imperial poets and novelists had turned the frontier into the most legendary strip of territory in the empire with tales of military glory, but the men who served there called it 'the Grim' because of the terror and cruelty of tribal warfare. Some sixty military expeditions were sent against the frontier tribes between 1848 and 1914, but never won more than temporary victories. An Indian Army handbook described the Pathans as 'brave to the point of recklessness', 'careless of human life', including their own, and 'capable of almost superhuman' deeds in the grip of religious fervour.[9] The British, sitting in frontier forts that resembled something from the Crusades, were fighting the tribes with tactics that had barely changed in decades when the RAF arrived on the subcontinent.

From the moment they appeared on the frontier, the air force played a vital role against the Pathans. Air power gave British forces an advantage that would have been unimaginable in the past to ground commanders whose forces had to slog their way blindly through the hostile mountains. And yet it was soon apparent that air power could only inflict temporary defeats on the Pathans. British forces still lost 639 dead and almost 1,700 wounded in a frontier campaign between 1919 and 1920 in Waziristan, despite strong air support that inflicted stinging losses on the local tribes.

Major General S.H. Climo's assessment of the strengths and weaknesses of aircraft in Indian frontier campaigns would remain relevant throughout the interwar era despite repeated RAF claims that air power alone could control the tribes. Aircraft excelled at reconnaissance and protecting ground units, and could inflict temporary defeats on the tribesman, Climo said, but the air force had not lived up to its main claim that air attacks would destroy the tribes' morale and permanently end resistance.

Climo also said that bombing was far less effective than the airmen claimed because most bombs missed the targets. During the Waziristan campaign, troops who entered the village of Kainguram in March 1920, after it had been hit with 16 tons of bombs, found that most of the projectiles had missed, and those that did hit the settlement caused only slight damage to a few buildings.

Turning the RAF's claims of waging cut-price war back on it, Climo said the cost had been 'out of all proportion to the material damage done'.[10]

The Pathans would be the most formidable opponents the RAF faced during the interwar era. The frontier tribes adapted to air attacks with a resilience and ingenuity that confounded the airmen's claims that 'primitive' people lost their will to fight after their first taste or two of bombing. While a Pathan tribe or war party invariably suffered serious casualties the first time it was attacked by air, subsequent raids generally had a diminishing impact as the tribesmen became accustomed to air raids and developed effective defences.

Every tribe on the frontier soon built air raid shelters of remarkable strength and sophistication. Captured pilots told of being held in dwellings that had been adapted to withstand air attacks by digging sunken floors lined with thick stone walls that barely shook when bombs exploded outside. Many villages developed labyrinthine air raid shelters in the caves that honeycombed the hills; hundreds of people could shelter safely in these spacious refuges for weeks at a time. It was almost impossible to lob a bomb into these caves and blast walls were often constructed at the entrance to deflect the explosions from any projectiles that detonated outside.

A highly effective air raid warning system was set up in some areas, with chains of lookouts on the peaks who could spot aircraft when they were still dozens of miles away and raise the alarm. Villages were evacuated and the inhabitants took cover well before the aircraft were overhead. Pathan marksmen took a steady toll on aircraft, even when they were flying thousands of feet above. Three Bristol fighters were shot down in one raid in January 1920, while a political agent who flew with a squadron to direct the bombing of a village he administered was shot and badly wounded by one of his charges.

Attacking the tribes' mountain villages was dangerous and taxing because of the vertical terrain, unpredictable weather, the limited capabilities of the aircraft and the Pathan defences. Success required superb flying skills, and a fair amount of luck. Aircraft often had little time and space for manoeuvring in the cramped sky over villages hemmed in by vertical mountain walls and the smallest misjudgement by a pilot could slam a plane into the sheer rock faces. The number of planes over a target at any one time was limited after a DH9A was hit in mid-air and obliterated by a bomb dropped from a plane flying above it in a December 1922 raid.

Arthur Capel, who had survived the aerial slaughter of the Western Front, was part of a disastrous 1924 raid. The formation of six planes lifted off into a serene morning sky only to be caught in the mountains by a wall of black cloud that descended without warning and blotted out the surrounding mountain sides. Two planes flew into the sides of mountains, killing all four crewmen, while Capel and another pilot crashed on the boulder-strewn valley floor. The overturned plane was ringed within moments by screaming men, women and children. The two dazed aviators were wrenched from the cockpits, and the furious crowd tore at their faces with their hands and ripped their clothing.

A frenzy erupted as the Pathans next tore the aircraft apart, shredding the fabric and smashing the wooden frame. But the airmen were treated almost as honoured guests after the initial anger had subsided. Capel's captors fed him hard-boiled eggs they insisted on peeling for him as a mark of respect, but their unwashed, begrimed fingers turned the gleaming white surfaces black. 'All very filthy and it almost makes you ill to look at it,' he later noted.[11]

Capel's gunner was soon ransomed, but he was held for several days while his captors haggled with British officials over the price for his release. Capel complained about the lack of knives and forks and the stringy chicken he was given to eat. Things improved when a box arrived from British lines with tinned tongue, sardines and other delicacies along with whisky, beer, warm clothing and something to read. After that the young officer treated his captivity as an impromptu holiday, reading and admiring the scenery over a whisky. He was embarrassed when the Pathans offered him a share of the ransom, and they only let him go when he accepted a revolver and bandolier as a souvenir. Capel, who was an air vice marshal in the Second World War, marvelled at how kindly he was treated by people he had been trying to kill, although he found the women 'vindictive and unpleasant'.[12]

Capel's adventure was not unusual despite frontier lore that captured white men were tortured to death. Flyers who fell into the hands of the Pathans were invariably well treated, partly because of the ransoms paid for their safe return, partly out of the tribes' admiration for brave men. Flight Lieutenant F. W. Sinclair, who was wounded when he was captured, was carried to British lines by tribesmen who later visited him in a military hospital. A group of solicitous tribesman with long black beards ringed the pale young pilot's bed like anxious uncles fussing over a favourite nephew.[13]

Captured airmen were sometimes used as human shields against bombing raids. More than one downed pilot was chained in the centre of a village as it was attacked by his own squadron. Flying Officer Foster wrote of his experience:

I was made to stand in the middle of the village when the warning signal of the approach of the aircraft was heard, while the villagers all retired to their funk holes. I was also given to understand that they would have no compunction in shooting me if the village was bombed.[14]

The air force refused to call off raids because of hostages, but senior officers worried that pilots might choose to miss a target rather than risk killing one of their own.

★★★

The RAF became increasingly concerned in the early 1920s as Air Control failed to tame the North-West Frontier, despite local successes. One anonymous staff officer fretted that it would 'bring bombing into ridicule'.[15] Air commanders imbued with inflexible notions of the inferiority of black people could not accept that natives were capable of withstanding, let alone adapting to, air attacks. Determined to prove that its methods worked, the RAF stepped up operations against the tribes with ever bigger raids and bigger bombs to break the Pathans.

The usual prescriptions of 'moral effect' and moderate bombing was replaced by talk of inflicting heavy casualties and damage. A 1922 directive said that 'half measures are of no value' and raids must inflict as many losses on the tribes as possible; anything less would 'raise rather than lower the enemy's morale and may induce a feeling of contempt'.[16] Squadrons were told that they had one or two days to break a tribe, after which the people would scatter. Squadron commanders were instructed to use every available plane when mounting raids. An officer who did not send out every plane from the available two squadrons in a 1924 operation was reprimanded for being 'supine'.[17]

Bomb loads steadily increased as colonial squadrons were issued with more powerful planes and heavier weapons. The Indian squadrons had a combined bombing capability of 4 tons of bombs in 1919; this rose to 8 tons in 1925 and 30 tons in 1930.[18] Increasing use was made of delayed-action bombs, which exploded up to thirty hours after being dropped, to extend the impact of raids. Night raids to catch the Pathans in their homes became routine. A captured pilot came back with descriptions of such tempting targets as a dwelling where he had been held overnight with ten people, more than 100 goats and six cows.

Night operations were difficult and dangerous in aircraft flown mainly by sight, however, and the chances of hitting a target were low. Capel said night bombing was never accurate, and the real aim was to terrify the population.[19] Drawing on lessons from Iraq, squadrons were told the ideal time to attack villages was just before dawn when people would be asleep.

Bombing techniques were crude and unreliable throughout the interwar period, and day and night raids saw far more misses than hits, despite unflagging RAF claims of precision accuracy. Just forty-nine out of 152 bombs fell within 100 yards of the target in a 1924 Indian training exercise held under ideal conditions over flat ground without bad weather or ground fire.[20] A series of raids on frontier villages in November 1928 saw 102 out of 182 bombs explode harmlessly far from the targets.[21]

The Bristol fighters used by many Indian squadrons in the 1920s were not fitted with bomb sights, and pilots had to guess the angle and speed at which to attack while dodging surrounding mountains and ground fire. The DH9A had only primitive crosshair sights clamped to the side of the fuselage; the bombing was done by the gunners, who received very little training for the role. Gunners would lean far out of the cockpit, steadying themselves against gusts of wind that tried to pitch them into the sky, and adjusting the plane's direction by pummelling the pilot's shoulders. Crews became used to watching glumly as their bombs exploded harmlessly on waste ground or plunged into empty crevices.

Raids were often given very specific targets, such as the houses of a tribal chief and his lieutenants, but actual hits were rare no matter how hard crews tried. Aubrey Ellwood said most pilots were content just to hit something in the general area of a target. 'If the bombs did just hit a number of mud huts, as they mostly were, then you'd done something,' he said.[22] Accuracy was further impaired when pilots were ordered not to bomb below 3,000ft after Pathan ground fire brought down several planes. At that height bombing could only be 'moderately accurate,' Capel said, but while 'you may not hit the target … you certainly hit the village'.[23]

Many bombs turned out to be duds that failed to explode, angering crews who complained that they had risked their lives to drop them. A captured pilot saw Pathan children using unexploded bombs for toys. 'Every child had an unexploded Baby Incendiary [bomb] to play with,' he said.[24] Some captured airmen were shaken when they saw how little damage bombing sometimes inflicted. Flying Officer R.J.M. St Leger, who was captured in 1923 when his DH9A crashed, became increasingly incredulous as his captors led him through the villages his squadron was attacking. Only one in eight of the houses seemed to have been damaged, he estimated, and most of that was fairly minor, with a few holes in roofs or the occasional crack in a wall. 'The damage did not appear as great as the intelligence reports would lead one to suppose', he said. St Leger insisted, nonetheless, that the tribesmen were 'impressed with the bombing'.[25]

★★★

Almost any tactic was considered permissible as the RAF tried to hammer the tribes into submission in these early years. A 1923 RAF guide declared, 'In warfare against savage tribes who do not conform to codes of civilized warfare, aerial bombardment is not necessarily limited in its methods or objectives by rules agreed upon in international law.'

Spencer Viles, who flew many missions as an air gunner and bomb aimer, said the only objective for many crews was to kill as many people as possible: 'We just went up and wiped out the village.'[26] A 500lb bomb was dropped on a mosque during one operation, even though religious centres were supposed to be spared, and 'we left it non-existent ... and we don't know how many people were in it', he said. Viles' abiding memory, years later, was of the time when he was promised two bottles of Dutch beer for every hit he scored in one operation; winning fourteen or sixteen bottles.

Civilian officials became increasingly worried about the number of people, especially women and children, being killed in frontier air raids, partly because of criticism from some quarters in India and Britain, partly because of their own feelings that the victims were at least nominally British subjects. This helped lead to the introduction in the early 1920s of the use of leaflets to warn villages of raids and minimise casualties. The RAF's India Command was particularly vocal in criticising the system, especially the requirement to tell villagers when bombing would begin. Commanders said this allowed the tribesmen to determine how much time they had to move their property and flocks before the bombers appeared overhead.

A 1925 RAF memo complained that a tribe warned of a raid had 'removed not only their women and children but everything else of value'.[27] Government efforts to restrict bombing to specific targets such as the chief's residence were also resented, with air commanders arguing that pilots must be free to use their initiative in selecting targets. Air force officers complained that civilian officials were always ordering pauses in bombing campaigns to see if the tribes were ready to talk or submit. The airmen said any let-up just gave the Pathans time to gather food, wash their clothes and settle back for more raids. Bombing must not stop, the airmen said, until the tribes had given in.

For all its pugnacious talk, the RAF was extremely sensitive about any criticism or adverse publicity about Air Control operations. Air Vice Marshal Philip Game, the RAF chief in India, was outraged when some civilian officials compared what was happening in India to German air raids on London during the First World War that caused many civilian casualties. A white woman could not be compared to a native, he said: 'I gather that a woman ranks among the .... [tribes] as a piece of property somewhere between a rifle and a cow.'[28]

Indian nationalists and some in the country's increasingly influential intelligentsia and professional classes also challenged the air raids. RAF commanders in India complained that bombing was being portrayed as 'a low-down ungentlemanly performance',[29] and fretted about critical reports in Indian and Afghan newspapers. Some civilian officials were especially unhappy about the use of delayed-action bombs after receiving reports that they had killed a number of women and children. Game admitted to Trenchard that such weapons were brutal, not least because Pathan children thought they were toys. 'The inevitable result of long delay action fuses would be blowing a lot of children to pieces. They apparently have a passion for playing with dud bombs.'[30]

There were claims that the abduction and killing of several British women by tribesmen in the 1920s was a retaliation for air raids. Denys Bray, one of the Raj's most senior civil officials, warned, '... we must expect not merely intensive raiding into British territory, as a retaliation for our continuous air raids, but intensive raiding against our women and children in retaliation for the victims among tribal women and children of our air operations.' He said the claim that British rule was justified because it was benevolent was being undermined by employing 'a ruthlessness that cannot be other than promiscuous'.[31]

Even the RAF had occasional doubts. Game told Trenchard he was uneasy at bombing a tribe '... who after all had only stolen animals and sniped a bit'.[32] The aircrews that bombed frontier villages deeply resented the way they were vilified by critics of Air Control and worried about how they might be seen at home by the general public. Ellwood said:

There were great misunderstandings … especially at home, people said it was a
very cruel thing to do, it was bombing civilians, especially women and children,
they always thought we could select women and children from the air (and
miss them) … which of course was nonsense. In point of fact, they didn't know
that all these people … had all been warned to get out of their villages if they
didn't behave themselves … [33]

While it might be uncomfortable about bombing its own subjects, or squirm
under adverse publicity, the Indian Government could not afford to renounce
a weapon that massively increased its reach and firepower for the budgetary
equivalent of pennies. Officials tried to end the dispute by simply declaring
that bombing was not inhuman and acting as if the issue was settled. There
was no danger, it was stated in 1925, of British rule 'acquiring a reputation
for the employment of methods of barbarism. For one thing, air operations
… are not in their actual effect inhuman.'[34]

Every effort was made, nonetheless, to cover up or play down the bombings and their impact. Indian squadrons were instructed in August 1925 to
stop publicly reporting the number and weight of bombs dropped in frontier
raids – the Air Ministry said such details were 'for many reasons undesirable'.[35]
A memo said the air secretary was keen to omit details about the deaths of
livestock to avoid upsetting a British public that was more protective of
animals than natives.[36]

★★★

It was not until 1925 that the RAF was given a chance to prove it could
handle an Indian frontier campaign without the support of ground forces.
Richard Charles Montagu Pink had exchanged the perils of the submarine
service for the equally dangerous uncertainties of airships before the First
World War. He was a large, vigorous man who concealed a melancholic streak
with an outward show of unfailing good humour. One of his many talents
was writing and staging amusing skits about military life.

Pink was given the task of subduing a group of tribes in South Waziristan
that had been attacking government posts. The culprits lived in one of the most
inaccessible parts of the frontier, and a ground expedition against them would
take months, be ruinously expensive and have only a modest chance of success.
The tribes lived in a region some 5,000ft above sea level so Pink's planes could
only carry 60 per cent of their normal fuel loads, otherwise they could not

gain sufficient altitude to bomb the villages. Some forty villages were selected as targets and most were given numbers because the British did not know their names. Pink took the then novel step of calling together his entire command, including the lowliest enlisted men, and briefing them on the operation. He blushed violently when the audience burst into applause at the end.

Pink's squadrons began bombing the villages on 9 March and kept up the attacks for fifty-four days until the last holdouts finally submitted. British newspapers in India gloated that the tribes had faced being devoured by fleas in the caves where they sheltered or being blown to bits by bombs. Editorial writers raved over the RAF triumph, and advocated increasing the size of the air contingent in India to keep the tribes down. One journal pointed out that the RAF had only some seventy planes in India whereas Siam, a native power, was said to have 250 aircraft. 'Is it not time that India took a leaf out of Siam's book?' it inquired.[37] The campaign went down in RAF legend as 'Pink's War' and Trenchard tried to portray it as conclusive proof that his men could control the frontier single-handed.

The notion that air power would crush the Pathans was never realistic even though the North-West Frontier saw the largest, longest and most concerted Air Control operations in the interwar period. The champions of air power argued that with a few more squadrons, a free hand and enough time they could subdue the tribes, impose British control across the frontier and clear the way for the government to axe dozens of expensive army regiments.

Trenchard waged a tenacious bureaucratic campaign for the control of India's defence, claiming that with just six more squadrons the RAF could subdue the frontier tribes, and the government would be able to disband up to thirty army battalions.[38] But Trenchard's grand plan was unworkable even if the Indian Government had been willing to give it a chance. The RAF would have needed hundreds, even thousands, of planes at enormous expense, and the whole rationale for Air Control was that it slashed defence costs.

Even if it had been given the resources, the RAF could only have pacified the frontier by killing huge numbers of Pathans in a massive and sustained campaign that could not have been concealed, and which would have appalled even the most vociferous imperialists and air strategists. The RAF's obsession with vindicating Air Control in India blinded it to the fact that while aircraft could not defeat the Pathans they did play an increasingly crucial role in shoring up British defences.

★★★

If the RAF was set on revolutionising the defence of India, it was equally determined to fit into the privileged and stuffy world of Anglo-Indian society. A young service that was still unsure of itself outside of the cockpit desperately wanted to be accepted as part of the empire's ruling elite. Making the right impression on society hostesses seemed almost as important as proving that bombing sorties could pacify the frontier tribes. Considerable time and effort went into ensuring that air force officers were prepared for their social as well as military duties in India.

A 1921 air force pamphlet coached officers going to India on every aspect of their new lives, instructing them on everything from how much to tip servants to where they should spend their leave time. Great stress was laid on budgeting salaries, with guidelines on everything from basic living costs to 'drinks at the mess and club, smokes, personal pleasures, recreations, saving for leave or other purposes'.[39] No one wanted a repeat of the unhappy wartime stories about air officers who didn't pay their debts or filched official funds.

Air force officers were expected to follow all the rituals of Indian service life, including leaving their calling cards at the homes of superiors after arriving at a new post. RAF commanders usually returned the cards so that they could be reused – it was still a service that had very few men with private incomes to subsidise their modest salaries.

The topee or sun helmet was the ubiquitous symbol of the white man in India, an indispensable if cumbersome emblem of authority, and the RAF developed a special version for aircrew to wear while airborne instead of the usual leather flying helmets. It was indistinguishable from the land-bound version except for a broad chin strap that could accommodate radio headphones.

India offered abundant privileges and comforts for its white rulers, although living conditions on airbases right after the war were often primitive because the Indian Government starved squadrons of funds. William Coryton and other officers bathed in cheap tin tubs at Ambala in the early years, there was no electricity and their quarters were lit by oil lamps and candles.[40] Aubrey Ellwood remembered having to learn to draw water from wells for the first time in his life.[41]

Things soon improved and Harris had a very comfortable lifestyle. He lived in a spacious bungalow with a dozen servants and there was polo, shooting, tennis and other off-duty recreations. 'You lived like a blinking minor lord in a minor way,' he said.[42] Most air force officers plunged happily into the social routine of Indian life with its endless dinners, receptions, sports and hunting.

One of the great differences compared to RAF stations in the Middle East was the everyday presence of white women and many air force officers brought their spouses out to India. Air force wives were expected to work as hard as their husbands at boosting the service's social image. The guide for officers bound for India said that spouses would need more evening dresses than in England and the creations of native tailors were acceptable, but that stockings were hard to get on remote airbases and adequate supplies should be taken.

Sport was the other hallowed area of Indian life – 'Sport is still the best thing India can offer,' the officers' handbook declared.[43] Games were not just for recreation or exercise; the RAF saw athletic prowess as vital to its prestige and a key battleground in its rivalry with the older military services. Unit commanders were expected to put a lot of time and effort into raising teams that could beat army and civilian rivals. Sporting activity was covered assiduously in the monthly operational reports to the Air Ministry, with scores reported as carefully as the number of bombs dropped on the frontier.[44]

Officers bound for the subcontinent were told to take saddles, guns, fishing rods and golf clubs in their hand luggage. Hunting was popular on frontier bases although there was always the danger of enthusiastic Pathans hunting the British hunters. Militiamen picketed the hills to foil attacks when Capel and other officers went bird hunting on the frontier.[45] Rivalries with the army were usually forgotten in the social clubs that were the centre of life in every British community. There was a general ban on talking about 'shop' (work), so professional jealousies were generally left outside. There were lots of inter-service friendships, and Ellwood said it helped if the airmen were interested in horses because of the soldiers' obsession with polo and other equestrian sports.

Life was less sumptuous, although far from spartan for the lower ranks. India seemed like a fairy tale when W.H. Lawrence arrived in Bombay soon after the First World War. The young enlisted man never forgot his first, bedazzled glimpse of the majestic white marble buildings gleaming in the sun, the markets full of rainbow coloured fruits and spices and gleaming brassware, and the throngs of people choking the streets and alleys. 'We only stayed one day but it was like a month's education,' he remembered.[46]

The country's poverty and filth was equally shocking to many; even those who had grown up in some of the grimmest slums in Britain were shaken by their first sight of hordes of stick-thin children and beggars covered with sores. Most men were apprehensive or slightly frightened at first because the country and the people seemed so very different. Old sweats took pleasure in teasing new arrivals with tales of the horrible fates that might befall them. Wilfred Page was told to be wary when he used the toilet because the Indian cleaners who removed the waste pans beneath the seats would try to castrate him.[47]

There were real threats. Wilfred Anderson never forgot how the coming of the monsoons at Ambala sparked an invasion of snakes seeking shelter from the rain. Cobras, kraits and other poisonous serpents infested the hangars and aircraft, and mechanics had to be careful about where they trod or reaching for a tool. Afternoon snake hunts were sometimes organised despite the dangers, and a snake charmer brought in to help rid the base of its unwelcome guests one year was bitten and died.[48]

The lower ranks lived in the traditional stone or brick barracks that the British military had inhabited for generations in India. Barracks had high ceilings for ventilation and fans provided a tepid draft in the summer. Thirty men generally occupied the large single space, with fifteen beds on each side. Meals were eaten at a large table in the centre of the room that was also used for games, writing letters and lounging in off-duty hours. Food was fairly good and abundant, although some men grumbled about constantly being given eggs.

Men had servants for the first time in their lives; half-awake airmen were deftly shaved in bed at dawn by Indian barbers, while bearers kept their clothes clean and ran errands. The most common complaint was of the crushing heat of the Indian summer; men suffered from the needle-jabbing pain of prickly heat and their skin blistered and peeled because of fungus infections.

Life on the bases was often monotonous with only the canteen and the occasional trip to the native bazaar to break the routine. Page, a mechanic, said the long days spent in hangars made it seem more like working in a factory than serving in a military force.

Sex was easier to come by than in Iraq or Aden because men could go to local brothels. Page said the warnings about the dangers of prostitutes and venereal disease began on the troopship – an officer told him to look out for women on the docks who tried to lure men behind train wagons for sex. White women, while numerous, were almost exclusively from the families of officers and civil officials, and contact across the class divide was as taboo as racial mingling. Masturbation was a common release; Page said some men indulged in group masturbation, with four or five men urging each other on.

Marshal of the Royal Air Force Hugh Trenchard, architect of Air Control, and an aide stride along a London street in the air force's elaborate full dress uniform.

John Salmond with Air Secretary Lord Amulree in 1930. Salmond led early Air Control operations in Iraq and India, and succeeded Trenchard as chief of the RAF.

Arthur Harris in 1946. As a young squadron commander, Harris led some of the first Air Control bombing raids.

John Slessor who, as a young pilot in 1916, bombed an army of medieval cavalry in the Sudan. He rose to command the RAF after the Second World War.

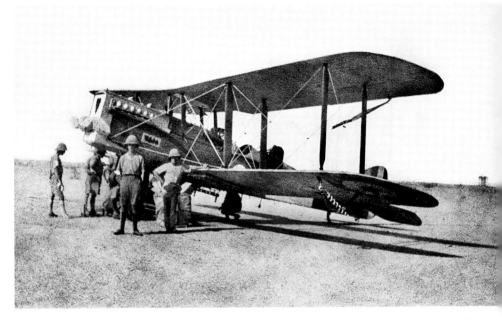

Ground crew with a DH9A in Iraq. Some regarded this light bomber as the true symbol of British imperial might in the early interwar era.

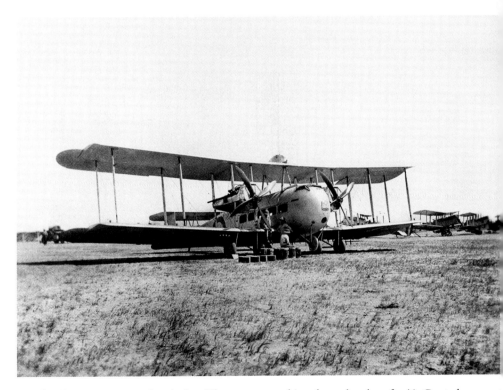

A Vickers Vernon transport plane in Iraq. They were turned into heavy bombers for Air Control operations by sawing an aiming hole in the cockpit and fitting bomb struts to the wings.

Sopwith Snipe fighters in Iraq shortly after the First World War.

Captain Robert 'Jock' Halley (left) and one of the crew of the four-engine Handley Page V/1500 that bombed Kabul in 1919. Trenchard claimed the attack ended the Third Afghan War.

Old Carthusian, the Handley Page V/1500 that bombed Kabul.

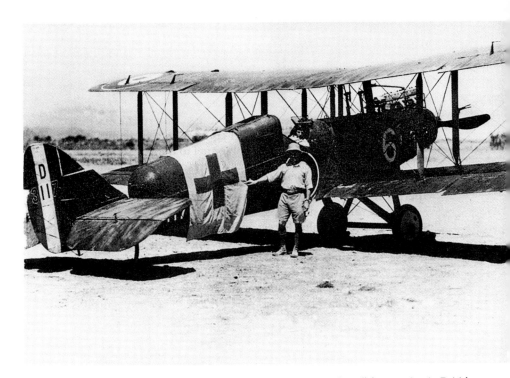

A DH9A that was fitted as a flying ambulance during the 1920 Mad Mullah campaign in British Somaliland. Wits dubbed it 'the flying coffin'.

Part of an RAF group diverted to Constantinople during the 1922 Chanak crisis. Legend had it their blue uniforms led to them being taken for Portuguese troops.

A DH9A squadron in Iraq takes off on an Air Control mission.

Kurdish prisoners taken during the RAF campaign to pacify northern Iraq after the air force took over the country's defences in 1922.

Air raids were used to enforce tax collections in Iraq despite frequent British government denials. This picture by an airman of a bomb dump at an RAF base was tellingly labelled 'Tax Pills'.

DH9As during night operations. Squadrons operated around the clock in bombing missions to break the will of rebellious tribes.

A bomber dips its wing over one of Baghdad's mosques. A British visitor who went on a routine air patrol chortled at the sight of people fleeing a mosque, saying that the British would not bomb a mosque, but the Arabs did not know that.

John Salmond's personal DH9A bomber while he was in command in Iraq. He often accompanied bombing raids, and its vivid maroon fuselage became a fixture in the Iraqi skies in the early 1920s.

A Westland Wapiti drops its bombs on a village on the North-West Frontier. It was the only plane specifically developed for colonial operations.

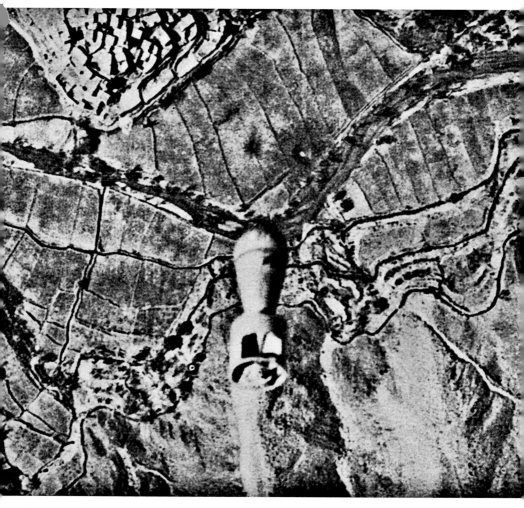

A bomb descends on a Pathan village on India's North-West Frontier. The Pathan tribes were the RAF's toughest opponents, enduring some of the fiercest bombing the world had seen up to that point.

A flight of Vickers Vernons patrolling over Iraq. Such shows of force were intended to discourage any resistance.

Civilians board an RAF transport at Kabul in 1929. The Western community was evacuated to escape an Afghan civil war in history's first mass air evacuation.

A Westland Wapiti flies over a British Army encampment during operations on the North-West Frontier against the Fakir of Ipi.

Mahsud tribesmen in the mountainous North-West Frontier during the 1930s.

The aftermath of a Pathan ambush of a British convoy on the North-West Frontier. A tank, the other technological innovation in colonial warfare, provides cover.

Indian Army survivors from a Pathan ambush in the 1930s. Air patrols frequently failed to spot tribal forces waiting to attack ground convoys.

Air Control was presented as a modern form of diplomacy, with aircrews visiting the most remote areas. Airmen take tea with Arab chiefs in Iraq.

Leonard Charlton, the senior RAF staff officer who opposed Air Control after seeing its results first hand in Iraq.

Crashes were frequent in the harsh conditions of frontier campaigns. The wreckage of a DH9A in Iraq.

A bad landing for a pilot in Iraq.

The remains of a DH9A bomber in the Middle East after a fatal crash.

A wrecked plane waits to be loaded on a river steamer in Iraq. The cash-strapped RAF insisted every possible spare part be saved, even laying down tables on how many camels and mules were needed to salvage each type of aircraft.

A desert funeral for two crewmen killed on Air Control operations in the Middle East.

The heavy, antiquated armoured cars could be ill suited to local conditions. A crew tries to get their vehicle across a narrow bridge.

Air Control doctrine belittled ground forces, but RAF armoured car squadrons were deemed indispensable to effective operations.

Armoured car squadrons had to operate for weeks at a time in the desert. A unit digs for water as amused Bedouin tribesmen look on.

Armoured car crews pose with a haul of wildlife. The crews often had to live off the land during long patrols.

The RAF recruited a private army of native troops in the Middle East. Assyrian Christians of the RAF Iraq Levies.

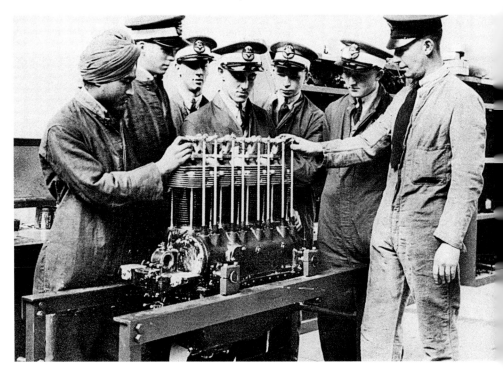

An Indian recruit at the RAF Cadet College at Cranwell in the late 1930s after the formation of a separate Indian Air Force. Non-whites were banned from the RAF for much of the interwar period.

An RAF detachment bound for the Middle East poses in England before departure.

The RAF might be the master of the air, but airmen still went out to colonial posts in decrepit troop ships.

After arriving in a foreign port, airmen invariably faced long trips by train and road to their air stations. Airmen trundle across Iraq in the 1920s.

Guard duty with the temperature at 126°F in the shade. Sentries took it in turn to stand in the summer heat.

Summer barracks in Iraq when the heat made life maddeningly difficult.

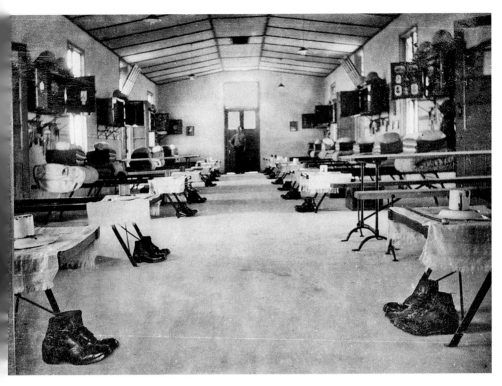

Winter barracks in Iraq when the cold made life almost as unbearable.

Guarding the empire usually meant endless military routine. Two airmen on cookhouse duty.

Comforts were few on remote desert airbases. The base shop offered little besides tinned food which was expensive, but it was a reminder of home.

A lone airman poses before the Great Sphinx in Egypt.

Most men rarely left colonial air bases except to visit the local bazaar to buy souvenirs to take home, or visit brothels despite strict prohibitions in many areas.

Sport was an important and popular part of RAF routine. A proud commanding officer accepts a trophy after his squadron triumphed at a fixture in Iraq.

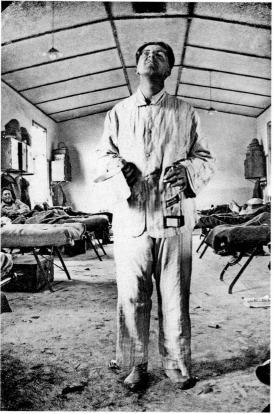

Alcohol was the easiest release for men trapped in the desert for up to three years. An airman clowns with a famous brand of whisky in a barracks, but drunkenness was a common problem.

Christmas was marked by up to two weeks of holidays on RAF colonial bases. A table prepared for Christmas dinner in a barracks hut.

Airmen and officers mix at a rare combined social event. The officers maintain their status in full evening dress despite the desert temperatures.

A coffin of an airman killed in Air Control operations awaits burial. The dead were buried within hours to encourage the survivors not to brood.

Race was the other great pillar of British life in India, and most RAF officers and men instinctively embraced the inflexible doctrine of white superiority and native inferiority. Indians were at best looked down on, and more often despised as weak, dishonest and detestable. One British visitor was told by a hardened memsahib that a native servant could not be trusted until he had been beaten sufficiently to have 'cuts on his back two fingers deep'.[49] Air force officers were encouraged not to whip their servants, however. 'Suffice to say that nowadays no servant will stay with a master who abuses him or beats him. Much real harm has been done in the past by youths coming out to India who regarded every Indian as someone to order about and shout at,' the RAF officers' guidebook explained.[50]

The cinema was one of the few areas where the races mixed socially in the subcontinent. Even the Pathans trekked in from the hills to the cinema in Kohat, although they had to leave their rifles at the box office and sit in a section fenced with barbed wire.

A few RAF men objected to this imperial apartheid, and tried to learn about India and its people. Page made friends with some Indian civilians and toured villages on a bicycle to see local life. He also learned about Indian art, dancing and architecture, despite the risk of being seen as odd by his comrades. He thought that his countrymen had more to learn from this ancient land and its people than they could ever impart. Most of the British, he said, were in India:

> ... to drink as many chota pegs [whisky] as they could, get as much money as they could and retire as early as they could and the last thing they ever considered was that they were serving a purpose to the Indian nation, helping to uplift them in any way at all.[51]

14

THE KABUL MIRACLE

The RAF's colonial squadrons achieved a triumph of a very different kind when they carried out history's first mass aerial evacuation, plucking hundreds of Western civilians from the middle of a civil war in Afghanistan. While such rescues have become almost commonplace, it was a remarkable achievement at a time when flying was hazardous and very few people had ever flown.

★★★

Amanullah, the Afghan ruler who attacked the British Empire in 1919 with an army of scarecrow soldiers and wild tribesmen, had not abandoned his determination to modernise the medieval kingdom. Goaded by his country's defeat in the war, Amanullah endeavoured to skip centuries of development and frogmarch his reluctant people into the twentieth century. Western schools were set up, a parliament was formed to give the populace a voice regardless of whether they wanted it and the king advanced women's rights, banning the veil and sending them into the classroom.

Amanullah returned from a visit to Europe in 1927 even more determined to transform the country, but many Afghans were outraged by photographs from the tour showing the queen in Western dresses and with her face uncovered. Ignoring advice to curb his zeal, the king cracked down on opponents, jailing and exiling many of his critics. Some of the tribes revolted and Amanullah turned to the tiny Afghan Air Force – one of his most prized innovations – to suppress the threat. Air raids failed to check the revolt, however. Some army units went over to the insurgents and the king soon lost control of much of the country.

Britain had no desire to be dragged into what London and New Delhi disdainfully regarded as yet another baffling Afghan mess, but British officials fretted about the hundreds of foreigners living in Kabul if the government collapsed. Britain, as the dominant power in the region, would be expected to protect other Westerners as well as its own citizens. Sir Francis Humphrys, the British ambassador in Kabul, made the novel suggestion of evacuating the foreign community by air if conditions became too dangerous. Humphrys, who had been a cricket star while a student at Oxford University in the 1890s, was the model of the imperturbable English diplomat. Unlike most establishment figures, however, Humphrys had a passion for aircraft. He had served briefly in the RAF during the world war, and liked to tinker with a radio transmitter purchased on a whim while on leave in London.

Humphrys warned in the autumn of 1928 that plans for a possible airlift should be drawn up after fighting cut the roads to India. The ambassador's idea of flying some 500 civilians out of a war zone without the protection of British forces would be a unique challenge. Individuals or small groups had been rescued by aircraft in Iraq or Arabia once or twice, but even the RAF's most visionary theorists had not anticipated flying an entire community out of a war zone.

Trenchard breezily assured the government that the RAF could easily evacuate Kabul's foreign community. In reality no one had any idea of what it might take to mount such an operation. The largest military transport planes could only carry twenty or so passengers and had limited range and endurance; officials were wary of entrusting the safety of scores of women and children to such fragile machines. Responsibility for the rescue was handed to Geoffrey Salmond, head of the RAF in India and elder brother of John Salmond. The older Salmond had been an army artillery officer, seen active service in the Boer War and Boxer Rebellion in China, and was given the unusual assignment of learning Japanese.

Salmond was drawn to flying rather than foreign languages, and enrolled at a private aviation school to qualify for the army flying corps before the First World War. His duties including clearing cattle from the flying school's grass airstrip every morning so that the planes could take off. He was a serious man who could seem curt compared to his gregarious and charming brother, and his career had lagged as John achieved one triumph after another. The older Salmond had taken over the India Command in 1926, when he became the first RAF overseas commander to fly to his new assignment rather than taking a ship.

Salmond's command had just one large transport plane, a two-engine Hinaidi that was ferrying an official on an overseas trip, when preparatory planning began on the Kabul operation. Front-line squadrons in India were still equipped largely with DH9As and Bristols that could only carry a pilot and a gunner or a solitary passenger. London ordered 70 Squadron, based outside Baghdad with Victoria transports, to assist.

The Victoria was a two-engine biplane designed to carry up to twenty-two troops. The crew sat in an open cockpit perched above the plane's bulging nose while the passengers rode in the enclosed cabin. It was not clear if the Victorias, which had only been used in desert conditions, could operate over the Afghan mountains in wintertime. London and Delhi had nightmarish visions of a plane crammed with white women and children slamming into a mountain side. Such a mishap, it was murmured, would damage British prestige among the empire's 'lesser' races. Secret tests were conducted hurriedly with a Victoria at Quetta near the Afghan border in December, and there was relief when the pilots concluded that the plane could cope with frontier conditions.

Amanullah had lost control of much of Afghanistan by late 1928 when Kabul was attacked by Bacha-I-Saqao, a brigand and the son of a labourer, who raised a private army to try to seize power while the royalist army was fighting the main rebel forces. The British Embassy, located in a large, walled complex outside the capital, was cut off as government troops and insurgent forces clashed in the surrounding countryside. Gunfire regularly peppered the embassy, smashing windows and shaking the walls. Hundreds of British and foreign diplomats and civilians were by now sheltering in the legation because of the growing lawlessness in the city.

Humphrys signalled on 17 December that conditions were too dangerous and all women and children must be flown out. To avoid any risk of being accused of meddling in Afghan affairs, British officials had RAF planes assigned to the rescue operation stripped of all of their weapons – the pilots even had to turn in their revolvers. Flight crews were given identity papers describing them as visitors or tourists despite wearing full uniform.

The evacuation ran into trouble as soon as the first plane, a DH9A piloted by Flying Officer C.W.L. Trusk and LAC G. Donaldson, flew over the city on 18 December on a scouting mission. Trusk had been told to reconnoitre the situation and drop off a Popham Panel, a signalling device resembling a Venetian blind in a box, to the embassy. As he approached, Trusk saw a message laid out on the legation lawn with large strips of cloth saying it was too dangerous for aircraft to land because of fighting around the compound. Moments later the plane was hit by Afghan marksmen, damaging the engine.

Donaldson managed to send a radio signal as Trusk made an emergency landing at the nearby airfield at Sherpur. The bomber was warmly greeted by Afghan and Russian pilots of the Afghan Air Force. The head of the Afghan Air Force said it was impossible to reach the embassy because of the fighting, so the two British flyers were given rooms at a seedy Kabul hotel called the Café Wali. A group of Afghan Government soldiers later managed to toss the Popham device over the embassy wall.

The RAF command in India reacted to the mishap by dispatching a second plane later that day, to fly over the Kabul embassy to demonstrate that 'the prestige of [the] Union Jack ... was being forcibly upheld' despite the loss of the first plane.[1] Trusk, a remarkably energetic and resourceful young man, decided to take over the evacuation. Without informing his superiors, he began talks with local officials.

A message arrived in India four days later stating he had negotiated an agreement with the Afghan Government for British planes to land at Sherpur and evacuate foreign civilians. Elderly government officials in India, steeped in iron-clad notions of seniority and protocol, were not used to young officers negotiating with foreign governments on their own initiative. A disapproving message was sent to Humphrys telling him about Trusk's unauthorised foray into diplomacy, and adding that nothing would be done without the ambassador's consent.

Humphrys, cut off in the embassy and with virtually no contact with any of the Afghan factions, insisted that all decisions should be left to him. Trusk, now on excellent terms with the Afghan foreign minister, moved with Donaldson to the embassy on 22 December. Royalist troops forced the insurgents back from the area the same day, and Humphrys decided it was safe to begin the airlift.

A flotilla of three DH9As, a Wapiti and a Victoria dipped onto the landing strip at Sherpur on 23 December and taxied grandly up to a waiting group of British and Afghan officials. Determined not to show any sign of panic, the British acted as if it was a sort of goodwill visit by the RAF, despite the occasional rattle of gunfire in the surrounding countryside. British and Afghan diplomats chatted amiably as the crews helped twenty-three women and children into the Victoria. The women were dressed smartly in coats, dresses and hats suitable for a winter day at the races or a country outing. Piles of suitcases and other belongings were squeezed into the cockpits and whatever other space could be found in the four smaller planes. Husbands and fathers waved as the Victoria loaded with their families thundered down the runway and began the steep climb to clear the surrounding hills. While no one appears to have checked, it is almost certain that none of the evacuees had ever flown before. Maud Hoare, the wife of the then air minister, Sir Samuel Hoare, had been the first woman to fly to India two years before; a feat for which King George V made her a dame.

A second group of twenty-eight women and children were airlifted out on Christmas Eve, most of them dependents from the French and German embassies. British diplomats had complained that their French counterparts were spreading false rumours that Britain was behind the uprisings against the king, but such ungentlemanly behaviour was put aside as the RAF crews helped the evacuees board the transport and stowed luggage. All operations were suspended on Christmas Day because the embassy was determined to keep up the façade that nothing exceptional was happening. A German woman was badly injured when she blundered into a spinning propeller as flights resumed on 26 December. A Hinaidi and two Victoria transports were now available, and by New Year's Day a total of 132 people had been rescued, including Germans, Italians, Indians, Turks and Syrians.

The return flights over the mountainous frontier in the primitive and heavily loaded aircraft taxed even the most experienced flight crews and terrified many of the evacuees. Too heavy and too weak to fly over the peaks that reached up to 15,000ft, the Victorias had to thread their way through the mountains. The passengers could only stare mutely at the towering walls of rock outside the cabin windows and the gaping, black gorges below. Afghanistan was experiencing one of its coldest winters in decades, and the British crews in open, wind-buffeted cockpits endured temperatures that fell to -20°C. The cold made flying even more difficult; the engines strained with the effort as the pilots coaxed the packed planes over the ridges and tried to dodge swirling banks of cloud and snow.

Most of the wives and children from the Western embassies had already been evacuated when Bacha-I-Saqao's forces drove the royalists out of Kabul. Amanullah abdicated on 14 January and fled south in a car after handing the crown to his brother Inyatulla in a last bid to save the dynasty. The new king reigned for three days, before yielding on condition that he and his family were evacuated by the RAF. Two Victorias flew them to India. Air force legend claimed that the prince flew out in one Victoria while his harem travelled in the second plane.

Bacha-I-Saqao declared himself king, but the main Afghan rebel forces soon moved on Kabul to topple him. Humphrys decided it was time to evacuate all foreigners from the city. The bandit king, not willing to antagonise the British, said the RAF could continue to use Sherpur, and he sent men to guard the airfield.

The final phase of the evacuation began on 28 January, only to be halted for days at a time by increasingly bad weather. Blizzards dumped up to 2ft of snow at a time on the airfield, making it impossible for planes to land and forcing frequent suspensions of the rescue flights. A fleet of seven Victorias and the sole Hinaidi took out the last thirty-nine evacuees on 25 February.

It was a much tenser scene than the first day of the airlift; the planes kept their propellers turning while they were on the ground, there was no time for small talk with Afghan officials, and evacuees were hurried on to the aircraft. Last to board were Trusk and Donaldson, who had been in Kabul for almost ten weeks, followed by Humphrys, clutching the British flag from the embassy. The last plane rumbled slowly down the snowy runway before pitching awkwardly into the leaden sky as the handful of airfield guards silently watched. Nadir Khan, the general who had commanded Afghan forces in the Third Afghan War, took the throne after defeating Bacha-I-Saqao, who was assassinated.

The evacuation was hailed around the world as a near miracle. Flying was still seen as extremely dangerous, the preserve of daredevils and lunatics, but hundreds of ordinary men, women and children had been rescued from the middle of a war in one of the remotest places on earth. The operation helped transform British public perceptions of the RAF, bringing it respect and affection after the odium of the post-war years. Government leaders proclaimed that the aeroplane was a great humanitarian instrument of empire as well as a formidable weapon.

A total of 586 men, women and children from eleven nations had been flown out of Afghanistan along with 24,000lb of luggage. The only mishap was the crash of a Victoria piloted by Flight Lieutenant Ronald Ivelaw-Chapman and Flying Officer A.R.S. Davies en route to Kabul on 29 January, when both engines failed.[2] Ivelaw-Chapman spotted what appeared to be a stretch of flat ground, and was coming in to land only to see at the last moment that the ground was littered with boulders that would smash the plane. He stalled the plane when it was at about 10ft, literally causing it to flop on the ground rather than fly into the waiting rocks. The impact broke the undercarriage and crushed the belly of the fuselage. The Victoria was immediately ringed by heavily armed Afghans who seemed to emerge from nowhere. A man claiming to be an Afghan general took the two pilots prisoner. He doubted that the aviators were British because of their blue uniforms; some of the tribesmen thought they were Russians from the Afghan Air Force.

Ivelaw-Chapman and his co-pilot were treated fairly well, although he complained of the stench in the tiny hovel where they were held at night with twelve guards. Eventually the two men were taken, first by mule and then in a decrepit Chevrolet van jammed with twenty-three people, to the British Consulate at Jalalabad. Davies was a morose man who irritated his companion by constantly humming mournful hymn tunes. The pair finally reached the consulate only to find that the consul had taken refuge with the Pir Sahib of Baghdad, an elderly Islamic leader from Iraq who had spent years exhorting the Pathans to fight the British.

The pair went to the cleric's compound, and the Pir Sahib beamed when he discovered the airmen's squadron was based in his hometown, as he put it. He ordered some of this men to build an airstrip so that the two aviators could be flown out. Work on clearing a stretch of waste ground was interrupted periodically by gun battles between two local tribes. One of the warring chiefs announced one day that he wanted to give Ivelaw-Chapman a gift to show he did not dislike the British. The young airman was told to dip his hand into a bulging leather bag and was stunned when he pulled out a fistful of gold Tsarist roubles.

Ivelaw-Chapman was less pleased when a Bristol fighter showed up to rescue them once the airstrip was finished. He had asked for a Victoria with its strong landing gear, and part of the Bristol's under gear promptly crumpled as it touched down on the rough strip. The Pir's carpenter managed to fix the plane with a leg from a broken chair and it took off with Davies. Ivelaw-Chapman went back to work to improve the airstrip, whiling away the evenings with a volume of Kipling's verses.

A Bristol made a successful landing a week later, and within an hour Ivelaw-Chapman was drinking cold beer in Peshawar. It was not his only spell of captivity; he was shot down in France in 1944 and spent two months on the run before being caught by the Germans. He returned to the subcontinent in 1950 as the commander of the independent Indian Air Force, and ended his career as an air chief marshal.

★★★

The RAF's most improbable recruit was caught up in the Afghan upheaval. Lawrence of Arabia, who had helped to secure the future of the RAF at the Cairo Conference and was an ardent advocate of Air Control, later enlisted as a common airman under the false name of Shaw to escape his fame. Trenchard, who came to know Lawrence well, initially resisted the idea of one of the most famous men in the world enlisting as a mere airman.

The presence of a living legend in the ranks was an open secret in the RAF. A wide array of officers and men remembered encountering this strange, reserved man who had little to say. S.T. Townson said everyone knew who Lawrence was despite his false name, especially because he was often seen at airbases in Britain walking along in deep conversation with Trenchard.[3]

Lawrence was sent to India in 1927 to bury him from public view, but William Dickson said that the hero's new role as a clerk at a remote RAF post on the Afghan frontier was the worst-kept secret in the empire. A stream of senior officials and generals began arriving unannounced in the hope of meeting Lawrence. An honour guard would have to be hurriedly assembled to greet the guest, after which the base commander would take the dignitary to his office and leave so that the visitor could chat with the clerk.[4]

Lawrence was hurriedly sent home in early 1929 after Indian newspaper reports suggested he was masterminding the unrest in Afghanistan. One report claimed Lawrence was roaming the frontier disguised as a Muslim holy man. A genuine holy man was attacked by outraged Muslims in Lahore and had to issue a statement insisting that he was not the famous English adventurer.

Salmond initially rejected demands for Lawrence's recall, saying a man who had served the empire so well was entitled to a refuge in the RAF's ranks. Humphrys insisted that Lawrence could not stay on the Afghan frontier, however, and pressure came from ministers in London to end what was becoming a diplomatic and public embarrassment. Lawrence was given the option of going to Aden, joining an RAF detachment of three men in Somalia or returning home. Lawrence opted to go back to Britain, where clamouring reporters met the returning hero, who tried to rebuff their questions by insisting that he was a 'Mr Smith'.

15

A British Air Service

A letter arrived at the Air Ministry in October 1925 from a postgraduate student at Cambridge University who was eager to join the school's air training squadron. The writer had been dazzled by an RAF flying exhibition the day before, and now wanted to do his duty as 'a loyal citizen of the Crown' and join what was clearly the finest of the empire's armed services. 'It was a magnificent show and influenced me very much. I felt quite sure that our Empire is absolutely safe for quite a long time to come in spite of the "Reds",' he wrote.[1] The young man's qualifications were as impeccable as his politics were soundly conservative – he had a degree in science from Cambridge, one of the best universities in the world, and had passed the entry exam for the Indian Civil Service that only a handful of candidates survived. His family background was equally impressive, with a father in the colonial police and a brother who had served in the army in the recent war. It was a letter from an ideal candidate that was read with increasing satisfaction by ministry officials – until they glanced at the signature. B.A. Bambawale was an Indian, and there was no place in the RAF's cockpits or workshops for black men.

★★★

It was assumed from the start that the post-war RAF would be both an imperial and an all-white service. Trenchard and his successors resisted admitting non-whites throughout the interwar era, claiming it would shatter the illusion among 'backward' people that pilots were gods. '"Familiarity breeds contempt", the effectiveness of the air arm must be to some extent diminished if aviation is mastered by these semi-civilised peoples,' Trenchard wrote in a 1926 memo.[2] There also was an emphatic insistence that non-whites were incapable of operating sophisticated machinery of any kind.

The notion of black men flying had disturbed whites almost since the first powered flights, and it was stirred with lurid predictions of doom. A hack 1923 novel, *The Collapse of Homo Sapiens*, was the tale of British universities educating African and Asian students, who promptly went home, built air fleets and bombed London. At the heart of the RAF's resistance was more than a touch of the petty racism that saturated and besmirched virtually every aspect of imperial life.

Bambawale was the personification of the empire's self-proclaimed mission to raise or civilise the 'lesser' races; he was brilliantly educated at a level far above that of most RAF officers, westernised and an ardent imperial patriot; as English as the English; a true son of empire. And that was the problem. Nothing frightened or stirred the contempt of the vast majority of British officials and military men who ran the empire at the grass roots more than a black version of themselves who expected to share their homes and clubs.

Bambawale's letter landed on Trenchard's desk in days, demonstrating the sensitivity and importance of the race issue in the air force. Bambawale may not have been wanted in the RAF, but he was one of the very few aspirants whose case was personally overseen by the head of the service, as the voluminous file generated by his application testifies. Trenchard personally ensured that the young Indian, and others like him, would not be accepted by the training squadrons which had been set up at the best British universities as part of the campaign to boost the RAF's prestige.

Wing Commander J.B. Bowen, the head of the Cambridge unit, had been sympathetic to Bambawale's request, noting that several professors backed the idea. H.R. Raines, his counterpart at Oxford, added a new twist to the age-old rivalry with Cambridge by saying its training squadron would not follow suit if Bambawale was admitted. 'Personally I am very averse to accepting undergraduates for enrolment who are not of pure European descent, and more especially Indians,' he wrote.[3]

Bowen's initial enthusiasm evaporated when he had to defend his views in a meeting with Trenchard. The air force chief gave Bowen highly unusual instructions to come direct to him on such matters in future, and told him that while the RAF would not formally ban 'Indian gentlemen'[4] from the university units, because of possible opposition from the school authorities, they must never be accepted. Trenchard's views were discreetly made known to the committee that vetted candidates for the Cambridge squadron and Bambawale's application was rejected without any explanation.

Bowen knew what to do the next time he got an application from another Indian student. Rabindranath Mukharji was also an excellent candidate – a gifted science student, with a father in the Indian judicial service. 'If matters are allowed to take their normal course in this case, I think I may say that Mr Mukharji will not be among those selected,' Bowen ingratiatingly wrote to Trenchard,[5] who replied that such men must never be allowed to become officers 'in the British Air Service'.[6]

★★★

By the early 1930s, the RAF's role as guardian of the empire played a large part in its new found pride and confidence, and it wanted officers who had been born and raised to subdue 'lesser' races. Britain's elite public schools, with their tradition of preparing boys for imperial and military service, were now prime RAF recruiting grounds and senior commanders visited them regularly to attract entrants.

Norman Bottomley gave a typical talk at Marlborough in 1931 in which he presented the air force as essentially a benign colonial police force, with only a passing reference to its ostensibly main function of defending Britain in a future war. Bottomley took his young audience on a simulated flight around the empire complete with an illuminated slide show featuring RAF stations in Iraq and India, native forts being bombed in Aden, and the tribesmen of Sudan and the Afghan frontier. The role of the RAF was to keep the peace among wild people, he explained, before giving an overview of Air Control that included the innate 'backwardness' of natives and the methodology of bombing:

> In this country we hope the big stick will remain in the cupboard, but in many parts of the Empire it is often brought out; because civilization is on such a low scale that we can keep order only by showing and sometimes by using the big sticks. There are several parts of our Empire – in Asia and Africa where this is particularly so … Certainly it seems that the more primitive a race is, the more it respects sheer power.[7]

It was a tenet of the colonial creed that natives could not be entrusted to rule themselves. A 1932 article in the *RAF Quarterly* celebrated the supposed natural gift of the British to rule others:

There are three outstanding characteristics in the British national character, a perfectly natural inclination to abide by the law, a sound and well-balanced judgment, and the capacity to rule. That sixty thousand Britishers are able to control three hundred million natives in India is due to certain qualities of character not possessed by others.[8]

Poor Bambawale and others like him could never be British, no matter how many degrees they earned or otherwise aped the empire's rulers.

★★★

The RAF's hostility to admitting non-whites was challenged from time to time during the interwar years. A proposal at the end of the First World War to train 100 Indians as pilots because of the dire shortage of aircrews came close to being accepted. One British commander, aware of the young RAF's reputation for drunken excesses, said that the Indians would make 'excellent pilots in view of their keen sight, and their abstinence and general temperament'.[9]

White officials in India opposed training Indians as pilots, however, saying that they might one day use their aircraft against the British. 'The danger of a mutinous native unit of the Air Force using its machines for revolutionary purposes will be seen to be one not likely to be faced,' a note from the Indian Government warned.[10] No one noted that such a remark made little sense, let alone was fair, at a time when hundreds of thousands of Indian soldiers were fighting and dying for the British Empire.

The end of the war made the issue of accepting Indians for flight training less than pressing, and Churchill, in his early days as secretary of state for war, was happy to rule that they could not be pilots. Air Force regulations in the interwar era stipulated that 'only the sons of British parents of pure European descent' could enrol in its ranks.[11] The appeal of aviation and the lure of flying could not be suppressed, however, and many talented Indians were determined to get into the sky and the RAF. Officials at the India Office in London made half-hearted attempts to breach the RAF's colour bar, but the most energetic efforts in the early years came from the Indian nobility, who had the wealth to buy and fly planes and were the one native group fawned on by the British.

Two native rulers who were keen aviators, Sir Taj Bahadar Safru and the Maharajah of Alwar, pressed for Indians to be accepted by the RAF at a meeting at the Air Ministry in 1923. Uncomfortable British officials ducked their queries. The pair had no more success when they suggested Indians with their own aircraft be allowed to form an auxiliary air service to support the RAF's Indian squadrons in emergencies. It did not help that the Indian Army had reluctantly opened its ranks to Indian officers after the First World War, and Indian officer cadets were being accepted in small numbers at Sandhurst.

Indians were also being admitted to higher positions in the Indian civil administration, despite claims by some outraged British officials that 'Indianisation' was deeply upsetting to most Indians, who were said to dread being ruled by men of their own race because they would be dictatorial and corrupt.[12] British officers of the Indian Army claimed that Indian soldiers would never follow officers of their own race into battle, and that British rankers would be humiliated if they had to take orders from black officers.

The RAF refused to follow even the half-hearted reforms of the Indian Army and civil service, saying it would be unnatural and perverse to have an Indian flying British officers. It was argued that admitting Indians would force the air force to accept Arabs or even Africans, and that taking black recruits would discourage white candidates. Much was made of Indians' supposed backwardness and inability to work with machines. Air Vice Marshal Edward Ellington, a future head of the RAF, told Trenchard in 1925:

> I have said that Indians as a race are wanting in determination and character, that they rarely have mechanical aptitude and have ideas and habits which are different to those of Europeans which make them out of place in all British units.[13]

RAF commanders threatened to stop a programme to train the Indian Army on air–ground co-operation if Indian officers were included. The India Office cravenly gave way on condition that there was no official ban that could be used by anti-colonial critics as proof of discrimination; instead, it was understood that no Indian officer's application for the course would ever be approved.

Some in the RAF and the government saw separate or segregated colonial air forces as the solution to the race issue. There was discussion as early as 1921 about creating an Indian air force run by British and Indian officers with Indian other ranks. Such a force would buy off the critics and liberals, it was argued, but it would be kept as small as possible to ensure both that it was never a threat to British control and that the RAF remained the linchpin of imperial defence.

A 1932 Act finally established the force, and its first squadron had four Wapitis and five Indian pilots under a British flight lieutenant. Places were reserved at the RAF's officer training academy at Cranwell in the later 1930s for Indian cadets from the force, but it still had just one squadron until 1941 when the Japanese onslaught in Asia forced rapid expansion.

The little air force was immensely popular with many Indians. Members of the Indian Legislative Assembly, who had lambasted the British for bombing Pathan tribes, approved its formation by unanimous acclamation. One of its first combat tasks was to attack the Pathans, earning praise from British commanders for meticulous bombing.

Non-whites were still not admitted to the RAF. It would take the dire needs of the Second World War to bring down that barrier. Occasional questions in Parliament as to why black applicants were barred from the air force were flicked aside by government spokesmen. Sir Philip Sassoon, the undersecretary of air, said in 1936 that airmen of any rank 'must be of pure European descent, must be British subjects and must be the sons of British subjects'.[14] Wilfred Page, an airman, said there was apprehension in the ranks when it was learned that officers of the fledgling Indian Air Force would be attached to regular RAF squadrons in the subcontinent for training. Men bridled at the idea of saluting a native, so they were told to salute the uniform and not the person wearing it.[15] Page's distaste evaporated as it became apparent that the Indians were superb pilots; others never got over their prejudices.

★★★

If loyal black subjects of the empire were not allowed to join the RAF, some of the native rulers whose lands were bombed by Britain had more success in overcoming British opposition and acquiring air forces of their own. It was a development that demolished British presumptions about the supposed inability of black people to fly or maintain aircraft and shocked the RAF, which had assumed it would always have a monopoly of the sky in the little wars of empire. Indeed, Air Control had smugly been built on the tenet that 'the enemy' did not have aircraft and 'are confronted with a weapon against which they cannot retaliate'.[16]

Although the RAF was never to face hostile aircraft during colonial operations, Trenchard repeatedly warned that allowing native states to have military aircraft was a threat to the aura of British invincibility, and the service tried to undermine such efforts.[17] Yemen and Afghanistan purchased aircraft from

Western governments or arms dealers and hired European flight crews and mechanics. Countries which were not friends of Britain, such as Italy and the Soviet Union, were ready to help, usually at a high price. Yemen obtained six planes and two pilots from Italy in 1926, RAF Intelligence reported, and two large aircraft were acquired from Germany in 1928.[18] The Yemenis struggled to keep the aircraft in working condition, however, and they rarely flew. Possessing aircraft was, if nothing else, a propaganda victory for Britain's opponents. Outraged British officials denied gleeful Egyptian press reports in 1928 that Yemeni aircraft had buzzed Aden and the governor had sent a delegation to Sana to beg the imam to stop.

Afghanistan, which had endured British bombing of its capital and other towns in 1919, was the most successful in creating an air force. London was torn when the Afghan Government approached it in June 1921 with a request to buy six planes. Some officials said that Afghanistan would turn to the Soviet Union if it was not given help, but the British Embassy in Kabul was adamant that the notion of Afghans flying was madness. Unperturbed, King Amanullah purchased planes from Russia and Italy and hired German mechanics, while ten Afghans went to Rome to train as pilots. Shaken by these developments and fearful of losing influence, London agreed to supply aircraft in 1924 when the king unveiled plans for an expanded force of forty aircraft.

British officials in India tried to stop the deal by saying the Afghans would crash the planes because natives could not fly and then try to cover up their incompetence by claiming they were sold defective machines. The king, impatient with British delays and obstructions, turned to the Soviet Union. By 1925 there were twenty-five Russian pilots and advisers in Kabul, and an equal number of Afghans went to the Soviet Union for pilot training. The Indian Government seethed that the fledgling Afghan force was a 'tool of Bolshevist intrigue' while the British Embassy in Kabul cryptically reported that it was doing everything it could to ensure the 'natural and unlamented death of the Afghan military air force'.[19]

The Afghans did not give up, and the king soon had a small, effective force that was used against his restless tribes in the same way British aircraft were bombing their kinsmen on the other side of the Indo-Afghan border. The little air force did not save Amanullah from being deposed in 1929, but his successors maintained and expanded the service.

Even efforts by allies and client states like Egypt and Iraq to purchase British aircraft and train pilots were opposed by the RAF. Trenchard, who was not interested in being the father of anyone else's air force, wrote in 1926:

We quite realize that in time we may be forced to have native air forces in countries which are under British influence, but we want to put off that day as long as possible and until such a contingency is absolutely unavoidable. This view is held not only by me, but by almost everyone here.[20]

Trenchard ignored government officials who tried to argue that his policies harmed the British aviation industry, which was struggling to stay alive because of a dearth of orders in the post-war slump, and that other countries would step in if Britain refused to help.

An Egyptian request to send five men to Britain for flight training was blocked after the RAF said the proposal 'was foredoomed to failure'. As an added measure, stereotypes of Eastern depravity were invoked with a claim that it would be unhealthy to send 'full grown Egyptians' to a school 'which is an establishment for training boys'.[21]

Saudi Arabia asked for British help in the mid-1920s to start a military and civil air service. An RAF officer and two mechanics were sent to Riyadh with instructions to find out as much as they could about the plan and try to scuttle it; the scheme failed to stop the development of a Saudi Air Force.

16

BOOM'S SWANSONG

Hugh Trenchard left the Air Ministry in December 1929 for the last time as head of the service he had guided and nurtured for the past decade. He had decided to retire several months earlier, even though he was just 56. T.E. Lawrence, still masquerading as an airman in the ranks, offered advice from his own experience of adjusting from commanding tens of thousands of men to long, empty hours. Governments were only interested in what individuals could do, he said, not what they had done.[1] The same caveat applied to the RAF, which, even if it no longer had to worry about being broken up, was to face challenges that would make its second decade as arduous as its first.

***

The 1930s are often treated simply as the era when the world tumbled inexorably into the abyss of the Second World War, but until the middle of the decade the RAF and the army continued to see colonial duties as their main operational role, and the best way to prove their worth. Successive governments had accepted that the country needed an air force, but saw no need to lavish money on it. Rearmament because of the deteriorating situation in Europe did not begin until 1935.

Air Control would see setbacks as well as successes in the new decade. The RAF played a vital role when uprisings and wars shook British rule in India and the Middle East in the 1930s, and the squadrons in the subcontinent carried out some of the biggest bombing operations the world had yet seen. Lord Londonderry, the air secretary, boasted in 1933 that the bomber had eclipsed the battleship as the traditional emblem of British might in some parts of the empire. 'As soon as the boundary of Asia is passed, the Royal Air Force becomes the symbol of British power,' he told Parliament with palpable pride.[2]

Buoyed by imperial successes, the young service began to outgrow its early sense of inferiority as a small but effective force emerged. Its new colonial role was vital in boosting its new sense of assurance. T.C. Traill said:

> We had begun to find a sense of unity with each other and a rather anxious pride in our new service: anxious because we were apt to feel new and callow in the presence of the army and the navy, a feeling they were sometimes pre-pared to encourage.[3]

Above all, the airmen were driven by the conviction that air power was the future, and Britain must have an outstanding air force. 'We all firmly believed in the fact that air power had come to stay and it had got to be developed,' Aubrey Ellwood said.[4]

Once widely shunned in the upper reaches of British society, the RAF's social standing improved in the later interwar years as the officer corps became more resolutely middle class. Arthur Capel[5] said it was clear things were changing when fox-hunting clubs, a leading arbiter of standards among the gentry, started to welcome air force officers. After a few years, he said, senior RAF officers and the instructors at Cranwell, the service's officer acad-emy, were being accepted on the same social level as the best army regiments. Trenchard declared in 1925 that the social tide was finally turning when he was invited to three social events on the same day.

Trenchard was determined to guide the RAF after he had stepped down. He spent his final months in command working on a plan to fulfil his dream of making the air force the dominant military service. For years he had advanced the notion of 'substitution' by which the RAF would take over any army and navy roles that could be performed more effectively and cheaply by aircraft. In reality 'substitution' was a Trojan Horse to turn the army and the navy into mere ancillaries.

Aides and colleagues referred to Trenchard's grand scheme as his 'last will and testament', while he called it his 'swansong'. Some air advocates went even further, imagining the day when aircraft would take over civilian policing in parts of the empire. An article in the *RAF Quarterly* a year after Trenchard stepped down outlined a plan to control India from the air and do away with all but a few soldiers and policemen. It envisaged replacing the 150 British cantonments or military bases in the subcontinent with just fourteen airfields to cover the entire country. Aircraft would quickly squash the demands of Gandhi and other troublemakers for independence, it claimed.[6]

The plan, entitled 'Fuller Employment of Air Power in Imperial Defence', was distributed to the Cabinet in October 1929. Trenchard began by saying he had become convinced as early as 1921 that air power provided the most 'effective, economic and humane control of undeveloped countries'.[7] Air Control had been a success from the Sudan to Afghanistan, he went on, strengthening and extending the empire, yielding huge defence savings and drastically reducing British casualties. The armed forces should now be transformed by substituting aircraft for infantry battalions and warships wherever possible.

Trenchard's plan called specifically for the RAF to take control of India's North-West Frontier, with the Indian Army being slashed by twenty-five to thirty battalions, ten artillery batteries and a wide range of support units. Africa would be taken over by the air force, with the elimination of local land forces, and aircraft would replace the Royal Navy's ships in the Persian Gulf and Red Sea, and take over the coastal defence of the British Isles.

Trenchard's proposal triggered a furious row. Aghast admirals and generals, who saw that the plan would only be a prelude to further RAF encroachments, denounced it as madness that would leave the empire defenceless. Air enthusiasts were just as quick to hail Trenchard's ideas, insisting that air power would decide all future wars. An article in the *Sunday Pictorial* newspaper accused the army's 'bow-and-arrow generals' of using underhanded methods to discredit the RAF. 'It is the ever-recurrent clash between youth and senility,' it thundered.[8] Even theorists who generally supported land power said that air power was transforming warfare. B.H. Liddell-Hart, one of Britain's leading military commentators, sympathised with the army and the navy but said that 'their future is a narrowing horizon'.[9]

Trenchard's decision to unveil such an ambitious plan as he was stepping down was a rare blunder by such a masterful politician. The scheme was far too ambitious for the times, and he would have no way to steer it through the inevitable tumult. Air power was still largely unproven and even politicians and officials who supported the RAF were not ready to entrust the defence of Britain and the empire to a single service. Nor was the British public, which had been raised on the notion that Britannia ruled the waves, and legends of Waterloo and other battles, likely to accept that the country no longer needed a large navy or a decent army. Even some of Trenchard's closest lieutenants questioned his final gambit. Slessor, who helped craft the plan, later said that Trenchard had gone too far. The government let the scheme slip into bureaucratic oblivion.

Trenchard, who had been made a viscount, made a half-hearted attempt to keep the plan alive from his new perch in the House of Lords. In a maiden speech in April 1930, Trenchard employed his usual disarming guile, insisting as always that he could not express himself clearly and deprecating his achievements. He scoffed at claims that he wanted to scrap the army and the navy, ingenuously insisting his only aim was to give the RAF more 'humdrum responsibility in peace time'.[10]

Retired admirals and generals who had fought Trenchard for years in government shot to their feet to denounce their old rival. A former chief of the army said the air force only knew how to slaughter women and children. A former Indian administrator insisted only diplomacy could pacify the North-West Frontier. He talked about how such efforts had resulted in British officers and Pathan tribesmen spending their time 'shooting, fishing and picnicking' together and going to 'sports and race meetings' – a claim greeted with astonishment by embattled British troops on the Afghan frontier.[11] Trenchard gave up his clearly doomed campaign when he was unexpectedly offered command of London's Metropolitan Police.

Trenchard's departure was the signal for a major reconsideration of Air Control within the RAF. A new generation of RAF leaders remained convinced that air power was the best way to defend and police the empire, and there was no slackening in the drive to boost the force's standing by increasing the number of colonies under its control. But while Air Control's basic doctrine that 'backward' regions could be policed from the sky remained unquestioned, some commanders and theorists had doubts about the military and political viability of simply blowing up disobedient natives – such tactics were less and less effective and drawing ever more criticism. Trenchard's former subordinates had cringed when he told the House of Lords that the natives did not really mind being killed. He had assured the chamber:

> The natives of a lot of these tribes love fighting for fighting's sake, and for the sake of the glory and the loot. They have no objection of being killed, some of them, if they can kill you and take your rifle, and, it may be, some domestic article like boots, but they do not like fighting if they may only lose their boots and have no chance of getting yours.[12]

The 1930s would see attempts to improve Air Control with tactics intended to break opponents' morale while inflicting fewer casualties. By the late 1920s colonial squadrons were achieving fewer successes despite mounting ever bigger bombing raids. Ostensibly 'backward' tribes were showing remarkable ingenuity and courage in withstanding air attacks.

A revised air policing manual issued in 1928 was one of the first indications of the RAF's changing views. It said that excessive bombing could be counterproductive because extensive casualties might create 'an attitude of sullen resignation' or resentment that made tribes determined to keep fighting.[13] A flow of reports from the field added to the growing sense that the days of easy victories were over. A pessimistic 1930 assessment from Somaliland said bombing was having little effect because tribesmen had learned to scatter or hide from air attacks and rebellious clans mixed their livestock with the herds of neutral tribes or drove them across the nearest border.[14]

Two senior commanders, Norman Bottomley and Edgar Ludlow-Hewitt, both of whom went on to become air chief marshals, emerged as the leading voices for the new approach to colonial operations. Bottomley was one of the foremost Air Control theorists, producing a stream of influential articles and memos. He was an urbane, witty man with the carefree charm of the dashing aviator. More unusually, he was an excellent talker and writer, as comfortable with ideas and books as with a drink at a soiree; his analytical skills had been polished by a spell at a French university before joining the army on the eve of the First World War. Bottomley transferred to the RFC during the war and saw service as a pilot on the Western Front. He first gained practical insight into colonial issues as a staff officer in Egypt in 1921, and held the key command of head of No 1 Group in India from 1934 to 1938.

Bottomley said that Air Control was misleading as a term because military force alone could not administer countries or replace everyday government. It 'is not a particularly happy or descriptive' term, he wrote 'One does not control these countries from the air any more than from the business end of an 18 pounder [cannon] or a service rifle.'[15]

While Bottomley still saw air power as the best way to prevent or suppress tribal unrest and win colonial wars, he declared in an influential 1932 paper that the mass killing and destruction which had been employed in many colonial air operations only embittered the tribes, and made it more difficult to secure lasting peace.[16] Aircraft should be used to isolate and suppress trouble with as few casualties as possible, he said, which would show native people that resistance was futile and persuade them to accept British rule as benevolent. 'The ultimate aim of our administration should be to bring ... a sound system of government, to foster peaceful arts, to promote commerce, and trade, and in the end to establish responsible government,' he wrote.[17]

The modernisers' main innovation was to be the air blockade. This involved driving rebellious tribes or other troublemakers from their homes and forcing them to live in the open with little or no food and shelter for weeks or months until their morale was broken by hunger, cold and the suffering of their families. People were to be forced out of their villages by leaflets warning that they would be bombed if they did not leave, and then prevented from returning by round-the-clock air patrols.

The new methods would counter the exasperating ability of the tribes to withstand bombing raids, it was said, and reduce, if not end, the casualties that provoked more tribal resistance and also criticism in Britain and elsewhere. The modernisers ignored or played down the fact that driving people into the wilderness, especially in the winter in the mountains, might inflict deaths, particularly among children and the elderly. 'One feature of our policy is very definitely the avoidance of casualties', one strategy paper stated, adding awkwardly that this proved Air Control was 'far from inhumane at least in conception'.[18] The new methods also promised to be cheaper since they would require far fewer bombs.

A 1935 RAF handbook on frontier tactics said:

> There is no useful object served in imposing wholesale material damage or heavy casualties on the tribes. Once a village is demolished we have lost our power to threaten its destruction and the tribesman has less incentive to save his village by submitting. It is to be borne in mind that if a Commander were to prolong unduly concentrated attacks on the property of a tribe not only would the cost of bombs be excessive, but these operations would rapidly reduce that tribe to a state of extreme poverty, which in itself is one of the causes of lawlessness on the Frontier.[19]

It was a long way from the brash assertions of the early 1920s that a sharp dose of bombing and severe casualties would break the most warlike and stubborn tribes. Squadron Leader G.C. Pirie flippantly told a course at the RAF Staff College in 1932 that the aim of air blockades was to bore rather than bludgeon a tribe into submission. Submission would be '... induced by the boredom, acute discomfort ... and above all by a feeling of impotence,' he noted.[20] Bottomley said the new methods meant that bombing now was all about shepherding people out of their villages without hurting them. 'Truly an artistic problem,' he enthused.[21]

Bottomley commanded one of the first major tests of air blockades with an operation in the winter of 1931 against Kurdish insurgents in northern Iraq. He called it 'air control … in the most humane manner possible'.[22] Air crews were instructed to use force only to drive the Kurds from their homes and then keep them away, and to avoid destroying homes and livestock. Bottomley wrote:

> I explained that it is only too easy to create a terrible state of affairs in a tribal area by the drastic use of air bombardment. Villages could be completely destroyed and all cattle practically wiped out of existence within a short time. The results of drastic action of that kind would be felt in the subsequent hardships suffered by the tribesmen over a period of many years. If destitution were caused in this way the area would remain disturbed and discontented for a long time.[23]

A Victoria bomber was fitted with loudspeakers to warn the Kurds about the raids and urge them to leave their homes. An Iraqi police inspector, perched nervously behind the pilots, read out warnings in the local dialect that were magnified by the speakers and the surrounding mountains:

> In the name of Allah, the Compassionate, the Merciful. O People of [the villages of] Barzan and Shirwan, listen. The Government has made humane proposals. The armistice will finish this evening. We are starting to bomb all villages tomorrow morning, until you make dakhalat [submit]. We will go on bombing day and night. Leave your villages and hide yourselves, your families, and your flocks. Until you come to make dakhalat, it is of no value to show white flags to the aeroplanes.[24]

Air force intelligence officers announced the experiment was a success when the Kurds, tired of living in the wilds, submitted despite suffering only minor casualties.

While modernisers said that the new methods made Air Control more effective, things did not always change in the frontier squadrons. Traditionalists, including some front-line commanders, scoffed at the new ideas, and championed unrestrained bombing, insisting that troublemakers were subdued by heavy casualties and the obliteration of homes and property. One senior officer in the Middle East in the 1930s ridiculed air blockades as unworkable, saying they were 'not a true definition of any air operations which has yet taken place (anywhere) so far as I am aware'.[25] Air crews were more interested in improving their bombing and fighting skills than minimising native casualties; they had enlisted to fight rather than disrupt a tribe's domestic routine. And even the modernisers supported all-out bombing to deal with major threats such as uprisings on the North-West Frontier.

★★★

Ludlow-Hewitt led a less successful fight within the RAF against the idea that air power alone could win wars, arguing that inter-service co-operation or combined operations were the key to military success. His lean, gloomy features had the look of a querulous clergyman or schoolmaster. He possessed a strong sense of morality that some contemporaries misconstrued as a lack of killer instinct despite his indisputable personal courage.

Ludlow-Hewitt was one of the early stars of British military aviation. He transferred to the RFC in 1914 after a decade in an Irish infantry regiment and won a reputation as an excellent pilot before ending the war a brigadier general. As commandant of the RAF Staff College between 1926 and 1930, he campaigned for co-operation with the other military services, and against what he saw as the delusion that land and sea forces were now irrelevant. 'This baneful influence insinuates its chill presence between the Services and lays its cold hand on every honest effort to advance the interests of inter-Service co-operation,' he later wrote.[26] He seethed at the growing number of smug RAF officers who 'again and again abandon logic and common sense in their attempt to maintain claims for the Air Force (and air power) which ought never to have been advanced'.[27]

Ludlow-Hewitt spent most of the 1930s in senior colonial commands, serving as chief air officer in Iraq, and then becoming RAF commander in India in 1935. Colonial experience confirmed his ideas that military success depended on co-operation with the other services. He refused to 'conform to the [air power] purists' fanaticism' that aircraft alone could win wars and advocated full co-operation with land forces.[28] Ludlow-Hewitt found some support among his crews in Iraq and India, many of whom knew from practical experience that soldiers were as important as airmen in defeating tough tribal opponents.

Flight Lieutenant C.E.N. Guest voiced the opinion of many junior men when he said in 1934 that even Iraq, supposedly the greatest triumph of air power, was never 'an example of air control pure and simple' and that the soldiers on the ground could be as important as the men in the air.[29] But pleas for inter-service co-operation did not go very far. Many in the RAF were wedded to the belief that air power would win future wars, and the rivalry between the leaders of the three military services was as bitter as ever.

It was not a coincidence that the drive to make air policing less bloody came at a time of growing unease, in Britain and across the empire, over the RAF's treatment of imperial subjects. There was rising criticism in India, where nationalists and loyalists alike questioned how blowing up some of their fellow subjects was consistent with British claims that the empire existed solely to protect and civilise the subject peoples. Fears that the air force were being seen as heartless killers prompted the Air Ministry in the 1930s to start a campaign claiming the RAF's humanitarian work far outweighed its military activities.

Sir Philip Sassoon, undersecretary for air, portrayed the RAF as a kind of guardian angel in a 1933 speech in the House of Commons, saying it saved many more lives than it took. He cited examples from the Kabul airlift and the protection of Iraqi tribes from Wahabi raids, to the airlifting of sick natives to hospitals and delivering supplies to stranded desert expeditions. Far from fearing the RAF, many natives saw it 'as their one protector, under the shadow of whose wings they can freely pursue their peaceful avocations,' he told the chamber.[30]

17

SWIFT AGENTS OF GOVERNMENT

Trenchard's 1929 plan to make the RAF the dominant military service envisaged bringing vast new stretches of the empire under its umbrella. His successors would spend much of the 1930s trying to take control of the defence and policing of territories and outposts from Africa to China. While there would be successes in this scramble for colonies, the airmen were to be frequently frustrated and blocked by new military, geographical and political obstructions.

Trenchard's plan envisaged the RAF taking control of virtually all of Africa, which seemed the perfect amphitheatre for air power. Aircraft promised to open up the continent, where there were very few roads and even fewer railways. An admiring colonial governor said that warplanes were destined to be the 'swift agents of government' across the continent.[1]

While some races had defied predictions that aircraft would crush their spirit, the RAF insisted that Africans would always be terrified of the white man's flying machines. 'The African native is in a far more primitive stage of advancement than the Arab or the North-West Frontier tribesman,' an RAF paper declared.[2] British air propagandists never tired of quoting a wartime account by a German officer of how natives in East Africa reacted when they saw an aircraft for the first time:

Seized with fear and terror, they ran away from their fields and concealed themselves in the huts and in the forest. Natives who were on the road to Taveta to work there for the Government, threw away their tools and did not return for many days. Women who were on their way to the market left their produce on the road, ran home and, by exaggerating what they had seen, spread terror in places far distant … They considered the aeroplane as a supernatural being [called] Muungu. This Muungu was endowed with great power. The route which he followed had now become spirited and the land was unproductive. The natives over whom he flew were now possessed of evil spirits.[3]

Plans drawn up in 1919 to set up the first RAF base in equatorial Africa had selected Nigeria, but this was changed to the Sudan after the success the following year of H Unit against the Nuer tribes. The British Government did not agree to basing a squadron in Sudan until 1925, however, and officials in London and Khartoum bickered over the cost. The problem was only solved when the Cabinet agreed to give Sudan an interest-free loan to build an airbase.

★★★

Khartoum seemed squalid and boring when the men of 47 Squadron inspected their new home. Sudan had a tiny British community and the only amusements were a solitary, seedy hotel, the cinema at the army base or trips to the city's reeking, rundown zoo. Moreover, the climate was atrocious, the food monotonous and many of the locals clearly resented British rule. Air force personnel grumbled about everything, including the language. 'The Arabic language, owing to its vagueness and lack of precision, is clearly unsuited to official correspondence of all kinds,' it was noted.[4]

Sudan's air wing was used mostly for patrols and assisting occasional punitive expeditions against tribes that raided their neighbours or failed to pay tax. Air force commanders told the civilian administration that rebellious tribes must be suppressed with devastating bombing raids. After such an apocalyptic experience, the airmen said, the tribe would never again defy British authority. When air power was used 'against ignorant and very superstitious savages it is desirable to achieve a great moral effect at the commencement of the operation by using aircraft in strength and continuously,' an RAF commander wrote.[5]

Civilian administrators were uneasy or appalled at the idea of bombing some of the most 'backward' people on earth, or they feared the criticism it might provoke. Air operations were generally limited to supporting ground units despite vociferous RAF protests that it was a scandalous waste. Frustrated RAF commanders reacted by ridiculing the government and army, describing the Sudanese police who controlled much of the country as 'savages without clothes' and complaining that their pilots were being used as taxi drivers by the army.[6]

Blocked from unfettered use of the killing power of their aircraft, the airmen laid on occasional displays for native audiences. Fake villages with grass huts and animal pens were constructed so they could be blown up in front of an audience of chiefs and tribal elders. A delegation of fifty chiefs was summoned from the south in 1932 to tour the Khartoum airbase and see aeroplanes up close. Crowds of locals in the streets laughed and jeered at the almost naked men from the south when they arrived on a river boat.

The airmen were eager to get a close look at people who, up until then, they had only fleetingly glimpsed from the air. Most of the chiefs were physically imposing men, strong and lithe, including some as tall as 6ft 5in. An RAF account of the visit said that the Africans 'appeared to have the mentality of children, and were most certainly savages'. Just three of the chiefs accepted an invitation to fly. 'An officer was detailed to each one with instructions to hold the native down and, if necessary, beat him on the head with a Very [flare] pistol if he showed signs of panic or a desire to throw himself out' of the plane, the account said. The three chiefs squatted on the cockpit floor, and saw nothing during the brief ascents.

A demonstration of bombing and strafing was laid on for the visitors, after which a young white officer told them their villages would be obliterated in the same way if they defied British orders. What seems to have really shocked the chiefs, however, was the revelation that the RAF men, who were not allowed to bring their wives to the Sudan, lived without women.[7]

Much of the airmen's time was taken up with air patrols to show the authority of the government and spot potential trouble. A network of 100 or so unmanned airstrips was scooped out of the bush across Sudan so that planes could operate over vast areas. Most of the strips had small stocks of petrol that were carted in by camel. A crew would spend several days on patrol, flying from one strip to the next and camping at nights in a tent; the flyers shot game for food and drank from rivers or waterholes. S.E. Townson said the water was usually a thick brown sludge that reeked like fish glue.[8]

Ferrying senior government and military officials around on visits was another routine chore. Pilots chauffeured the Bishop of Sudan on visits to his far-flung parishes. Flight crews complained that local officials seemed to regard the RAF as a sort of aerial public works department. Townson was asked to build a scaffold to hang a murderer, because the local district officer was squeamish about using the traditional method of tossing a rope over a branch – the airman declined.[9]

The Pyramid War of 1927 was a rare chance for the RAF to demonstrate how Air Control should work. Gwek Wonding, a chief of the Nuer people who was described by colonial officials as a witch doctor, refused to acknowledge British authority. Much of the chief's power over his followers was said to stem from a great earthen pyramid in the centre of his village. The hand-built mound rose some 60ft and was decorated with coloured stones, bits of bright metal, carvings and other talismans; it was visible for miles in the surrounding swamps.

British officials decided to bomb the pyramid to discredit Wonding's authority. Bombers tore gaping holes in the mound, but failed to flatten it as Nuer marksmen fired at the planes and one pilot was wounded in the thigh. Nuer warriors fought back as columns of troops and police moved into their territory, and did not submit until the RAF killed some 200 people and large herds of cattle in a series of bombing raids.[10] Troops finally occupied Wonding's village in February 1928 and blew up the pyramid in front of a sullen audience of local chiefs.

The RAF liked to crow with the military's usual schoolboy humour that its brand of magic was superior to any 'juju' the natives could conjure up, but local superstition vanquished Western technology on at least one occasion. A demonstration flight was arranged in a remote area after the local British administrator said the tribes refused to believe that white men could fly. A couple of bombers duly buzzed the tribes' villages at roof level, sending people fleeing into the surrounding bush, after which the planes flew back to Khartoum, the crews confident they had made a profound impact. The tribe responded by sacrificing several bulls to persuade their gods to protect them against these terrible sky machines. Instead of praising the RAF's efforts, the administrator complained the natives were boasting their magic was superior because the planes had not returned.

The RAF did not regard Sudan as a great success for Air Control even though aircraft greatly extended British authority in the vast country. Local officials refused to let the air force take command of the territory's defences and sharply limited the use of bombing. Civilian administrators regarded the Khartoum squadron more as a defence against a revival of Mahdism, the Islamic revivalist movement that briefly ruled the Sudan in the later nineteenth century, or a mutiny of their own black troops. They also saw the little air detachment as a way to intimidate Khartoum's 'petty municipal [Arab] intelligentsia', which opposed British rule – a role that did not impress the RAF crews.[11]

A lack of funds frustrated the RAF's ambitions in Somaliland, despite the triumph against the Mad Mullah in 1920. Churchill approved the basing of two planes in the territory in 1922 after tribesmen killed a British official, but London was only willing to pay for a derisory fifty hours of flying a year and the local administration said it could not afford any additional time. The RAF detachment consisted of just three men, a pilot and two ground crew ,and a pilot was sent from Aden to fly the detachment's spare plane if there was trouble. Funds were so limited that the governor wrote personally in 1931 to the Colonial Office about purchasing plates and cups for the three men.[12]

★★★

The RAF had much greater hopes for the rest of Africa and the airmen campaigned and schemed for much of the 1930s to extend Air Control south of the Sahara. There were no white troops in East or West Africa, and the RAF was confident that it could persuade officials to scrap the African regiments which served as the local garrison. Britain's East African territories, covering a million square miles, were the main target: their vast plains were ideal for air operations, and the prosperous local economies could help fund large air detachments.

The RAF threw itself into the campaign to take over the defence of Kenya, Uganda, Nyasaland and Tanganyika with its usual thoroughness. The first step was to send out flotillas on 'air cruises' or goodwill tours. The cruises established new air routes, demonstrated the versatility of air power and sought to build support among the local settlers.

Staff officers in London scoured newspapers and other sources for reports of African unrest to bolster the case for upgrading local defences and 'air mindedness' notes were kept on colonial officials to show whether they were friends or opponents. Almost every conceivable tactic was tried or considered. A 1930 memo suggested mounting a 'buy British' campaign to show the patriotic value of replacing black African troops with white aircrews.[13]

The airmen became so wrapped up in political manoeuvring that they almost neglected the excellent practical reasons for using aircraft to control such a vast region. Kenya, for example, had only a few hundred African soldiers to guard the 800-mile frontier with Abyssinia, and air patrols would be far more effective against cross-border raiders who attacked villages in British territory for cattle and other loot – raiders slaughtered 117 men, 233 women and 6 children in the spring of 1929 alone.[14]

No one was more energetic than Arthur Harris in pushing for Air Control in Africa. Having spent part of his youth in Rhodesia, he was the perfect man for the mission with his fervent sympathy for the white colonists, passionate belief in air power and withering contempt for the army. He told his superiors 'my acquaintance with British East Africa and the substitution problem is no superficial one.'[15] Harris worked hard to establish close ties with the leaders of the white settlers. He said the settlers detested local British officials, who they saw as 'ill mannered, over-bearing, over paid [at their expense] autocrats, put over them by the Colonial Office'.[16]

The colonists complained that the government always favoured the black majority. They vehemently objected to arming Africans and feared that the black soldiers of the King's African Rifles, the only local army unit, could be used against them by London or might mutiny. Harris told John Salmond, now chief of the RAF, that the settlers were enthusiastic about his idea of disbanding the black troops and turning defence over to the RAF and the settler's own part-time defence force. 'As regards internal security, their attitude is that the all-white Kenya Defence Force could "skin all the n[★★★★★]s in the country in a week", and I for one am not disposed to refute that argument,' he wrote.[17]

Harris proposed feeding confidential government information to his local contacts to help them campaign for the RAF to take over Kenya's defence. He also advocated giving leading settlers free flying lessons and making some of their sons RAF officers to boost local political support.[18] The hyperactive Harris also courted the local press, giving interviews freely and briefing editors privately.

In 1932 Harris led the first air cruise to East Africa. The formation of Fairey IIIF bombers was applauded by an enthusiastic crowd of white settlers when it landed at Nairobi's ramshackle little airport. Sumptuous hospitality was lavished on the crews as they toured the colony. Airmen used to meagre RAF pay and the skimping of the Depression were inundated with alcohol, admiration and more than a few amorous adventures. Kenya's white settlers were legendary for their disdain of anything that smacked of restraint, and one approving airman later wrote that, 'A Kenya Gentleman is a fellow who lays down his wife for his friends.'[19] A post-tour report said the endless parties had been a 'serious strain on the personnel of the flight'.[20] The cruise came to resemble an ancient Roman triumph as the airmen were showered with gifts, including two cheetahs, monkeys and a lion that caused 'alarm and despondency' in various hotels along the way.[21]

Showing off the intimidating power of aircraft was seen as one of the best arguments for Air Control. On Harris' 1932 air cruise, bombers terrified the black population by roaring at low level over native villages and tribal gatherings. Harris said that the sight of the black locals fleeing chased by aircraft delighted white settlers, who had been invited to watch, but he wanted future tours equipped with bombs to stage 'proper demonstrations'.[22]

While there were no protests about terrifying black people, nature lovers complained vehemently that the RAF was frightening African wildlife. The Earl of Onslow, chairman of the influential Society for the Preservation of the Fauna of the Empire, said low-flying pilots caused stampedes in which calves were separated from their mothers and perished. Harris took the complaints seriously; he told the *East African Standard* newspaper that the RAF had determined how high planes should fly to avoid causing distress to animals.[23]

There were also complaints about flight crew hunting animals from the air for sport. Trenchard had favoured aerial hunting as a way to hone the crews' marksmanship, and John Salmond protested that trying to restrict the shooting of animals was ridiculous. Still, guidelines were introduced to try to avoid protests from the public. Pilots were instructed to select individual animals and not to shoot at random into herds; an aerial hunting session was not to last more than ten minutes; and wounded animals were to be tracked down and finished off to avoid suffering. Some crews ignored the rules: Arthur Gould Lee said some pilots enlivened routine patrols by blazing away at any game they saw with the planes' heavy machine guns.

The RAF's campaign to take over East Africa had only limited success despite the keen support of the colonists. Even Harris could not counter the fact that there was rarely any trouble, and the modest force of 12,000 black troops in West and East Africa along with the local police easily controlled an estimated population of 40 million people at minimal cost.

Local British officials were appalled at the idea of using bombers against the local people. A meeting of East African territorial governors in 1935 concluded that bombing could only be used if there was a major uprising, and only if everything else had failed – something they clearly deemed virtually impossible.[24] Air force hopes soared when the army's chief in East Africa, Brig. Gen. C.C. Norman, suddenly agreed in 1935 to scrap three of his seven black infantry battalions to fund a permanent air contingent. Norman and Air Vice Marshal Cyril Newall, a future head of the RAF, had concluded in a joint study that the cut would improve local security by freeing up money for transport aircraft to ferry troops to trouble spots, giving them a far greater reach. The Committee for Imperial Defence in London rejected the plan, however, because it thought that a large number of black troops would be needed in any future regional or global war.

Civilian officials also reiterated their objections to maintaining British rule with aerial bombs. The Tanganyika administration said the black population was too backward to comprehend what aircraft could do:

> The East African native is docile and unimaginative; he is familiar with the askari [native soldier] and sees him frequently in the guise of soldier or policeman, and he knows full well the power of troops. With aircraft he is less familiar, and he has no standards, nor the mental capacity, by which to form any idea of their power. Aircraft may be effective to kill or terrorise him if he revolts, but cannot compare in tranquilizing and steadying effect with the regular infantry ... [25]

A full squadron was only moved to East Africa in December 1936 following Italy's occupation of Abyssinia, although smaller formations had operated in the region on temporary assignments. 'Wings Defend Africa' was the grand motto of 223 Squadron when it moved to Nairobi, but the men lived in tents at the city airstrip and worried about encountering prowling lions at night.

The squadron's first priority was agitating for an increase in its foreign living allowance. Long lists detailing the cost of everything from fruit to lady's underwear were sent to London to back claims that local costs were prohibitive, although it was noted that RAF personnel got a reduced rate at Nairobi's two cinemas except on Saturdays and public holidays.[26] The Air Ministry was not sympathetic to the plea for more generous allowances or a request to pay the hefty fees for the squadron's officers to join both of Nairobi's white clubs; the squadron said the officers must have a place to relax, and joining only one club would offend the members of the other institution.

There was little for the airmen to do in East Africa beyond routine operations. There were regular border patrols, the occasional breaking up of anti-British protests by flying low over crowds and a few bombing operations against cattle raiders. The biggest operation was the use of aircraft to ferry troops to put down strikes by black copper miners in Northern Rhodesia in 1935. Officials agreed the RAF had been helpful, but concluded that the incident proved the need for stronger land forces.[27]

Efforts were also made to establish RAF detachments in West Africa, although the vast tracts of jungle made the use of aircraft more difficult, and the RAF seemed less enthusiastic about a region that was still notorious for its lack of comforts, sweltering climate and deadly fevers. Several flights were based in West Africa by the late 1930s, mainly to ferry troops or police in the event of unrest.

South Africa, which largely ran its own affairs, had been quick to see the potential for aircraft to intimidate the black population and created its own air force at the end of the First World War. South Africa asked the British Government in 1919 for the loan of a bomber for trials. Local officials assured London that the plane would not be used against whites: 'the machine will not be used against the white population of Johannesburg but will be held in reserve mainly for demonstration purposes and consequent moral effect [bombing] against the natives ... should they become out of hand.'[28]

The South African Air Force was used in the interwar years to suppress occasional black unrest – records show there were bombing attacks on native villages in 1922, 1925, 1930 and 1932.[29] Questions were raised in the British Parliament in 1922 after reports that South Africa had attacked villages in its South-West Africa protectorate. It was claimed that forty bombs were dropped on a settlement in 1922, killing and wounding many of the esti-mated 500 inhabitants. A Johannesburg newspaper gave a dramatic account of the attack, 'Bombs were dropping from 100 feet. Machine-gun fire was opened. Many of them tumbled into the gorge ... scores were killed ... The aeroplane, the natives may find, has made war an impossible thing for them.'[30] Churchill told Parliament it was a purely South African matter.[31]

Ironically, some black South Africans looked to the skies for salvation, and South African officials fretted about rumours circulating among the black population in 1930 that black Americans would soon arrive by air to help end white rule.[32]

★★★

Trenchard's grand 1929 plan also envisaged extending the RAF's reach into the Far East, and the air force drew up plans for a network of bases and air routes extending beyond India to Burma, Malaya, Singapore and China. It would complete the air chief's vision of an arc of air power reaching from the west coast of Africa across the Middle East and India to the Pacific.

The small amount of money available for Far Eastern defence in the inter-war era went mostly to constructing a new naval base at Singapore, however, and the government opposed funding large-scale RAF expansion in the region. The navy wanted to defend the Singapore base with long-range guns. Trenchard presciently predicted that it would be better to use torpedo bombers, attacking an enemy fleet while it was still hundreds of miles away. British admirals, who loathed any suggestion that aeroplanes could sink their battleships, ridiculed the plan. Eventually it was decided to shield Singapore with a few guns and some obsolete aircraft – a feeble compromise that failed to save it from the Japanese in 1942.

A torpedo bomber squadron was based in Singapore, and gradually added to during the 1930s. A 1938 incident revealed how the increasingly confident RAF was starting to show some of the arrogant rigidity that the airmen claimed blinkered the army and navy. British Intelligence lost track of the main Japanese fleet, and a military alert was ordered amid fears that it was a prelude to an attack on the Singapore base.

Astonishingly, a plan had not been drawn up to co-ordinate the settlement's air defences; the RAF controlled the air raid alert system as well as its aircraft, while an army unit manned the anti-aircraft batteries. Moreover, there were no telephone lines between the main military operations centre and the anti-aircraft batteries scattered around the island. A portable telephone exchange with lines to the batteries was set up on a veranda that was the only spare space at the operations centre.

But supercilious RAF officers refused to let the army gunners into their operations room from where the approaches to Singapore were being monitored. The airmen either declined to share information or relayed it in handwritten messages. Each note was recorded in a register for security reasons before being carried to the gunners on the nearby veranda, where it had to be signed for and a receipt sent back. Exasperated army officers claimed it sometimes took hours for a message to move the few yards from the RAF room to the veranda. Things did not improve when the switchboard was put in the corridor outside the RAF room with army runners standing just inside to wait for messages. Annoyed RAF officers eventually were forced to provide space for the switchboard in the room, and let an army officer stand at the plotting table.[33]

A 1931 revolt in Burma was a serious setback for the RAF's hopes of extending air policing into the Far East. British officials were caught by surprise when hundreds of nationalists wearing crude blue uniforms took over villages and attacked army and police outposts. Many rebels had tattoos of a mythological bird, which they believed made them invulnerable to gunfire.

Aircraft from Singapore were flown in to help hunt down the insurgents, but the crews could see very little as they flew over the vast tracts of jungle where many of the bands were hiding. Tony Dudgeon, a pilot with a Singapore-based squadron, said the jungle canopy concealed whatever was going on hundreds of feet below the overarching vegetation, and the notion that anything could be seen from an aircraft was pure fantasy:

> The hills, with occasional clouds in the valleys, looked as though they were covered with giant parsley gone mad. Rolling greenery as far as the eye could see with never a glimpse of the ground. It had a beauty, of a sort; in fact it was an unending counterpane of branches and leaves reaching for the sunlight at the tops of trees with bare trunks 200ft high.[34]

Air commanders advocated carpet bombing of suspected rebel strongholds, but civilian officials refused to allow random attacks for fear of hurting innocent Burmese. Instead the planes dropped leaflets urging the rebels to surrender and mocking the idea that tattoos and spells could protect them from British bullets. 'Don't believe those persons who profess to be able to make you bullet proof with charms, amulets and incantations. There is no drug and no charm that can cope with the guns of Government,' a typical leaflet read.[35]

Senior air officers were furious over subsequent claims by government officials that aircraft would be of limited use in putting down unrest in the Far Eastern colonies because of the terrain or the relative sophistication of the natives. The airmen said the real problem had been the feeble refusal of the civilian administration to authorise bombing raids. One pilot insisted that a few bombs would have ended the revolt. 'The moral effect of an attacking aircraft on people so superstitious and credulous that they believe their leaders are able to make them bullet proof can well be imagined,' he wrote.[36]

Some lower ranking civilian officials had enthusiastically supported bombing rebel areas regardless of the risk to any innocent bystanders. One robust district officer wanted to use bombers like beaters in a tiger hunt with a curtain of exploding bombs driving the insurgents to the guns of waiting infantry units.

★★★

Things did not go well for the RAF when it tried to carve out a niche in China. Foreign powers meddled ceaselessly in China's chaotic affairs in the interwar years, and British and other businesses operated from so-called 'treaty ports' free of Chinese control. The British Army's China Command had garrisons from Wei-Hai-Wei in the north to Hong Kong, the only formal British outpost, while a powerful Royal Navy flotilla patrolled the main rivers as well as the coast.

The RAF believed it had to play a role in the region to keep up with the other services. Envious air officers studied guides for army officers going out to China. Married officers were told they must have four servants, and preferably six, to run even a modest household; hunting was poor, but the excellent local polo more than made up for its shortcomings; and it was best to have any dental problems fixed before leaving Britain because reliable local dentists were exorbitant.[37]

Shanghai, which was largely controlled by British interests, was the jewel of the treaty ports and the sixth largest city in the world. A full British infantry division was sent to protect the settlement in 1927 when it was threatened by a power struggle between local Chinese warlords – an extraordinary show of power underlining the importance of the city and its trade to Britain. A squadron of Bristol fighters was included, along with two aircraft carriers and other warships. The Bristols operated from Shanghai's racecourse; the planes took off from the grass paddocks to patrol the settlement and its hinterland. In the end, Chinese forces did not attack the city.

Shanghai was celebrated as the 'Paris of the East', and thousands of British soldiers, sailors and airmen from the force wandered wide-eyed through its teeming streets and markets. Many of the men were drawn to the city's brothels, and venereal disease soon afflicted one in fourteen of the force. An army chaplain toured the red light district, vainly imploring the men to desist, and the military authorities asked the European ladies of the local United Gospel Mission and the Moral Welfare League to help persuade the troops not to be 'beastly'. A plan to buy film projectors for 'rational entertainment' failed to eclipse the men's interest in sensual pleasures, and the military eventually set up medical facilities at twenty-one brothels.[38]

The RAF did not remain in Shanghai as part of the British garrison when the emergency force was withdrawn, and it only managed to establish a small presence at Hong Kong. The RAF had more success when its units operating from Royal Navy aircraft carriers were used to chase Chinese pirates, who preyed on British and other foreign shipping along the coast. A typical incident was a June 1934 attack on the British cargo ship SS *Shuntien*.

Pirates masquerading as passengers seized the vessel and abducted several British and Chinese citizens from the first-class section. The hostages were taken to a coastal village, where they glumly watched the pirates divide up their belongings. The pirates showed a particular taste for European evening dress, and several paraded about in dinner jackets and patent leather shoes as others, unaware of the irony, played 'Rule Britannia' on a looted gramophone.

The aircraft carrier HMS *Eagle* and four destroyers found the pirates' village four days later. A patrol of Fairey IIIF planes were fired at as they flew over the settlement. A navy report complained that pirate leaders let their men blaze away unchecked at the planes, 'Any man who thought he would like to take a pot shot did so without asking any-one's [*sic*] permission.'[39] Several bombs were dropped, inflicting about a dozen casualties, after which the impudent firing stopped.

Alarmed by the British flotilla off shore and the planes buzzing over their village, the pirates released two abductees, a British insurance salesman and a Chinese official, with an offer to release all of the foreign hostages if the air attacks were halted. Two British seaplanes spotted the pair in a sampan waving a white flag and landed next to it. The insurance salesman boarded one of the planes, but the Chinese official, 'who had never ceased bowing from the hips', had to be hurled onto the other plane by the sampan crew, where he lay on the wing 'in a confused heap continuing to take off and put on his hat and shouting, "Ah, my dear friend, the brave English"'. All of the Westerners were released after planes dropped messages warning the village would be bombed.[40]

★★★

Air Control made a token appearance in the necklace of islands and atolls in the South Pacific that marked the eastern fringe of the empire. A solitary plane of the New Zealand Air Force helped put down unrest in Western Samoa in 1930 after a policeman and several civilians were killed in a riot. Local officials called for reinforcements. A Moth seaplane was strapped to the deck of the cruiser *Dunedin* for transport to Samoa, where it had to be manhandled ashore through the surf because there was no harbour or jetty. Once ashore the little air detachment happily lived like beachcombers, growing beards, wandering around in shorts and unbuttoned shirts and sleeping in grass huts.

Having got the Moth into the air, the enthusiastic little air detachment offered to subdue the population with some displays of aerial firepower. The plane was armed only with a Lewis gun, the expedition did not have any bombs; the pilot had a pistol for self-defence and 'shooting down coconuts in the event of a shortage of rations'. Civilian administrators, horrified at the thought of sleepy little villages being attacked, opposed any use of violence. The Moth was instead put to work flying reconnaissance patrols and dropping leaflets on hamlets urging people to obey government orders.

The air detachment's hopes of seeing action jumped when a stone was thrown 'dangerously close' to the plane as it flew over some huts. The pilot circled 'to learn the exact intentions of the stone thrower', and fired a flare when a second stone was flung skywards. A subsequent inquiry noted the flare set fire to the home of a local official, who had nothing to do with the stone throwing, and that his alarmed wife barely managed to douse the flames. In justifying the attack, the air force said it was well known that the Samoans were adept at throwing stones.

Flare guns were also used to fire warning shots to turn back canoes suspected of conveying some of the rebels to nearby islands. Tired of such restraint, the navy made a crude bomb consisting of 3lb of gun cotton in a metal tube. It was dropped near a group of suspected rebel canoes and exploded without causing any damage. It turned out that the boats were only carrying an Australian missionary and his peaceful flock. The New Zealand air contingent went home to boast of its exploits in reports that parroted its British parent's teachings about backward native mentalities.[41]

★★★

Air Control never had a serious chance of taking over the policing of British territories in sub-Saharan Africa and the Far East. The African possessions were remarkably peaceful, and local officials were horrified at the idea of replacing village policemen with bombers. Efforts to build up the air force in the Far East only started in the late 1930s because of growing tension with Japan. Such setbacks made little difference to RAF fortunes. Uprisings and wars in India and the Middle East in the 1930s meant the airmen were needed more than ever to buttress the empire.

18

BATTLE FOR THE RAJ

I n the early interwar era many in the British military saw the battle to control the North-West Frontier of India as the greatest threat to the empire.
The storm clouds that began to envelop Europe were barely noticed by
the tens of thousands of troops tied down in the seemingly unending struggle
with the frontier tribes. Squadron Leader A.J.Young, who served as a bomber
pilot, described it as a war against 'two million Iron Age tribesmen armed with
modern rifles'.[1] While its campaign to take over India's defences made little
progress in these years, the RAF was increasingly vital in propping up British
control of the frontier with a series of unprecedented bombing campaigns.

★★★

By 1930 life in India for the RAF had improved immensely from the penni-
less days after the First World War when planes had been held together with
rope and wire and squadrons inhabited derelict army barracks. Officers and
men still complained, only now it was the usual military grumbling about
the heat and dust, poor pay and slow promotion. The airmen had adapted to
the rhythm of life in the Raj with all of its trappings and privileges. When
squadrons moved to new bases, the long railway trains of men and gear
invariably included two or three freight cars carrying that ultimate symbol
of British India – the officers' polo ponies.

Indian civilians dubbed 'flight coolies' did much of the heavy work on
airbases. Sweating gangs of labourers pushed planes back and forth from the
hangars as British NCOs bellowed orders in a mix of English, Urdu and
Arabic punctuated with colourful profanities. 'Puckaroo that bleeding tail

gharry and push the *burra sahib's hawajahaz* on to the *mutti bort jeldi*' meant 'Wheel out the commanding officer's plane as quick as possible'.[2]

The airmen continue to cultivate their own, informal style to set them apart from what they saw as the stuffy formality of the Indian and British armies. Officers sported an eclectic range of formal and casual clothing – shorts, riding breeches, bush shirts, tunics and brightly coloured silk scarves, in and out of the cockpit – to emphasise the service's taste for individuality. Norman Bottomley, who was a senior commander in India in the 1930s, had to rebuke his officers for a lack of military smartness: appearances were vital, he said, to maintain British prestige in front of the natives.[3]

The RAF's main role in India throughout the 1930s was policing the North-West Frontier and all but one of the eight squadrons in the subcontinent were based in the frontier region by 1930. Air power was one of the most effective weapons against the tribes, even if RAF claims that bombing would end resistance permanently had long since been discredited by Pathan resilience. The frontier squadrons were always busy. When there was no fighting, units flew regular patrols to keep watch on the Pathans; carried out aerial photography to produce and update maps; escorted army and supply columns; and ferried political officers around their 'parishes'. Every part of the frontier was supposed to be flown over at least once a month, partly to remind the tribes they were being watched, partly to familiarise crews with the targets of the next campaign.

Flying was much safer by the early 1930s because of major improvements in aircraft and supply inventories, and there were far fewer accidents and perilous forced landings amid the jagged peaks.

The Westland Wapiti, which was as legendary in colonial operations as the Spitfire would be in the Battle of Britain, began in the late 1920s to replace the DH9As, Bristol fighters and other veterans of the First World War in overseas squadrons. A tough, versatile biplane with open cockpits, it was the first plane expressly designed for the heat and dust of colonial operations.

The Wapiti resembled the loyal DH9A, although parts of its fuselage were metal and its radial air cooled engine gave it much greater lift and reliability, especially in the high altitudes of the North-West Frontier and northern Iraq. The Wapiti was more agile and stable than its predecessors, which made bomb aiming much easier for an observer leaning over the side, squinting at a village 3,000ft below in a narrow mountain valley. Nonetheless, costs were kept to a minimum – the rear cockpit lacked a proper seat and the observer either stood or squatted on a kind of folding flap.

The Wapiti had a number of problems, including a heavy nose that made it prone to flipping over on landing, as well as a tendency to lurch sideways taking off or landing. Many pilots struggled initially to master the plane – three Wapitis crashed in the first week after 30 Squadron in Iraq was issued with the plane in 1930.[4] But crews came to cherish this stolid aircraft with its ability to withstand almost any amount of rough handling, atrocious weather and dirt landing strips.

The Hawker Hart, a fast, manoeuvrable biplane bomber, and its army co-operation variant, the Hawker Audax, equipped some Indian and colonial squadrons in the later 1930s, although 5 Squadron was still operating Wapitis on the frontier as late as 1940.

Trenchard's 1929 master plan had singled out the North-West Frontier for the biggest 'substitution' or replacement of army units with air squadrons. Geoffrey Salmond, as chief air officer in India, fleshed out Trenchard's proposal with a 1930 memo ponderously entitled 'Air Staff Proposals for the Fuller Employment of Air Power on the North-West Frontier of India'.[5] It made the usual claim that aircraft could put down trouble before it became more than the mutterings of a few mullahs. It was therefore 'a logical step', it continued, to pull the army off the frontier altogether, and give the RAF full control. Salmond proposed cuts in the army of twenty-five infantry battalions, a cavalry regiment, twelve and a half artillery batteries and a wide range of support troops. At least 30,000 troops would be axed for an estimated annual saving of £2 million. There would be no regular soldiers in the tribal belt; only the lightly armed tribal militias and paramilitary police would be retained under RAF command.

Salmond's scheme would have given the RAF control of the most important theatre of active military operations in the empire, and been a major victory in the struggle with the army to dominate imperial defence. The scheme predictably outraged the Indian Army, which denounced it as dangerous lunacy. It also alarmed many government officials and observers, who did not see how aircraft alone could control the vast and dangerous stretches of the frontier.

Lieutenant General C.J. Deverell of the Indian Army said that the RAF had yet to prove it could control the tribes, despite more than a decade of air operations on the frontier. The RAF, he added, always exaggerated the ability of aircraft while grossly minimising the importance of land forces. Salmond's predictions of vast savings were mocked as the 'exchange of 20 shilling bombs for five penny [infantry] bullets'.[6] There was a nasty jibe at the airmen's courage when Deverell said their methods worked only as long as the tribesmen and their families were willing to sit helplessly and be slaughtered. Air Control, he concluded, was a betrayal of every justification for British rule in India. He fumed:

> The only offensive action open to Government would be bombing of villages, and any Government which relied solely on this method of keeping order amongst a large section of its own subjects would present its enemies with a very potent weapon with which to attack the good faith of its humanitarian declarations.[7]

The two services and their supporters had barely begun ripping into each other when a major uprising unexpectedly erupted on the frontier.

India appeared largely peaceful to its British rulers at the start of 1930. Gandhi's calls for Britain to leave aroused only moderate concern. There was some unease about his unlikely ally on the North-West Frontier – Abdul Ghaffar Khan, a charismatic Pathan leader who headed a movement known as the Red Shirts because of their paramilitary uniforms. The group operated in the settled areas of the province that were under British control unlike the tribal territories along the Afghan frontier. Government officials, unnerved by the Red Shirts' taste for marching and other pseudo-military activities, arrested Ghaffar in April 1930. Within hours protesters took over the provincial capital of Peshawar, a medieval labyrinth of tightly packed houses, streets and alleyways. The city's small police force failed to disperse the riots, and troops brought in to deal with the riots opened fire, killing at least thirty people and wounding thirty-three others.[8]

Trouble erupted across the province and the tribal belt as lurid rumours spread of British troops slaughtering defenceless civilians in Peshawar. Red Shirt agitators toured villages, waving rags they claimed were the blood-stained clothing of men, women and children mercilessly gunned down by the army and police.[9] There were rumours that the British had abandoned Peshawar or were pulling out of India altogether. Unrest erupted in the tribal belt, where the Haji of Turangzai, a tribal chief and an inveterate British opponent who was also Ghaffar's father-in-law, called for an uprising. His three sons, nicknamed Badshah Gul I, II and III by the British because they had the same name, raised a *lashkar* or tribal army.

Badshah Gul I led a force of 700 men towards Peshawar. Colonial officials were stunned when people in the settled areas, who were supposed to fear and despise the tribesmen as looters and murderers, welcomed the *lashkar*. Trouble erupted in other parts of the tribal belt as other *lashkars*, some armed with homemade cannons, captured several government militia posts on the frontier.

The RAF was called in to put down the unrest as the army hurried reinforcements to the frontier. Salmond's squadrons were employed around the clock against the tribal forces threatening Peshawar. Any village in the tribal belt or the settled areas suspected of aiding the *lashkar* was bombed. A formation of nineteen Wapitis and five DH9As dropped 10 tons of bombs and incendiaries on settlements on May 14 alone. Flight crews said that conditions were hazy and it was hard to see the villages, but claimed that they had hit the targets repeatedly.

Many of the tribes and clans did not support the uprising, but more than one pro-British village was bombed because aircrews did not find the right target or could not tell one settlement from another. British officials shrugged off such mistakes. A political officer said an attack on a friendly village in his area was an 'error ... of little consequence'.[10]

The frontier squadrons were reinforced with anything that could be got into the air. A Hinaidi transport plane, which had been used a few months before by the viceroy for a goodwill tour of the frontier, was converted into a rudimentary heavy bomber by stacking bombs in the passenger cabin and tossing them out by hand. A newspaper correspondent, who showed marked sympathy for the army over the RAF, gave a rather jaundiced account after flying on one of the Hinaidi's bombing missions. The plane took off at night and seemed to circle aimlessly until the first rays of dawn illuminated a drab, brown landscape. Its target, the correspondent wrote, was 'a miserable, abandoned collection of mud huts' badly damaged by earlier raids. Two 500lb bombs painted yellow missed the target on the first pass. 'The taxpayers' money had made two nice craters for the tribesmen to take cover in,' the writer mockingly wrote, adding that the next pass created holes and bumps which the tribe's children would be able to use as a playground.[11]

A far more serious threat emerged when some of the Afridi clans, regarded by the British as the most powerful and fearsome tribe on the frontier, joined the uprising. An Afridi *lashkar* advanced on Peshawar in late May and was welcomed by people in the settled areas. Air patrols failed to stop the bands of warriors streaming down from the hills behind red banners. The *lashkar*, said to number 7,000 men, occupied the Khajuri Caves outside the city. Showers of bombs exploded impotently in flashes of white and yellow flame on the surrounding hillsides as the RAF tried to dislodge the tribesmen from their deep subterranean shelters.

A part of the Afridi force advanced on Peshawar on the afternoon of 4 June. British Army and police units failed to intercept the tribesmen and the RAF was ordered to stop the Afridis entering the city. Every available aeroplane was ordered into the air with the first flights roaring into the sky as dusk settled over the Peshawar Plain that evening. The planes blindly pounded the tracks the Afridis were thought to be following but some 1,500 tribesmen reached the outskirts of Peshawar, where they hid in the lush gardens and orchards ringing the city.

Planes from 5, 20, 27 and 60 Squadrons bombed and strafed the bands from dawn until dusk the next day. Bombers dived on the belts of trees and bushes where the Afridis were sheltering, pockmarking the green vegetation and brown earth with 20lb bombs and machine-gun fire. A cavalry brigade with armoured cars tried to drive the Afridis onto the guns of a waiting infantry brigade as if they were hunting tigers, but the horsemen were driven off by tribesmen entrenched behind stone walls. The Afridis only retreated after hours of withering air and artillery attacks. Over the next few days many of the tribesmen left the Khajuri Caves and returned to their villages. Tribal losses were put at between 150 and 200, with the RAF claiming most had been killed by air strikes.

A second Afridi *lashkar* marched on Peshawar in July, eluding the air patrols that bombed their route to the city. Some 5,000 warriors were soon sheltering in the Khajuri Caves. Only a few of the frontier tribes had joined the uprising, but British officials knew any sign they were losing control could bring hundreds of thousands of well-armed fighters pouring down from the hills. Two infantry brigades with more than 6,000 troops moved out to shield Peshawar on 5 August as ninety planes from six squadrons bombed the tribesmen's positions and villages suspected of aiding them.

The RAF made 144 sorties alone on 7 August, with pilots attacking anything that moved on the Khajuri and Aka Khel plains. It was not enough to stop large parties of Afridis reaching the city's southern outskirts that night. Cavalry and air patrols swept the surrounding plains and villages on 8 August, and an infantry brigade fought running battles with the tribesmen after dark on the edge of the city. Some British newspapers were astonished by events at Peshawar and the military's inability to crush the uprising. The RAF was singled out for criticism in several scathing editorials, with the *Daily Telegraph* asking why the dropping of 6,000 bombs by the air force had failed to stop 'backward' tribesmen getting to the walls of a major British city.[12]

Peshawar showed signs of resembling a besieged fortress by 9 August as roads and the railway line were impeded, telephone and telegraph lines were cut and bad weather interrupted radio links with the rest of India. A cavalry unit was attacked outside the city by some 200 tribesmen concealed in a dried-out river bed and angry army officers accused the RAF of failing to spot the gunmen. The tribesmen next attacked a major army supply base on the edge of the city, surging over the walls and bursting through the gate before being driven off by the guards. Alarmed British commanders launched a major sweep to drive back the Afridis. Virtually all restraint was dropped as bombers and artillery pounded the villages around the city despite the risk to civilians. One exasperated army officer said that when 'tribesmen could hardly be distinguished from presumably peaceful villagers, it is no wonder the odds were heavily in favour of the Afridi gangs in their game of hide and seek with the troops and the air force'.[13]

Finally, superior British firepower began to tell, and air and ground patrols reported on 11 August that the Afridis had pulled back. Air commanders claimed the tribesmen had been broken by the bombing and were now sitting in dark caves, trading accusations over who was to blame for their losses. An armoured train reopened the railway line on 12 August. Three days later the *lashkar* began to disintegrate and air patrols spotted bands of tribesmen streaming home through the hills.

The events of the summer, nonetheless, shook the British establishment. With notable understatement, military commanders conceded that a tribal attack on a major city was 'a departure from the normal methods of [frontier] warfare', and a worrying sign of what lay ahead.[14]

The uprising was still raging when the RAF and the army had begun bickering over who deserved the credit for putting it down. Salmond told London in July that only swift intervention by his squadrons had prevented a general uprising.[15] One of his aides exulted, 'The tribes are at our mercy … we have countered the attacks, and now the whip is in our hand.'[16]

Army assessments of the RAF's performance were far less flattering. Ground commanders claimed that air patrols frequently missed tribal forces and repeatedly failed to disperse the *lashkars*. The air force's only effective tactic was the 'intensive punitive bombing of villages' that indiscriminately slaughtered women and children, the army said, omitting it had clamoured for the raids.[17] Whatever the army claimed, bombing was vital in defeating tribal attacks, but the growing ability of the Pathans to endure air attacks undermined RAF claims that Air Control could pacify the frontier – air power checked the tribes, but it did not stop them from making further challenges to British control.

Tribal forces had long known that air patrols could be eluded, especially in bad weather or at night. Their positions could easily be concealed from aircraft and most of the bombing was imprecise. Even Salmond admitted that the tribes had adapted, 'in spite of every form of surprise and harassing air attacks adopted by day and night'.[18] The RAF defended its performance, nonetheless, saying it only had 100 planes and air operations had been hobbled by civilian interference. With more planes and a free hand, the airmen insisted they could handle any threat on the frontier.

Despite Salmond's assertions about having too few aircraft, his squadrons had unleashed a staggering 23,826 bombs with a total weight of 583 tons, 80,853 incendiaries and countless machine-gun bullets in little more than three months.[19] It was some of the most intense bombing the world had yet seen. Air force records refer vaguely to 'exemplary punishment' of rebel villages and of hundreds of dead and wounded, but give very few details on the destruction the avalanche of explosives and metal had inflicted. Instead, the bombing was played down because of British fears of inflaming Indian and international public opinion.

Air commanders inspected bombed villages in the tribal belt when British troops occupied some areas later that year. Wing Commander H.V.C. de Cresigny of 2 (Indian) Wing said that in one bomb-riddled settlement the raids had destroyed 25 per cent of the buildings and damaged another 30 per cent. Roofs, floors and interiors had been obliterated by bombs exploding inside buildings, he noted, but the stout exterior flint walls generally had not collapsed. The report made no reference to casualties or to the damage to food stocks and other possessions which caused serious hardship for the generally poor inhabitants.

De Cresigny was surprised by the elaborate bomb shelters he found in the villages, and he marvelled at the engineering skills of these ostensibly 'primitive' people. Bunkers were deep and well shielded, walls had been built in front of cave mouths to deflect bomb blasts and skilful camouflage concealed the entrances. De Cresigny said one cave complex he inspected could shelter 600 people, and had good ventilation and a spring for drinking water; he conceded that it was invulnerable to any bomb in the RAF's arsenal. He cheerily insisted that the villagers did not resent the bombing because he was offered cups of tea wherever he went.[20]

The Indian administration set up a committee of political and military experts to study frontier control in the wake of the 1930 unrest. Its final report foresaw a gloomy future of dwindling British strength and rising challenges, 'It is idle to expect conditions will ever be normal again.'[21] Salmond, who had been named to the committee in a sign of the RAF's growing influence, argued that air power was the key to the effective and affordable control of the frontier. Army leaders replied that bombing would only create hatred of the British and lead to more unrest in the future. 'We cannot bring ourselves to believe that the casualties, suffering and hardships of the women and children which so frequently occur with air action, can fail to arouse bitter resentment,' the Indian Army's General Staff said.[22]

Air officers shot back that the army was peddling a false picture of mass slaughter, and asserted that aircraft reduced casualties by swiftly suppressing uprisings. 'In similar conditions in Iraq, Transjordan and Aden the spread of civilization under the protection of the aeroplane has been very marked,' the RAF insisted.[23] The committee concluded that the unrest had proved the value of aircraft and the RAF might one day have the power to control the frontier, but it would be dangerous under existing conditions to replace army units with air force squadrons.

Air force commanders tried throughout the 1930s to persuade the Indian Government that air power was the best way to control the frontier tribes. They insisted that air blockades of villages would crush any resistance without inflicting serious casualties. Hunger, cold, sleep deprivation, lice and other discomforts would wear down the tribes and force them to submit to British authority. 'Gradually, existence in these uncomfortable surroundings becomes almost unbearable,' declared an RAF paper prepared for the Indian Government.[24] It might take time 'before a particularly stiff-necked tribe gives in', it added, but a blockade required only modest effort and expense.[25]

Air blockades were used in a number of small operations on the frontier in the 1930s with varying results. In a typical action, a belt of Mohmand villages was blockaded off in the autumn of 1935 after tribesmen attacked work parties building roads for the army. The tribes submitted after two months, but forty-five people, including nineteen women and children, were killed, despite claims that blockades caused few casualties.[26]

The RAF always complained that it was never given a chance to prove that Air Control could work in India because of the hidebound and timid attitude of the Indian Government. Edgar Ludlow-Hewitt wrote at the end of his tour as RAF chief in India in 1937 that civilian officials could not understand how air blockades and other tactics worked and instead frittered away air power by allowing only limited operations.[27] And yet RAF claims that it could control the entire North-West Frontier if it was given just three more squadrons seemed delusional. A blockade of one or two villages that might last for months required at least a full squadron; cutting off the entire tribal belt with millions of tribesmen would have required scores or even hundreds of squadrons. The empire could not afford such an enormous extravagance and it would have undercut the prime justification of Air Control that it could control the empire at a fraction of the cost.

The tussle for control of the frontier during the 1930s deepened the already strong enmity between the RAF and the Indian Army, with each side accusing the other of being ready to use any deceit. A memo to the Air Ministry from RAF HQ in India said that '… relations between us and the General Staff can scarcely be more strained, and the opposition to all RAF proposals is extremely bitter'.[28] A 1936 RAF memo claimed the army saw the air force, rather than the Pathans or any foreign power, as their chief foe. 'No enemy balks larger in their minds than does the Royal Air Force. If they could defeat that they would be satisfied that they had served their country well.'[29] Army officers shot back that the airmen would stoop to anything to get their way. A senior army officer said he never missed any opportunity in official reports to point out the air force's shortcomings or mistakes:

> I wish to emphasise any causes of failure on the part of the RAF. They are never fair to us, and as long as I am satisfied that my statements are true … I wish to include them however unpalatable they may be to the RAF … you can have no idea of the extremes to which the Air Staff will go to make their points.[30]

Some air officers claimed the army refused to share intelligence during frontier campaigns because of inter-service animosity.[31]

For all the talk of air blockades, bombing was still the main response to any serious threat on the North-West Frontier. Bomber squadrons were used routinely to punish rebellious tribes, often inflicting severe casualties and destruction to check the 'danger of the infection spreading'.[32] Warnings were dropped before some raids to try to minimise casualties, but with varying success. The RAF accepted that sixty-five people were killed or wounded, more than half of them children, in the bombing of a village called Massozai in 1930, even though warnings had been dropped beforehand.

The air force blamed the inhabitants, saying they had ignored warnings, although it claimed that 'as a result of the air action, we were now on better terms with them than we have ever been before'.[33]

Some squadrons said that warning the tribes was a waste of time after leaflets were sent back 'with rude messages inscribed thereon'. Aircrews complained that it put their lives at risk because planes had to fly over villages to scatter the warnings and the inhabitants rushed to 'the roofs to get a better shot'.[34] British officials knew most unrest was the work of a few militants or brigands, but the entire clan or village would be bombed under the notion it forced the community to curb troublemakers. British officials knew, however, that all too often the tribe had no control over the militants. Some Mohmand chiefs who pleaded in 1935 for a halt to raids on their villages were sent home because they 'did not possess full power of attorney' to speak for the entire tribe.[35] Efforts were sometimes made in air raids to single out the compounds of rebellious chiefs and their main lieutenants to minimise damage, but such attacks only temporarily discouraged the more determined insurgent leaders – the Haji of Turangzai and his sons led a series of uprisings despite regular attacks on their compounds.

Air force crews still had few, if any, qualms about bombing villages or women and children despite growing criticism from political and religious leaders in Britain and other parts of the empire. Most aircrews claimed, then and later, that it was all just a game enjoyed equally by both sides. If pressed about the rightness of what they were doing, many airmen said the natives only had themselves to blame for defying British authority and that the warnings dropped before raids gave them every chance to stop. One squadron leader said:

> If they went on being troublesome, we would warn them that we would bomb an assembly of people. An assembly was normally defined as ten people ... I can remember actually finding nine and saying 'That's within ten per cent and that's good enough' so I blew them up.[36]

Most airmen assuaged any doubts by insisting that bombing raids did not cause much damage or hurt only those who deserved it, something they held up as proof of the uniquely benevolent nature of British colonial rule. 'Of course we could have dealt ruthlessly with the whole population as certain other nations have done with undeveloped people, but this is not the British way and we were prepared to have a drawn game and return match,' Basil

Embry wrote.[37] Anyway, these young men had joined the RAF to fight. Even senior officers regularly left their desks for the thrill and occasional terror of combat missions – de Cresigny, the commander of 2 Wing, sometimes flew in the back seat of a Wapiti, doing the work of an enlisted man so that he could take part in dive-bombing attacks.

Flying crews were far more likely to question what they saw as misguided or outdated operational methods. Pilots complained about being forced to use tactics designed for European battlefields – formation flying and high-altitude bombing were often useless against guerrilla forces in wild countryside. Bottomley said his crews railed against a ban on flying below 3,000ft, intended to avoid ground fire, because it made it difficult to make out targets such as a lone gunman concealed in the rocks.[38] Crews often ignored the height restriction. Slessor helped pioneer new low-level bombing techniques on the frontier, including the 'VBL' method, in which a diving plane raked the terrain with its forward machine guns to suppress ground fire, dropped its bombs at the bottom of the dive and then climbed steeply as the gunner in the rear cockpit laid down suppressing fire.[39]

Crews that excelled at dive-bombing were picked for especially difficult tasks. Squadron Leader S.B. Harris and Corporal W.R. Ellis were assigned to bomb the Haji of Turangzai's fortified compound at Gagh in March 1932 with orders not to hit the nearby tomb of a Muslim saint for fear it would inflame the entire frontier. The house was sheltered by a cliff that rose almost vertically behind it and the two men made eighteen attacks over two days in a Wapiti, plunging down the side of the cliff while Ellis tossed out 20lb bombs by hand and used the Lewis gun to suppress ground fire, before Harris unleashed a 230lb bomb and then hauled the plane into a heart-crushing climb. The heavy bombs were fitted with fifteen-second fuses so the plane could escape the blast. Ten bombs hit the compound, two of which failed to explode, and the structure was badly damaged.[40]

The general accuracy of bombing continued to be derisory despite the RAF's dogged insistence that most bombs found the target. Of the 19½ tons of bombs dropped in frontier operations in March 1932, only 48 per cent were reckoned to have fallen close to the objective, which was probably an extremely generous estimate.[41] Even in practice exercises, usually held under ideal conditions with good weather and no ground fire, less than 50 per cent of bombs fell within 100 yards of the target.

At least there was now money for regular bombing exercises and other training: five frontier squadrons dropped 1,250 bombs of varying sizes and fired 24,000 machine-gun bullets in June 1935 exercises.[42] Not that the RAF had forgotten Trenchard's mantra about the need to impress the government by keeping costs to the minimum. Squadrons had to use up stocks of obsolete bombs before new models could be ordered, even if that made things more risky for flight crews. India Command was instructed in 1935 to use up 9,000 Mark VI 112lb bombs to clear the way for the new Mark VII model. Crews complained that the First World War era Mark VI's tended to fall off in mid-flight because of weak couplings. The air force's response was an instruction to avoid flying over areas inhabited by British personnel.[43]

Efforts were made to improve squadrons' knowledge of the frontier to make bombing attacks more effective. Detailed photo surveys produced better maps, lists of potential targets with accompanying details were compiled in a 'Doomsday Book' and crews were given 'Where's Where' cards with photographs and locations of the villages they were sent to bomb.[44] There was some concern about using paid tribal informants to select targets because of fears they settled personal vendettas rather than identifying real troublemakers, but the practice was never abandoned.

Remarkably few airmen were killed or injured in Indian frontier campaigns in the 1930s despite the size of the operations – Air Control proponents had always argued that saving the lives of British servicemen was one of its main justifications. Even when there was no fighting, however, it was not unusual for planes to return from routine patrols with a bullet hole or two in the fuselage.

Even some friendly Pathans could not resist testing their marksmanship if a plane crossed the sky. David Lee, a pilot, once asked his Pathan servant what he was going to do during his upcoming leave in the tribal belt. Lee was horrified when the man, who had been with him for several years, said he would join the other men of the village and shoot at RAF planes. An incredulous Lee asked the bearer if he would shoot at him, to which the Pathan replied that he would never shoot at his employer, just his plane.[45]

Airmen who were captured after being shot down or making emergency landings continued to be treated well despite the legends about the ghastly fate that supposedly awaited captured white men. Flight Lieutenant Sinclair and his gunner, Aircraftsman Watson, crashed during a 1934 patrol. The aeroplane clipped several trees as it careened down a steep hillside, rolling over several times before ending up in a mangled heap among some boulders. Local tribesmen took the injured men to a nearby house, where a crowd of wildly shouting people gathered outside arguing over what should be done with the captives. A government medical orderly arrived to treat the airmen (native medical workers and messengers working for the British were generally allowed to come and go) and a Sikh government doctor also arrived only to be sent away after the tribesmen decided that the Muslim orderly could handle the situation.

Some of the tribe wanted to sell the crew to their Afghan neighbours; a second group thought a *jirga*, or tribal conference, should consider the issue; while the third wanted to take the men back to the British lines and claim the reward they knew would be paid for their safe return. The last group triumphed and Sinclair and Watson were carried on beds for almost fourteen hours across 70 miles of mountain wilderness to the nearest road, where an ambulance was waiting. The tribesmen carrying the beds refused to share the load and lugged the two men all of the way. Sinclair told an inquiry he was fairly sure the plane had been hit by ground fire even though the area was at peace. Tribal elders, when asked if this was true, said it was difficult to control some of the local shepherds.[46]

★★★

Bombing became increasingly controversial in India in the 1930s as Indian politicians, religious leaders and some British officials questioned the morality of bombing imperial subjects, especially women, children and other non-combatants. The RAF command grumbled that its methods were being maligned as 'bomb rule'.[47]

Government officials tried unsuccessfully to choke the criticism by releasing as little information as possible about raids. Air force files from the 1930s often carry warnings that any operational reports which might be made public were to be toned down and all gory details omitted. It helped that very few independent observers got to the tribal belt because of official restrictions and the danger of being abducted or killed by the tribesmen. But unsettling reports of raids emerged from time to time.

A 1935 story in the *Manchester Guardian* quoted an army officer's description of the aftermath of recent raids:

> When our troops entered a bombed village the pariah dogs are already at work eating the corpses of the babies and the old women who have been killed. Many suffer from ghastly wounds, especially some of the younger children who … are all covered with flies and crying for water.[48]

It turned out the officer had never seen such things and was citing what others had told him, but the report caused an uproar.

In spite of the mounting public criticism, the British and Indian governments believed that the bombing was indispensable and refused to stop it. Many officials had deep personal reservations about bombing, especially since they knew that most of the people subjected to it were pawns caught between the militants and the British forces, but they saw no alternative.

Few were better qualified to understand the dilemma than the commander-in-chief of the Indian Army, Field Marshal Sir Philip Chetwode. He said that the bombs often fell on helpless people who had not committed any offence but he felt compelled to sanction attacks when his own commanders argued there was no other way to put down revolts and avoid high British casualties. It was, he told the viceroy in 1935, 'indiscriminate air action against thousands of people who are not now, and never would' resist British rule:

> I loathe bombing, and never agree to it without a guilty conscience. That, in order that 2,000 or 3,000 young ruffians should be discouraged from their activities, dozens of villages inhabited by many thousand women, children, and old men, to say nothing of many who have refused to join the lashkars, should be bombed, and their inhabitants driven into the wilderness while the Air Force conduct a leisurely month or more bombing … is to me a revolting method of making war, especially by a Great Power against tribesmen.[49]

And yet civilian administrators on the frontier who dealt with the Pathans often were the most vehement supporters of bombing, arguing that in many situations it was the only thing that worked. District officers working and living in the tribal belt criticised the central administration, located in Delhi far from the dangers of the frontier, for wanting to limit bombing.

Olaf Caroe was given the task, in 1933, of protesting on behalf of the frontier administration when Delhi tried to halt the use of large bombs as a sop to the growing criticism of Air Control. Caroe said even a moderate reduction in bombing would ensure that:

> … the whole military and political balance of our relations with the tribes is altered. [British control would be] most seriously impaired.
>
> There can be no doubt that the tribes up and down the frontier now regard with the utmost dread a force which can search out their most remote and jealously guarded sanctuaries, and can deal out the most prompt and effective

punishment [inflicting] … heavy losses … in personnel and material … This
position has been achieved by the Royal Air Force almost solely by the bombing of villages of recalcitrant tribes.[50]

London and Delhi acquiesced in the face of stark warnings that the frontier
could only be held by bombing. All they could do was implore the RAF to
limit the damage, or at least ensure that distressing details of raids did not
leak out.

Part of Embry's duties as a staff officer in India in the mid-1930s included
handling, or rather smothering, queries about air operations. A not untypi-
cal parliamentary request from London asked how many bombs had been
dropped on the frontier since 1919, the number of people killed and the
value of the property that had been destroyed. Embry promptly made up a
figure of how many bombs had been used, said one person had been killed,
adding that it may have been due to army action, and concluded by saying it
was impossible to estimate property losses because 'there was no value placed
on a mud hut and no house agents existed on the frontier'.[51] His glib and
completely misleading response was never queried or challenged.

19

'WHAT A MESS WE HAVE MADE'

A formation of British bombers circled helplessly over the ancient heart of Jerusalem as Arab mobs rampaged through the narrow stone streets below, attacking and looting Jewish businesses and homes. The DH9As dived on the rioters now and then to try to disperse them, but the pilots were under strict orders not to attack – British officials cringed at the thought of the global uproar that would ensue if the RAF bombed the holiest city on earth. The events of that summer's day in 1929 were the start of a struggle that would see Air Control's greatest setback.

Hugh Trenchard had said that Air Control could not be used to police 'semi-civilised' areas such as the ancient cities and towns of the Middle East, but the RAF assumed responsibility for Palestine in 1922. It was a sleepy region that seemed content under British rule and the air force wanted to grab as much territory as possible from the army. In the 1920s the mandate had a reputation of being the RAF's dullest colonial assignment; the tiny air force contingent merely patrolled the borders and left internal matters to the police.

Most RAF men were not interested in the local people. One airman, W.H. Lawrence, said the few who did mingle generally found it easier to get along with Jews from Europe and America.[1] Arabs were caricatured as backward, dishonest and rapacious, although some in the military preferred them because the westernised Jews did not instinctively bow to the British. The torpor of the early years of British rule crumbled as a growing influx of Jews seeking a new homeland alarmed the Arab population. British officials were befuddled by the territory's increasingly complex sectarian and political polarisation. 'God, what a mess we have made of this Palestine affair,' British Major General H.R. Pownall lamented in his diary.[2]

Deadly sectarian riots erupted on 23 August 1929 in Jerusalem and other towns. The RAF's first response was a bumbling attempt at scaring the rioters by sending bombers to buzz riot-torn areas. It took only minutes for the rioters to grasp that it was an empty threat and the planes would not attack. A solitary plane haplessly flew in circles over Nablus as some 3,000 Arabs attacked the police station and dozens of Jews were killed in the surrounding streets.

Unable to halt the protests with empty threats from the air, and with no army units in the mandate, the RAF assembled scratch ground units to reinforce the police. Mechanics, cooks and other ground crew were formed into makeshift riot squads, but they were far too few and hopelessly unprepared for such a task. A little convoy with just fifty men was sent from Amman in neighbouring Transjordan with instructions to restore order in Jerusalem where thousands of Arabs had seized parts of the city.

Even the RAF's armoured cars were of little use after government officials ruled out using their machine guns for fear of civilian casualties. Leo Hetherington of the 2nd Armoured Car Company was part of a squad of four cars sent into Jaffa to help police break up a mob of 6,000 Arabs. The stunned airmen watched as the small police detachment was overwhelmed and beaten by swarms of rioters wielding clubs, iron bars and rocks. The crews, forbidden to fire, twirled their gun turrets around in a forlorn attempt to frighten the protesters, but the jeering Arabs pelted the vehicles with stones and pounded on the iron sides with clubs and bare fists. Hetherington peered helplessly out of a turret slit at the sea of contorted, screaming faces just inches away; the mob's hatred seemed literally to buffet him in the face. A few days later, Hetherington's armoured car was destroyed when an Arab woman splashed petrol on the back and set it ablaze; the crew had to leap clear and run to another vehicle.[3]

Army units were rushed to Palestine to stop the spiralling violence. Two platoons of Welsh infantry flown in from Cairo were the first to arrive. 'The going was very bumpy and most of the men got rid of their dinners,' an RAF report laconically noted.[4] An army unit that reached Haifa was shocked by the devastation they found. Murdered Jews lay in the streets and the soldiers rescued terrified Jewish women and children from buildings set on fire by rioters. The railway station was crammed with Jewish families trying to flee.

Control was not regained until a British battleship arrived in the port. Confusion, inadequate equipment and petty bureaucracy hampered the fumbling efforts to end the unrest. The military's ageing radios frequently failed, regulations stipulated all messages had to be translated and transmitted in code even though it meant interminable delays and the navy and RAF bickered furiously over whether to use GMT or local time.

Trouble spread as Arab mobs attacked isolated Jewish settlements in rural areas. A small force of bombers was all that could be spared to protect the outposts, but the crews were given permission to use their machine guns in open areas. Two planes on 25 August strafed marauders leaving the burning settlement of Bir Tobia and claimed to have hit at least ten of the attackers. Pleas from pilots for permission to use bombs and incendiaries were rejected by officials worried about hurting the settlers.

Arabs took to attacking the settlements at night to evade air patrols. Planes flying over Bir Tobia at dawn two days later saw huge spirals of black smoke rising from a string of burning Jewish settlements stretching across the plain. Two planes fired at people moving through the wreck of Bir Tobia, although an RAF report later admitted the crews could not be sure if they were shooting Arab looters or Jews trying to douse their burning homes. 'Owing to the difficulty of distinguishing between Moslems and Jews [on the ground], air offensive action is very difficult,' it complained.[5] Worried about victims of the mobs being accidentally shot or bombed by the RAF, the British administration imposed such tight restrictions that it became almost impossible for the aircrews to intervene.[6]

Air Vice Marshal Hugh Dowding arrived in September as head of British forces in Palestine and Transjordan in a routine change of command. His first task was to find out why the RAF had lost control during the recent riots and mend the damage to the service's reputation. Dowding came from the same template as most of the early RAF leaders: an army officer with a string of colonial postings in India, Hong Kong and Gibraltar, an enthusiasm for flying that saw him become a pilot on the eve of the First World War and led to his success and rapid promotion in the air force during the conflict. He held a number of senior posts after the war, including serving as chief staff officer in Iraq in the mid-1920s.

Dowding, who would find his own moment of immortality during the Battle of Britain as head of RAF Fighter Command, was one of the service's rising stars when he arrived in Jerusalem. His appointment to the Palestine Command was another illustration of how the Middle East was a nursery for the RAF's best and brightest. For all his abilities, Dowding could find no way around the simple fact that aircraft could not surgically suppress riots since air attacks would kill and injure victims of the mob as well as the lawbreakers.

An RAF post-mortem on the riots complained that there had been 'no military enemy'. Its impotence was underlined by the fact that the Palestine squadrons had only used their machine guns nine times and had not dropped a single bomb during four weeks of nationwide unrest.[7] Dowding did what he could to salvage the RAF's reputation, insisting that it had helped end the riots by limiting border incursions and forcing Arab marauders to mostly attack at night.

In London, the Air Ministry brazenly tried to shrug off any responsibility by insisting that it had always said that aircraft could not handle this kind of trouble: ' … it was of course perfectly apparent to the Air Ministry that communal rioting and racial murder in towns and villages could not be dealt with by the bomb'.[8] The army tried to use the RAF's failure to take back control of Palestine's defences. A government committee set up to study the issue only ensured future problems by leaving the RAF in charge while boosting the garrison with two army battalions under a semi-independent commander.

Clumsy British attempts, in the wake of the riots, to find a political solution to the growing sectarian tension satisfied neither side. Arab unease increased as Jews continued to flood into the territory, and there were sporadic riots and clashes in the early 1930s. Still, the British were caught by surprise when the disturbances turned into a full-scale Arab revolt in 1936 that became one of the biggest challenges to British control anywhere in the empire in the interwar era.

The RAF was still in control of Palestine's security when the trouble began in the spring with demonstrations, strikes and riots. Two unarmed RAF men were shot by a gunman as they walked along a street in Jerusalem, and one later died.

Air Vice Marshal Richard Peirse, the military commander, was another RAF star who held a series of senior posts until he caused a major scandal by eloping in the 1940s with the wife of General Claude Auchinleck, one of the leading British generals of the Second World War. Peirse knew the little garrison was totally inadequate to deal with the uprising. It did not help that most of his air contingent was not even in the mandate – an army report subsequently pointed out that the only air formation assigned to Palestine was based in Egypt, mischievously implying this was so the crews could have more comfortable quarters. Peirse hastily called for harsh measures to suppress the protests, including martial law, censorship, forced labour, curfews and, above all, air raids on selected villages to cow the population. He proposed randomly picking a large Arab town and heavily bombing it to show the Arab population what would happen if it resisted British authority.[9]

Sir Arthur Wauchope, head of the British administration, was horrified. He rejected Peirse's draconian plans, and army and navy reinforcements were brought in. Bomber crews were sent out to blizzard Arab villages with leaflets saying that Britain was their benefactor and friend, but the RAF felt humiliated at being relegated to such a role. British forces lost control of large areas to bands of Arab fighters. By midsummer, the British had deployed twenty-two infantry battalions and two cavalry regiments in the territory. London recognised that RAF control of the mandate now made little sense. Responsibility for Palestine's defence was transferred to the army on 15 September 1936 and Peirse was replaced by Lieutenant General John Dill (who would briefly command the British Army in the early stages of the Second World War). It was a humiliating loss of face for the air force, if not the disaster that some smug army officers imagined.

The uprising faltered in the face of the massive military build-up and Arab leaders were persuaded to wait while a British commission studied the territory's future. Sardonic aircrews now had to scatter leaflets across the countryside extolling the wisdom and good intentions of the committee's British members. A new revolt erupted in the autumn of 1937 when the commission recommended the creation of separate Arab and Jewish states. Volunteers from across the Arab world flocked to Palestine to aid the uprising. Arab army officers and veterans from Iraq, Syria and elsewhere helped organise the anti-British forces. Bewildered British Army reports conceded that the Arabs were brave and resourceful fighters, not the cowardly figures normally conjured up by British imperial propaganda. Samuel Wentworth, an airman who had shared the general view that Arabs could not fight, changed his mind the day he saw two British soldiers come down from a hilltop observation post to fetch tea. In a few minutes Arab guerrillas deftly planted a bomb that killed both men as they trudged back up the well-guarded path.[10]

Arab forces became increasingly effective and the insurgency turned into a full-blown guerrilla war. British forces struggled to respond to fleeting attacks by guerrilla bands that melted into the civilian population or faded into the hills. Ambushes and snipers shot up British traffic on the highways; saboteurs blew up train lines, mined roads and cut telephone wires; and government supporters and informants were assassinated, depriving the British of information about the insurgents. Scores of British soldiers and policemen were killed and injured.

Aircraft were invaluable under these conditions and the three Palestine squadrons, soon reinforced by a fourth, were used for reconnaissance and ground support. Aircrews could make free use of their armaments against insurgents in the open countryside, although there was a strict ban on bombing buildings. In September 1938 alone, 6 Squadron expended 797 bombs and 63,000 machine-gun rounds, and claimed to have inflicted hundreds of casualties on the Arab forces. Aircraft generally were used singly or in pairs to patrol and support ground units, but there were mass operations such as a 15 September 1938 clash around Deri Ghassan against a force of 500 Arab fighters when dozens of planes from 6, 80 and 211 Squadrons claimed to have killed at least 130 insurgents.

In a sign that the air attacks were inflicting serious losses, Arab leaders complained that the airmen were merciless killers. Stories appeared in regional Arab newspapers claiming that British planes dropped poisoned sweets on villages.[11] Air operations boosted the morale of the local British population, which saw bombing as the best medicine to dish out to the Arabs. 'A terrific battle is in progress all round the Safed hills, the aeroplanes have been passing backwards & forwards all day from Samakh – do hope they'll get another good haul – one can't help feeling the more A's [Arabs] that are killed the better!' a British woman wrote home.[12]

The conflict between the airmen and the elusive guerrillas was fleeting and anonymous. Crews flying over the villages and fields could not tell if a figure below was a toiling peasant, a harmless traveller or a gunman. One pilot complained about the difficulty of identifying a few rebel fighters 'amid a million similarly-clad inhabitants'.[13] British infantrymen in khaki uniforms could also be easily mistaken from the air for insurgents, but a proposed solution of having soldiers wave their sun hats proved useless when pilots frequently failed to see the gestures. Despite the danger of ground fire, planes generally had to fly at 500ft or lower to have a chance of spotting the insurgents, who usually hid in the olive groves and thick shrub that covered the countryside.

Pilots said 112lb bombs were the best way of winkling snipers out of olive trees with their thick, sheltering branches. The insurgents responded by building tough, effective bomb shelters, forcing the RAF to attack at ever lower levels. Pilots generally found it best to work in pairs with the lead aeroplane flushing insurgents out with a bomb and its wingman finishing them off with machine-gun fire. There were some extraordinary feats. A South African pilot, with the improbable name of Marmaduke Thomas St John Pattle, became an overnight legend when he shot and killed three

Arabs hiding in a well by vertically diving on the tiny target in a Gloucester Gladiator fighter. Pattle became a top RAF fighter ace in the early part of the Second World War before being killed in 1941.

Palestine saw the RAF suffer some of its worst losses in the interwar years. A growing number of aircraft were damaged or shot down as Arab marksmen became more proficient, and their armouries swelled with modern weapons, including machine guns donated by Arab sympathisers or purchased from profiteering British servicemen. In all, 6 Squadron had forty-one planes damaged, of which six were destroyed, as well as five crewmen killed and two wounded during the uprising. In the last four months of 1938, 33 Squadron suffered two dead and two injured along with seventeen planes damaged, including three destroyed.

The army also struggled to defeat the insurgents despite the vast disparity in manpower and weaponry between the two sides. Some officers clung fanatically to the belief that the bayonet was the best way to cow the Arabs, but more imaginative commanders achieved successes with motorised columns, armoured vehicles and radios. The insurgents hit back by turning old artillery shells into improvised bombs that were hidden in roads or on country paths – these devices were the crude forebears of the deadly Improvised Explosive Devices (IEDs) of modern Iraq and Afghanistan. British forces used increasingly harsh and indiscriminate methods to crush resistance: collective fines were imposed on villages, tanks and explosives were used to demolish the homes of anyone suspected of sheltering guerrillas and there were cases of soldiers and police indiscriminately killing Arabs.

Tanks flattened slums in Jaffa that were anti-British bastions, and army engineers blasted two corridors through the labyrinth-like centre of the old city. Such tough measures heartened the mandate's British civilians and servicemen, more than a few of whom wondered why they were risking their lives in this bizarre conflict. Morale was especially shaken when Edward VIII abdicated to marry an American divorcee. 'It seems to me that it is the beginning of the end of the British Empire,' one disillusioned patriot wrote.[14]

★★★

British forces had some of their greatest successes when aircraft worked in close co-operation with army ground units. Arthur Harris and Bernard Montgomery, who were to play such momentous roles in the Second World War, were instrumental in developing air co-operation tactics.[15] Harris had returned to the Middle East as chief air officer for Palestine and Transjordan in June 1938, while Montgomery commanded an army division in the territory. Harris, his young wife Therese and aide James Pelly-Fry lived in a large, comfortable villa outside Jerusalem. Pelly-Fry, whose father had died when he was 5, was enchanted by his welcome into the family. Harris read voraciously, and Pelly-Fry recalled sitting for hours as his commander, relaxing in the privacy of his own living room, talked passionately about politics, history, art and a dozen other subjects. It was a world far away from the usual bland officers' mess chatter and a respite from the official social round of interminable cocktail parties, gymkhanas and government receptions. When time allowed, Harris and his domestic entourage occasionally toured the countryside in an open car with a picnic basket and an RAF armoured car trundling along behind as an escort.[16]

Harris was as thrusting and acerbic as ever. He advised junior officers to avoid postings that involved putting down civil unrest because they were likely to be punished for using too much force, or too little. Harris raged against the restrictions on bombing as idiocy and weakness, and advocated tough tactics of the kind he had helped develop in Iraq in the early 1920s. He said the uprising could be ended with 'one 250-pound bomb or 500-pound bomb in each village that speaks out of turn … The only thing the Arab understands is the heavy hand, and sooner or later it will be applied.'[17]

Harris and Montgomery developed tactics employing air cordons to isolate a settlement or area and trap insurgents. Aircraft arrived at dawn, or 'first shooting light',[18] and dropped leaflets warning people to stay indoors until the army and the police arrived to search for wanted men, weapons and other contraband. 'You are hereby warned to remain in your houses. Any person who may endeavour to leave the village or to go to the fields surrounding the village will be liable to be shot. You will be told when you can leave your houses in safety,' was a standard warning.[19]

A growing number of insurgents were cut down by planes as they tried to flee from surrounded villages. Air cordons were employed more than 100 times between late 1938 and the spring of 1939 when the revolt petered out – they had no similarity to air blockades which were intended to keep people out of settlements and might last for months. Co-operation and inter-service cordiality improved further as RAF squadrons repeatedly came to the aid of beleaguered army and police units. Ground units trapped in ambushes tapped out an emergency 'XX' signal, and RAF radio stations relayed the calls to loitering aircraft. The army praised the aircrews' 'gallantry and efficiency' for rescuing their troops again and again.[20] An army report said that aircraft often accounted for more than half of the monthly totals of insurgent losses. However, improved inter-service relations did not stop Montgomery ending the last vestige of RAF control when he cancelled its operational command of the Jordan Valley, handing the task to the cavalry.

On the ground the RAF's increasingly dilapidated armoured cars helped the army sweep rural areas and patrol the towns. By reputation, at least, the armoured car companies were still a dumping ground for second-rate officers; it was a slur on men who often faced greater danger than the air-crews. Armoured car crews, many of them younger than their vehicles, were exposed to hideous risks in the cramped, sweltering interiors of these relics of another age. The cars constantly broke down and the armour did not always fend off modern machine guns and rifles. Mines were the deadliest threat, and even a small device could wreck the poorly protected vehicles.

A lack of money and equipment meant that damaged cars had to be repaired and reused rather than replaced with new vehicles. Squadron Leader Ernest Ford spent six months in 1939 with an armoured car company hunt-ing for insurgents or keeping Arabs and Jews apart. Most British servicemen could not understand why they were risking their lives in this perplexing squabble. Ford said that units called to intervene in clashes between Arabs and Jews increasingly preferred to stand back and watch the two sides kill each other.[21]

★★★

The RAF continued to play a major role in other parts of the Middle East during the 1930s. In Iraq, air power was crucial in maintaining a large degree of British control after the territory became independent in 1932. A large RAF contingent remained in the country to prop up the government and ensure that it remained part of the British imperial sphere. Two squadrons were based at Basra in the south and two squadrons at Habbaniyah, some 50 miles west of Baghdad.

Air force officers and men acted as if nothing had changed. Alfred Earle remembered that the British lived in their closed-off bases, rarely mixing with the Iraqis except for occasional trips to Baghdad or Basra.[22] And yet the Iraqis were no longer so submissive. Charles Batchelor, who had served in the country in 1919 with the army before returning in the 1930s with the RAF, was dismayed to discover that a British uniform or a white skin was no longer an automatic mark of authority. Some Arabs now shouldered British servicemen aside on the street rather than deferentially making way.[23]

The RAF detachment helped the Iraqi Government with regular summer campaigns against Kurdish independence forces. Iraqi officials had no inhibitions about bombing civilians they despised as rebels, and the RAF dutifully followed requests to flatten Kurdish villages and support Iraqi ground offensives. Ernest Folley recalled that the seasonal operations were looked forward to as 'summer sports', when aircrews and mechanics operated from forward airbases, sleeping six or eight men to a tent.[24]

The British detachments enjoyed life in the open in the northern uplands. The cool, bracing weather and lush grasslands were a blissful escape from the sweltering summer heat of their bases. Mechanics worked on planes in the open, and air patrols set out every morning to search for Kurdish fighters or attack suspected rebel positions. Few Kurds were seen, except for an occasional horseman galloping across the hills – the Kurds had long since learned to take cover when they heard the drone of an approaching aeroplane.

Despite helping the government, some airmen tended to sympathise with the Kurds, who they saw as more manly than the supposedly weak and deceitful Arabs. Folley and others insisted, rather improbably, that the Kurds liked the British and did not blame them for the air attacks, even though they shot at planes and some crewmen were injured.[25] British airmen were scathingly contemptuous of the new government, especially as it began to be torn apart by power struggles and coups in which the Iraqi Air Force took part; it all just seemed to confirm the general British prejudice that natives could not rule themselves.

Trenchard had resisted the creation of an Iraqi air force because of his opposition to coloured pilots and aircrew, only giving way when the British Government insisted that the new state must have an air force if it was to survive. A small force equipped with Dragon and Moth aircraft was built up with the begrudging help of the RAF. Many British officers and airmen shared Trenchard's contempt for black airmen. Earle trained at Cranwell with the first Iraqi cadets, and remembered them as able and pleasant men, but deplored their involvement in Iraq's acrimonious and bloody politics.[26] The British lower ranks bitterly resented having to defer to black officers. Spencer Viles, an air gunner, said some of the Iraqi officers attached to the RAF for training were good pilots, but he would only fly with them if given a direct order by his British superiors. It was widely claimed that Iraqi airmen, although British-trained, were cowards; an Iraqi pilot supposedly would bail out at the first sign of trouble.[27]

When it became clear that British rule in Iraq was coming to a close, the RAF made the astonishing claim that only white men could enforce Air Control and the Iraqis must be discouraged from employing it. Senior British air commanders said that an independent Iraqi Government would misuse aircraft to impose tyrannical rule and indiscriminately slaughter its own people. 'It is most important that bombing should be treated more and more as a last resort for punishment ... and every endeavour made to mete out the necessary punishment without using air action,' it said.[28] The RAF did not see this as a contradiction because of its smug belief that only Westerners could rule 'backward' people fairly and be trusted to administer punishments humanely and with minimum casualties. Moreover, the RAF was concerned it would be blamed if it carried out bombings for King Feisal's government and things went wrong. A memo spoke of 'unpopular acts of repression or punishment by aircraft as the result of British highhandedness which he [the king] is powerless to control and which he has earnestly deprecated'.[29] London agreed, and insisted that the complicity of the king and his ministers in any British bombing operations be made clear.

★★★

Aden, at the tip of the Arabian Peninsula, remained undisturbed as a bastion of Air Control throughout the 1930s. A succession of unapologetic RAF commanders used muscular methods despite calls from London to cut down on bombing. It helped that the rest of the world had little idea, and even less interest, about what happened in Aden and that there were few, if any, local politicians, nationalist groups or Western busybodies to challenge air assaults on anyone who resisted British authority.

Charles Portal, who would command the RAF in the Second World War, became chief of Aden's defences in 1934. A former Oxford law student, he had been marked for high command since joining the air force during the First World War after a brief spell as a dispatch rider in the Royal Engineers. One of his first challenges in Aden was countering raids on caravans in the interior by a confederation of tribes known as the Quteibi.

The subsequent air campaign made little headway despite weeks of raids on villages. British political officers sent in discouraging reports that the tribesmen had become uncannily skilful at judging where bombs fell, rather like fielders gauging the fall of a cricket ball, and easily evaded the blasts. Portal's planes responded by dropping leaflets insisting the RAF could keep up the attacks indefinitely so the tribes should accept the inevitable and give up. 'This is a small matter for compliance in comparison to the discomfort you have already suffered, and will continue to suffer if you do not comply,' the mostly illiterate tribesmen were sonorously informed.[30]

The British were not as confident as the leaflets suggested. Their maps of the deserts were almost useless, tribal boundaries used to determine targets were mostly a figment of British imagination and hostile tribes were 'inextricably intermingled' with innocent neighbours.[31] An RAF report admitted that several tribes which had not committed any offence were bombed.

Portal was worrying about the growing strain of continuous operations on his crews when rescue came in the form of the short spring rains in May. It was the tribes' one brief chance to plant crops in the few tiny areas where anything would grow, and to miss it meant starvation. An umbrella of aircraft stopped the Arabs from working in their fields by firing on anyone. The tribes soon surrendered and met all the British conditions.

Portal told the Air Ministry that the tribes had behaved as if it had all been a good-natured sporting match. After meeting tribal chiefs, he said they were 'in cheerful mood and showed a praiseworthy sense of humour, apparently feel no resentment against His Majesty's Government for their recent punishment', despite being hit with 28½ tons of bombs, 40,000 machine-gun rounds and 26,386 incendiaries. His report showed the tendency of RAF commanders to keep making the same arguments for Air Control as if they were the first to discover them, including the idea that its effect was almost entirely moral and comparing the RAF to the friendly, neighbourhood bobby:

> The aeroplane ... seems to have been regarded as the quite impersonal agent of Government control, and by merely playing the part of constable on his beat, ready to check disobedience of the law but otherwise displaying no force or animosity against the tribes, isolated the Quteibis and put them to a certain amount of ridicule, and eventually produced a good humoured submission.[32]

His report was praised as a model of colonial operations by the Air Staff and held up as an example to other commanders.

Portal was followed in Aden by Wilfred McClaughry, the ex-Australian mounted infantryman who commanded the first RAF detachment in the outpost in the 1920s. McClaughry thought the tribes should be bombed for even minor offences. He insisted that the Arabs only respected tough methods, although like Portal he insisted the tribes held no grudges. 'When his bluff is called, he is amused rather than resentful, his attitude being one of respect and admiration rather than resentment,' he said.[33]

McClaughry ridiculed suggestions from London that he employ air blockades to discipline malefactors, arguing that they were far more cruel than bombing because they cut tribes off from water supplies and led to the deaths of children and other innocents. He told the Air Ministry:

> I agree that in theory the so called air blockade sounds delightfully humane, and to the ignorant may sound as though the RAF can achieve wonders without hurting anyone, or in other words can make omelettes without breaking eggs. In practice I am definitely of the opinion that not only is air blockade the weaker method of applying air control, which may have to be resorted to when other methods fail, but it is less humane than the method of hitting hard for a short time.[34]

McClaughry asked if the RAF leadership was 'inclined to think it necessary to apologise for our successful methods of controlling vast territories'. The Air Ministry chose not to argue. One official, noting that the world had little idea of what was happening in Aden, wrote to McClaughry, 'I do not think you have any cause to worry about your methods and we suggest you carry on as before.'[35] McClaughry's crews did just that, and he suffered no apparent damage to his career, rising to the rank of air vice marshal.

In the late 1930s, Aden's little force of bombers spearheaded the last campaign of conquest in the history of the British Empire, although it went almost unnoticed at the time. British influence over the desolate interior and much of the coast was traditionally exerted through local Arab rulers in return for subsidies and other support. It had never been a dependable system, and a series of power struggles in the interwar period saw the collapse or weakening of several pro-British rulers, prompting the authorities in Aden to intervene with aircraft, the only force available.

Tribal clashes in the Wahidi region in 1937 saw the RAF bombing an insurgent group for four days. Air power was used the following year further to the east in the Seiyun region to support the local sultan, followed by fifty-four raids in fifteen days early in 1939. It was like the heady days after the First World War, as Arab fighters who had never seen an aircraft fled in terror or gave up after the first bombing raid.

The onslaught gave Britain de facto control of the region for the first time, with political officers, backed by the threat of air attacks, controlling things from behind the scenes. Local RAF officers were ecstatic at this demonstration of how air power could acquire vast stretches of territory without a single British soldier on the ground. A network of airstrips extending up to 350 miles from Aden was established to control this new slice of empire.

Aircrews who fought in these campaigns remembered a strange little war of hunting elusive opponents and villages built of desert stone that merged almost unseen into the surrounding rocks. Large poisonous snakes and spiders were a constant menace; voracious red ticks feasted on the airmen's bodies at the desert airstrips; and the desert waterholes were filled with black, putrid water that pulsed with neon green bacteria. Heat-dazed men sat on the beaches, looking longingly at the sparkling water, but not daring to plunge in because of sharks and sea snakes.

★★★

The loss of the Palestine Command did not inflict any lasting damage on the RAF's overall colonial role or its claims that Air Control was still the best way to subdue lawless regions. Air power was as vital as ever to the empire, especially as military resources were diverted to the defence of the British Isles because of the darkening situation in Europe. This was especially so in the Middle East, where a squadron or two of bombers could handle most threats. Just how vital police bombing had become was made starkly clear when Britain risked international opprobrium to defend it.

20

BOMBING FOR POLICE PURPOSES

Anthony Eden, undersecretary of state for foreign affairs and a future prime minister, hurriedly returned to London from the Geneva Disarmament Conference in May 1933 to discuss an unexpected difficulty. Enacting a universal ban on bombing was one of the great hopes at the gathering of some sixty nations. Britain, one of the main proponents of disarmament, had tried to end months of deadlock on a ban by tabling a motion calling for 'the complete abolition of bombing from the air (except for police purposes in outlying regions)'.[1] The proposal caused uproar rather than the expected applause. What, a puzzled Eden asked a meeting of ministers, was bombing for police purposes? The ministers explained the term before adding, in a rare show of unanimity, that keeping the right to bomb unruly natives was essential to the preservation of the British Empire.[2]

★★★

Britain's reliance on air power in the empire became an international embarrassment in the 1930s. British leaders were caught between wanting to ban bombing as part of the effort to prevent future wars and its near indispensability for colonial policing. Lord Londonderry, the air secretary, told Cabinet colleagues in 1932, before the Geneva talks began, '... the real fact of the matter is that we cannot possibly give up bombing from the air by reason of our responsibilities in the East.'[3] At the same time, Britain was haunted by the spectre of the bomber and fears of the destruction of its own cities in any future war.

Articles, books and speeches by pessimistic politicians predicted an impending apocalypse in which aerial armadas would obliterate London and the other great cities of Europe in hours, killing and maiming millions of people. Civilisation would collapse in these nightmarish scenarios, and the ragged, dirty survivors would lead a brutal existence in its ruins, fighting for food and shelter. But while eager to prevent the future bombing of Britain, the government and the great majority of people did not see any connection between bombing 'backward' tribes and their opposition to air attacks on 'civilised countries'.

The RAF viewed the Geneva talks as a threat to its existence with its plans to eradicate the bomber and make air forces little more than aerial border guards. The airmen believed that the bomber would win future wars and saw no point in a future where they buzzed around in a few under-gunned aircraft on aerial sentry duty. Above all, the RAF was determined to keep using bombers in the colonies: imperial policing was still the armed forces' only active operational role.

The RAF Air Staff in London made strenuous efforts in the run-up to the talks to persuade colonial administrations in India and elsewhere to oppose any ban on police bombing. 'If villages are not to be bombed, the capacity of the RAF to control semi-civilised countries will be jeopardized,' warned John Salmond, as head of the RAF.[4] Pressure from the RAF and colonial officials pushed London to come up with the proposal at Geneva to ban all bombing except for imperial policing. The Air Ministry suggested the proposal would be accepted on the grounds that countries were entitled to bomb their own territory.[5]

There was strong support within the British Government and the armed services to continue using aircraft in colonial policing. Even the army backed the RAF for once. 'We oppose bombing in London because of the terrible mischief to its civilian population. In Asia and Africa an aeroplane with a loudspeaker and a few bombs does very little harm,' a 1933 army memo stated.[6] Londonderry gave the Cabinet an almost mystical description of Air Control as the panacea for small wars:

> I only wish the Cabinet as a whole could take advantage of the twentieth-century version of the flying carpet of the Arabian fairy tale, and see for themselves the absolute indispensability of the Royal Air Force, if the pax Britannica is to be maintained – and that at relatively trivial cost – throughout wild and turbulent territories ... Just as the Navy polices the Seven Seas, so to an ever-increasing

extent the aeroplane, the modern 'ship of the desert', covering hundreds of square miles in the course of a single patrol, is policing the Middle East, restraining the activities of the lawless and bringing succour to the distressed. The Royal Air Force is indeed, in the opinion of the competent political authorities, the sole means of keeping in check the forces of disorder, which if ordinarily latent, are all too near the surface and ready to break out the moment the strong hand and vigilant eye of the watchman are withdrawn. The air arm has proved itself to be the one instrument which can deal effectively with those little wars which there must always be in backward countries until we achieve the millennium.[7]

The Foreign Office, while avoiding Londonderry's hyperbole, agreed that British control over nations such as Iraq could only be maintained by air power, and that it was essential to retain the 'unfettered right to make full use of aerial bombardment'[8] in 'backward' countries. It unblushingly echoed the stance of other government departments that it was absurd to compare the bombing of an Iraqi village with an attack on a European town. A memo stated:

Again the term 'civilian population' has a very different meaning in Iraq from what it has in Europe ... it is far the most humane as well as inexpensive method of punishment that can be employed in these regions ... bombing from the air is regarded as an act of God, to which there is no effective reply, but immediate submission.[9]

The Indian Government warned London that a ban on bombing would lead to major unrest and threaten British control over large parts of the subcontinent. Air raids were cheap, it added, and had enabled the Indian exchequer to save a fortune on medical bills and pensions for army widows and crippled soldiers. It would be folly to give up a weapon that 'has proved itself a remarkably effective, economical and humane way of keeping the peace in certain parts of the world', an Indian Government memo said.[10] London accepted Delhi's position, but suggested it refrain from bombing villages during the Geneva talks to avoid unpleasant publicity.[11]

There was strong support in Parliament for Air Control. An all-party parliamentary defence committee unanimously approved a resolution saying Britain must reserve the right to keep on using police bombing:

That this Air Committee supports HM's Government in urging at Geneva the retention of air bombing for police purposes to carry out our Empire and mandatory obligations, believing that this use of the air arm in the territories for which HM's Government is responsible is not only an unusually effective deterrent, but also the most expeditious, economical and humane method of maintaining law and order.[12]

Air Control was just one of many issues at Geneva over which the delegates and assorted experts wrangled. Efforts to outlaw or limit bombing floundered for many reasons, not least the impossibility of working out a ban on bombing that did not also outlaw aircraft.

Britain was attacked repeatedly for its attempts to retain police bombing; critics, some of whom were British, accused London of the worst kind of hypocrisy. George Lansbury, the Labour politician who had led the fight against Air Control from the start, told Parliament that any attempt to defend such a murderous policy was 'a scandal on the lips of an Englishman'.[13] A government spokesman responded that 'the aeroplane as a fighting machine is the most humane instrument that you can employ'.[14]

British officials eventually indicated they would give in on air policing as the talks bogged down, but the conference collapsed when Hitler pulled the German delegation out in October 1933. Still, some thought that the British Government's dogged attempts to cling on to police bombing helped ensure failure. Lloyd George, who had played a key, if unwitting, role in the birth of Air Control after the First World War, sardonically commented that a workable agreement at Geneva was possible, 'but we insisted on reserving the right to bomb n[*****]s'.[15]

★★★

Air Control faced more criticism in Britain during the 1930s than in its early years, although it was little more than an irritant to the RAF and the government. Some left-wing and religious groups challenged the use of war planes for colonial control, and a few activists and writers tried to expose the casualties and suffering being inflicted on native populations. Even some imperialists believed that air policing was inhumane and incompatible with British claims of paternalism or benevolence. One pro-British Indian newspaper said:

> If bombing is to be abolished it must be abolished everywhere. For a country like Britain, with its population crammed into overcrowded cities, peculiarly

vulnerable from the air, to insist on the right to 'bomb and be bombed' is, apart from ethical considerations, sheer madness.[16]

Much of the criticism came from members of the Labour Party, even though it had not curbed Air Control during its brief spells in power. In the House of Commons in June 1933, Clement Attlee, another future prime minister, denounced the hypocrisy of trying to outlaw the bombing of European cities while continuing to blow up Indian villages and Arab nomads' camps. He blamed the double standard, with penetrating insight, on the 'demands of the Air Force to be put into a position of equality with the sister Services, and of its desire to get independent commands'.[17] Another Labour MP, Neil Maclean, sarcastically suggested that the British desire to avoid the bombing they inflicted on others reflected an excess of Christian zeal:

> We send our missionaries to convert the people to our religion, and we send our bombers to send them to that Heaven which we are trying to convert them to believe in, more speedily than they would go in the natural course. We think so much of our religion that we want them to be there first.[18]

Outraged government MPs asked how many natives the previous Labour Government had sent to heaven.

British anti-war groups campaigning for a ban on bombing paid surprisingly little attention to RAF operations in colonial territories. A Christian movement, the Oxford Group, that drew its members mostly from well-educated young people, called for 'God control' in an apparent rebuke to Air Control, and one of its speakers at a 1936 rally asked, 'Does God need a big air force or not?'[19] Some conservative anti-war groups tried to argue that police bombing was acceptable; Lord Robert Cecil said it was a legitimate form of self-defence.[20]

If British pacifists gave police bombing only passing attention, there was growing criticism in the colonies, particularly in India, where nationalists and an increasingly confident local elite protested at what they saw as the slaughter of their fellow citizens or used it to embarrass their foreign rulers. India's raucous nationalist press challenged and frequently castigated RAF operations on the North-West Frontier. Observing events in Geneva, the *National Call* newspaper mischievously stated, in September 1933, 'If a frontier village can be bombed and destroyed no objection can in principle be raised to the destruction of London or Paris or Berlin in a future war.'[21]

The outraged RAF Indian Command kept careful notes on these attacks, but its protests to the civil authorities, and demands that the press be curbed, went mostly unanswered. An RAF staff officer complained that the press seemed to imagine that every bomb dropped on the frontier was marked 'for women and children only'.[22]

***

Air policing faced occasional criticism in other parts of the world in the 1930s. India's colonial administration was especially worried about adverse comments in the United States, where there was strong sympathy for Indian independence.

The harshest attacks appeared in the Italian press, and were rightly seen by London as retaliation for its own criticism of Mussolini's actions in Abyssinia. Italian newspaper headlines on RAF operations on the North-West Frontier in 1937 included: 'Since yesterday aeroplanes sow massacre in Waziristan' and 'Humanitarian England in India; all Waziristan bathed in blood by bombardment'. A commentary in *La Tribuna* said, 'England, imperturbably icy, pitiless, continues her old methods … English history is rotten with the slaughter of entire unarmed populations.'[23] Agitated officials at the India Office in London asked the Rome embassy to distribute detailed explanations to show that British methods were humane, but it made no difference to the officially orchestrated campaign.

The British Government fretted, nonetheless, about international criticism of police bombing and the effect on British prestige. There was acute discomfort when RAF operations in India were compared to Japanese air attacks on Chinese cities or the bombing of Guernica during the Spanish Civil War. A 1938 British statement said it was an 'illusion that there is any sort of analogy between police bombing as practised by the RAF on the [Indian] Frontier, and the recent indiscriminate bombing of civil populations [in Spain] which has rightly aroused the indignation of all decent people'.[24] Police bombing, it added, was an exclusively British method that 'has frequently resulted in the unique combination of achieving a military end with no loss of life whatsoever'.[25]

Prime Minister Neville Chamberlain was asked in Parliament if it would be a 'splendid gesture to the world' if the RAF stopped its police operations since they were being used by Japan and fascist forces in Spain to justify their aerial excesses. 'No, I do not think it would be a splendid gesture,' an irked Chamberlain replied.[26]

Air force commanders thought better public relations would persuade most critics that police bombing was humane. The RAF India Command urged the Air Ministry to persuade journalists to write articles pointing out there were no comparisons '… between the methods of less civilised nations when bombing open towns and our extremely humane procedure for applying pressure to the tribesmen'.[27]

21

THE LAST OF THE
GENTLEMEN'S WARS

The Fakir of Ipi was a messianic Islamic leader who led the last great revolt against the British Empire on the North-West Frontier. Although he lost every battle, the fakir remained unbeaten and defiant until the British left the subcontinent. Ironically, John Slessor, whose solitary duel in 1916 with the horsemen of Darfur marked the advent of Air Control, played a leading part in the last of the RAF's interwar campaigns.

Beneath the usual military veneer of carefree charm, Slessor had intellectual tastes. He took volumes of poetry on campaigns despite the ribald teasing of other officers, wrote prizewinning essays on history and strategy and would be a leading theorist on air power. Slessor shared Trenchard's belief in the future of air power, but, unlike his mentor, he believed that Britain also needed a strong army and navy.

Such talents would lead Slessor to high command during the Second World War, and the ultimate pinnacle of chief of the RAF after the conflict. Slessor had been agreeably surprised in 1935 when the Air Ministry asked what he would like to do after a spell as a staff college instructor; the RAF bureaucracy rarely inquired about the hopes and aspirations of even the brightest officers. Noting that most of his experience had involved Indian and army co-operation duties, Slessor modestly suggested it might make sense if he did something new. He was neither surprised nor disappointed when he was promptly assigned to an army co-operation unit on the Indian frontier.

It was enough for Slessor just to be in the air force. He had been rejected by the army because of a childhood bout of polio, but a family friend secured a place for him in the air corps during the First World War. Four months later, in October 1915, the 18-year-old Slessor, with just thirty-five hours of solo flying, had his first taste of combat when he encountered a Zeppelin in the night skies over London. The gigantic German airship loomed over Slessor like a whale about to crush a solitary swimmer. While the intruder got away, Slessor believed he was the first pilot to intercept an enemy aircraft over Britain.

Slessor's new assignment was command of 3 (Indian) Air Wing based at Quetta in Baluchistan, at the western end of the North-West Frontier. Slessor first served in India after the First World War. He had flown a dilapidated fighter pockmarked with wartime bullet holes which could not be repaired because of the Indian Government's refusal to fund the local air contingent adequately.

He and his wife arrived in Quetta in 1935 with crates packed with glasses, cushion covers, curtains and the other adornments needed to turn a thread-bare government bungalow into a model English home. The Slessors had just given their first dinner party and gone to bed, when Quetta was hit by a massive earthquake before dawn on 31 May. Planes at the RAF base were tossed around like tiny wooden toys. Slessor's command suffered more than 100 dead and dozens injured when barrack roofs slammed down like iron presses on the sleeping men; it was the biggest loss of life suffered by the RAF during the interwar years. Bernard Montgomery, who was an instruc-tor at the local army staff college, helped dig dead and wounded out of the concertinaed buildings. Anywhere between 30,000 and 60,000 people were killed in the nearby city.

Slessor's wing was rebuilding when trouble erupted in 1936 in Waziristan to the north. It was a 'backward' and desolate region even by the bleak stand-ards of the North-West Frontier. The tribes who lived amid its lunar-like wastes said it was where God had dumped debris left over from the building of the universe. British officials and soldiers regarded the local Wazir and Mahsud tribes as among the deadliest and most troublesome of the Pathans.

Olaf Caroe, the British chronicler of the tribes, likened the Wazirs to the panther for their deadly guile, and the Mahsuds to the wolf because of their ferocity.[1] Each tribe was a loose patchwork of scores, and even hundreds, of clans and extended family groups that spent much of their time fighting each other. Raiding and blood feuds were as much a part of daily life as working in the stony fields where, even in the better years, the tribesmen only eked out a slender harvest of parched wheat or barley. People lived in tiny fortified hamlets huddled around stone war towers which kept a sullen watch over the arid landscape. A British visitor to one of these fortified hovels was appalled by the airless, reeking rooms submerged in permanent gloom and a blanket of blood-sucking fleas enveloped him as he stepped through the door.[2]

Attempts by the Indian Army since the previous century to pacify Waziristan had achieved little. Still, British officials were not perturbed when a Muslim teacher, Sayyid Ali Shah, eloped with a 15-year-old Hindu girl, who took her lover's religion and was renamed Islam Bibi. Her enraged family had the couple detained by the police because she was a minor, and a British court in April jailed the bridegroom for two years for abduction. Muslim tribal and religious leaders denounced the sentence as an attack on their faith. An obscure cleric, Mirza Ali Khan, who would become renowned as the Fakir of Ipi, led the denunciation of the British, and was soon calling on the tribes to fight the Christian interlopers.

Like the Mad Mullah of Somaliland, the fakir emerged from complete obscurity with little more than a reputation for profound piety and a remarkable ability to unite the tribes with his religious fervour. The son of a poor cleric, Khan spent his childhood at religious schools in India and Afghanistan. He had no early interest in politics, opting to become a fakir (holy man) who followed an austere life of prayer and wandering. An American journalist, who trekked to the fakir's stronghold in the 1950s after the British had left India, wrote the only known description of him:

> The Fakir was slight of body and had a thin face – brown, ascetic, even spiritual – with many fine lines in it. His spare black beard was streaked with gray ...
> He was quite motionless as he sat there, his brown eyes gazing somewhere else, but his presence was compelling.[3]

Revolt flared across Waziristan after the bridegroom in the Islam Bibi case was jailed, and the British authorities refused to hand the young bride over to Muslim elders as a ward. Pathan raiding parties attacked Hindu villages and British military outposts. British forces demolished the fakir's house as punishment and he fled into the mountains with a few followers.

It was around this time that the fakir began to claim he possessed supernatural powers. Tribal mystics often claimed they could make their followers invulnerable to bullets, but the fakir showed a distinctly modern touch by saying he could turn aerial bombs into paper. It was a claim that seemed true because the mostly illiterate tribesman had never understood why the RAF dropped warning leaflets before air raids, and they readily believed that the papers descending on their villages were bombs transformed by the fakir.

Two army columns were sent up northern Waziristan's Khaisora Valley in November 1936 to awe the tribes. A wit said that Helen of Troy's face had launched a thousand ships, but the rather plain Islam Bibi was worth just two columns of sweating infantry. Army chiefs breezily predicted there would be no trouble after tribal elders promised the columns would not be opposed. Norman Bottomley, commanding 1 (Indian) Air Group, was astonished when the army said the force did not need air cover. The force was assailed by thousands of tribesmen as it entered the valley and forced back after just two days with twenty-nine dead and 106 wounded.[4]

Army and air reinforcements were poured into Waziristan as the government belatedly realised the extent of the unrest. Slessor, riding a borrowed army horse, accompanied the 2nd Infantry Brigade to co-ordinate air and ground operations. Every sight and sound delighted his senses on what some regular British officers regarded as the last of the gentlemen's wars of empire. He relished the clear early mornings as the weak rays of the winter sun illuminated the lines of men and animals against a backdrop of snow-capped mountains. Wapitis and Harts flitted back and forth over the column like bees tending a garden, suddenly diving to inspect a hollow for snipers or rising to glimpse over the next hill.

Soldiers wore drab khaki to blend with the landscape, but there was a touch of heraldry in the coloured flashes on caps and epaulettes: red and blue for the artillery; green for riflemen and Gurkhas; slate blue for the RAF. Communications were primitive, and the column's antiquated radio frequently produced only a splutter of static. The most reliable link was a telephone line that was laboriously unwound for mile after mile from a spool carried by a mule. Strips of white cloth laid out on the ground were still the most reliable link between the ground forces and aircraft: X denoted all was well; V that opposition had been encountered with the apex pointing to where gunfire was coming from; T was the signal for a unit in danger of being overrun.

The Indian Army campaigned as if it was the high noon of Victorian Empire rather than the eve of the Second World War. Most officers saw no reason to be uncomfortable just because they were fighting ragged tribesmen in the middle of nowhere. Slessor's baggage included a camp bath, table and chair, books and a favourite oriental rug to add a touch of colour in his tent.

Evenings were the best time after the long days of marching. Hissing hurricane lamps illuminated the tents amid the comforting sounds of men and animals settling down for the night. Slessor and other officers gathered around the blazing camp fires, chatting and gossiping in a haze of blue tobacco smoke as orderlies served whisky and coffee. As a protection against the evening chill, most wore a mix of civilian blazers, native sheepskins and wool hats over their uniform shirts and shorts. Occasionally a Pathan sniper would pepper the camp, but a bigger danger were mules who occasionally broke loose and careened through the tents, stomping on sleeping men.

There was little resistance, and it all seemed like glorious fun until the column started to blow up buildings in the villages of Dalai Kalai and Mohammed Ziarat to punish the inhabitants for aiding the insurgency. The force of three infantry battalions, which should have been strong enough to awe the tribes, was suddenly attacked by swarms of Pathans. A battalion of the Hampshire Regiment on the west side of the valley was hit by heavy rifle fire. The II/2nd Punjabis became bogged down to the south amid heavy scrub and gullies that provided excellent cover for the Pathans.

The tired and confused British and Indian infantry could not see the marksmen pinning them down. There was unease as the column realised it was now the hunted. Slessor and the brigade commander could hear heavy firing to the south, but still had no clear idea of what was happening when the Punjabis messaged that their situation was desperate. A pair of circling Audaxes were ordered to blindly bomb areas where the Pathans were thought to be hiding. It did little good, and the Punjabis were forced to pull back, violating the cardinal command of the frontier to never leave wounded and dead behind. The 2nd Royal Sikhs, the brigade's third battalion, later counter-attacked under a shield of air and artillery fire to recover the slain Punjabis. After hours of jarring uncertainty, the brigade eventually extricated itself and pulled back.

The days when a few aircraft could rout a tribal army were long over. Air patrols had spotted the Pathans only twice in the Dalai Kalai clash, even though the column had been attacked by hundreds of tribesmen, and the seventy-three bombs and 1,750 machine-gun rounds expended by the six available aircraft seemed to have little effect. The RAF, nonetheless, insisted that air power alone could crush the uprising. Slessor and other air commanders said the tribes could be broken by air blockades of their villages and the army must be pulled back to give the air force a free hand. The Indian Government, rattled by the growing unrest, refused to stake the control of the frontier on the RAF's claims.

Additional reinforcements arrived and British forces began a major ground and air offensive. Columns operating under an air umbrella occupied the

Khaisora Valley in December, methodically burning and tearing down the villages of hostile tribes and 'flushing' Pathan fighters out of the hills with heavy artillery and aerial attacks.[5] The fakir's supposedly miraculous powers failed to turn British bombs and shells into harmless confetti, and his dispirited followers soon melted away. Informers said that the holy man was hiding with a few followers at Arsal Kot, high in the mountains near the Afghan frontier. It was described by the British as a village, but consisted of just half a dozen small shelters on a hilltop little bigger than a soccer pitch. Slessor jocularly described the bleak eyrie as the fakir's country shooting lodge.

The RAF was instructed to destroy the refuge. Planes first dropped leaflets to let women and children get clear, which read 'Government do not wish that your women and children should be harmed. So you are warned to remove them at once. You are also warned that it is most dangerous to handle unexploded bombs.'[6]

Wapitis from 60 Squadron plastered the hilltop on 30 December with 230lb bombs and air force intelligence estimated the crews scored twenty-eight direct hits on the buildings. A second raid on New Year's Day dropped seventeen bombs and 1,200 incendiaries that set fire to the sparse mountain vegetation, shrouding the hill in yellow flames and plumes of white smoke. The fakir escaped the bombing by hiding in a nearby cave complex. The RAF bombed the settlement for a full week after the fakir and his followers tried to return in early January.[7]

The vastly expanded British forces appeared to have suppressed the uprising by early 1937. The fakir's followers were said to have dwindled to less than 200 men, and British Army commanders confidently predicted that he would soon be hunted down or would surrender. The fakir's defiance had turned him into a legend, however, and fighting resumed in the spring on a greater scale than before.

The British lost control of much of Waziristan as tribal bands attacked road convoys, loyalist villages and military outposts, killing soldiers and civilians. Afghan tribesmen, as indifferent to international boundaries then as they are now, poured over the border to join the fight against the British. By April some 46,000 soldiers, militia and police – the equivalent of three army divisions – were tied down by the revolt. Seven of the eight RAF squadrons in India were operating in Waziristan, and air reinforcements had to be sent to the subcontinent.[8]

Tribal ambushes forced British and Indian troops and civilians to travel in convoys, often with air escorts. A column with a strong escort of infantry and armoured cars was trapped on 9 April in a gorge at Shahur Tangi by

200 tribesmen who had dug concealed positions in the steep sides of the defile the night before. Air patrols checking the route ahead of the convoy had failed to detect the gunmen. It took rescuers more than a day to reach the survivors huddled in the line of bullet-riddled, burned-out vehicles. Forty-seven soldiers had been killed and fifty wounded, while even the normally generous British estimates of their own successes put Pathan losses at no more than sixteen dead. Air attacks had failed to dislodge the attackers and a Wapiti was shot down.

Frustrated by the Pathans' skill at evading detection, British commanders gave aircrews orders to fire at anything suspicious in the operational area. Like many airmen, Wilfred Page never saw a Pathan fighter, despite flying dozens of missions as a gunner in an Audax bomber. In a typical experience, Page once spotted movement in the bushes and fired 100 rounds into the scrub with his machine gun, but he had no idea if he hit anything or if it was just a gust of wind rustling the leaves.[9]

It became an increasingly savage war, with no mercy shown on either side. British troops were enraged at the killing of captured soldiers and the mutilation of corpses. A patrol found the butchered body of a Scottish soldier:

> They cut the top of his head off and they took all the brain out and all the bone out and everything. And they just refilled it with earth and stones and they put the top back on … they shoved lit cigarette ends up his nose. They cut his privates off and they stitched them in his mouth.[10]

There was no more carefree talk around campfires about gentlemen's wars. Army units rarely took prisoners when tribal bands were run down. Aircrews were told not to waste ammunition on warning shots and to hit anything suspicious with as 'heavy and intense a volume of fire as possible'.[11]

The RAF unleashed some of the heaviest bombing attacks the world had seen as frustrated British commanders ordered raids to inflict wholesale casualties and damage on the tribes. In March, aircraft from 27 and 60 squadrons bombed two villages that refused to give up men suspected of killing two British officers. Almost 17 tons of bombs, including 148 230lb bombs and two giant 520lb bombs, fell on one village and 14 tons of bombs badly damaged all but eleven of the ninety-three buildings in the second village. 'Standard of bombing was of a high order,' an RAF review noted.[12]

A few weeks later there would be global consternation when German planes dropped 35 tons of bombs on the Basque town of Guernica in one of the twentieth century's most dramatic moments, killing hundreds of men, women and children. The British Government shrilly rejected comparisons between the frontier air raids and the attack on Guernica. Air force reports insisted that raids on the two Wazir villages had not caused any casualties because the inhabitants were warned to leave their villages, but there was no way to confirm the claim.[13]

A confidential RAF report conceded that the usual restraints to avoid or limit casualties were blurred in Waziristan: 'a state of affairs arose where bombing was carried out over whole areas, villages, wells, fields, caves, etc. ... There is no doubt ... a number of unnecessary casualties must have been inflicted.'[14] No word of the bombing was released except for vague references to general military operations.

Punitive bombings intended to inflict severe casualties increased as frustrated British commanders struggled to put down the uprising. Three villages were obliterated in raids on 1 and 2 June for failing to return three abducted Hindu girls – a torrent of 104 heavy bombs and hundreds of incendiaries destroyed 90 per cent of the settlements.

A raid in mid-June that destroyed the village of Tali Palosi was not preceded by warnings. British officials claimed tribal elders had been told to stop supporting the uprising, and that was sufficient warning. Some of the air raids appear out of all proportion to the size and importance of the targets: 10 tons of bombs were dropped in September on what was described as the village of the chief who led the ambush of the British column at Shahur Tangi, but the settlement seems to have consisted of just two buildings.[15]

As with Osama bin Laden in the next century, much of the military effort was poured into the hunt for the elusive fakir. Each vague report of the fakir's latest hiding place in the hills was the signal for intense bombing of the area. Air force statisticians calculated by mid-1939 that planes had clocked up an astonishing 4,470 hours of flying time 'harassing Ipi'.[16]

The scale and intensity of the bombing campaign put the RAF under immense strain, threatening to exhaust both aircrews and supply chains. Front-line airfields regularly complained that they had exhausted their stocks of bombs, and there were times when the main RAF depot at Rawalpindi could not provide more. Commanders at the Miranshah airbase asked for the station's reserve of 360 bombs to be increased to 1,000 bombs to meet the incessant demand. Shortages of delayed-action bombs became so acute by June 1937 that the entire Indian Air Force was rationed to just six a day.[17] There were also concerns that constant operations were wearing out aircrews, especially the enlisted men who served as observers and air gunners, but were still expected to perform their main duties as mechanics or fitters. Replacements had to be brought in from other training units, depots and elsewhere.[18]

Some RAF leaders wanted to curb the bombing, believing the scale and intensity made no sense. Edgar Ludlow-Hewitt, who tried to reform Air Control methods in the 1930s and was now the RAF chief in India, criticised what he saw as the growing number of needless air raids ordered by panicked civilian officials. While saying the occasional destruction of a village was useful, he told the viceroy in April 1937 that air power was being squandered on indiscriminate bombing:

> … the temptation for the Political authorities to use air bombing as a punitive weapon is obvious – it is such a simple and quick way of hitting back at the tribes-men. All previous experience proves, however, that, beyond the damage and loss sustained by the tribesmen, little effect towards the attainment of the main aim is to be expected from purely punitive bombing. If carried too far, such operations become wasteful and relatively an ineffectual way of using our resources. The destruction of a complete village now and then may have an excellent effect where the hostile movement is confined to a small locality or small beginnings. In the present instance, however, the trouble has got beyond that stage and is far more widespread than can be effectively dealt with in this manner.[19]

Only a systematic campaign of air blockades to drive the tribes from their villages and force them to subsist in the wilderness could end the unrest, he argued. Political officials replied that the best use of air power was to inflict casualties and severe damage. Whether or not the civilians were right, the trouble was too widespread and the RAF squadrons too few to have any realistic chance of countering the unrest with blockades, so the bombing continued.

The India Office in London fretted that word of the bombing might leak, and lead to 'charges of inhumanity' against Great Britain.[20] It made its usual pleas to the military to water down official reports on the campaign and expunge details about bombing and casualties to reduce the risk of a public outcry. The RAF had no objections to censoring official bulletins, but wanted the government to make a public statement that bombing 'is not only not inhumane, but probably the most humane form of applying military pressure that has yet been devised'.[21]

British forces gradually regained control of most of Waziristan in the autumn of 1937 as the tribes were worn down and their meagre food stores ran out, but the military never managed to end all resistance. There was little jubilation in the British High Command. It had taken the best part of three divisions more than a year to break a revolt by a few thousand lightly armed tribesmen who rarely operated in bands of more than 100 men. Military and civilian officials wondered what would have happened if other areas or the entire frontier had risen, and the armed forces had been faced by more than a million Pathan warriors. A July 1937 Air Staff review expressed serious concern about the 'unhappy ... situation on the Frontier' and evident British military weakness.[22] Army and air commanders were in no doubt that air power had been vital in holding the frontier.

British and Indian Army losses were severe, with 312 dead, 893 wounded and dozens more dead from disease.[23] Army reports claimed that up to 2,000 tribesmen had been killed and wounded, a disappointing toll for the British given the huge disparity in firepower between the two sides; moreover, there were the usual doubts about the figure, given the military's habit of inflating tribal losses. One of the few bright spots was the RAF's minimal casualties – Bottomley said only four airmen were killed despite intense ground fire.[23] One crew shot down by ground fire landed near a besieged British outpost, and spent a month with the garrison of local militia, whiling away the time learning the local Pashto language.

The fakir fought the British until they left India in 1947. British commanders in the final years on the frontier, knowing they would soon leave, increasingly relied on air attacks to hold back the tribes. Their aim now was to avoid losses to their own forces rather than any thoughts of defeating the tribes.[25] The fakir did not lay down his weapons when the British finally departed. He refused to accept the new state of Pakistan, denouncing its government as secular and a tool of foreign powers. Pakistani Air Force planes bombed the fakir's mountain base several times. He did not give up his lonely struggle for an Islamic state until he died in April 1960 in a cave that still bore the marks of RAF attacks. His death was marked by a long obituary in *The Times*.

22

LEGACY

Air Control ended on 3 September 1939 when Britain declared war on Germany in the wake of the Nazi invasion of Poland. Air policing was forgotten overnight as the RAF became indispensable to the defence of the British Isles. Trenchard's dream of airmen controlling the empire like celestial puppet masters was shrugged off like some youthful exuberance.

After the war, the RAF barely gave another thought to the colonial campaigns that had occupied it so much during the interwar years and helped to ensure its survival, nor did it ever again claim that air power alone could police territories. Colonialism crumbled swiftly after 1945, and the British preferred to forget the often brutal methods with which the empire had been ruled. Political and military leaders brushed over the use of bombers against former subjects it now wooed as friends and allies.

Air Control, when mentioned at all, lived on mostly in the tales of ageing veterans about wooden biplanes, outlandish tribes and comic book capers in the Hindu Kush. Only in the United States, heir to Britain's role as global policeman, would air policing be studied and held up by some strategists and airmen as a model for controlling unruly regions.

Although its memory has been all but erased, the importance of Air Control in the history of the RAF and the twilight years of the British Empire is undeniable. Britain's faltering grip on its empire between 1919 and 1939 would have been more severely tested without the vast and inexpensive firepower provided by the air force. Without Trenchard's handful of squadrons, large tracts of the Middle East might have been abandoned and much larger land forces would have been required to hold down India's North-West Frontier.

Indeed, it was fortunate for Britain that Air Control was only a limited success. It would have been disastrous in the Second World War if Trenchard's dreams of supplanting the army and the navy had succeeded. His plan to replace troops with planes in India, for instance, would have led to the scrapping of dozens of Indian Army battalions, perhaps fatally weakening a force that barely survived its initial encounters with the Japanese in 1942. British naval aviation, even though it frequently blundered in the Second World War, would have fared even more miserably if the navy had not snatched back control in the late 1930s.

For all its military success, air power could not solve the empire's dilemma. Military force, no matter how effective or innovative, could only delay the growing demands for independence. Moreover, the use of military might to prop up British rule only sharpened the clamour for freedom by undermining the empire's political and moral legitimacy, and eroding or destroying the trust of colonial subjects. Army critics of the RAF, forgetting their own 'butcher and bolt' methods, had made a telling point in the 1920s when they argued that although aircraft 'can spread chaos in any enemy's country, they cannot build up law and order in one's own'.[1] And despite its many tactical successes, the RAF never lived up to its claim that it could bring permanent stability to the most lawless areas such as the North-West Frontier.

Most historians agree that the small wars of empire did little to prepare Britain's military for the Second World War, and might have contributed to their initial shortcomings. It was almost a maxim in the armed forces at the time that colonial wars, with their low-key operations against poorly armed opponents, were not a training ground for modern warfare. Indeed, the main function of many imperial service units was not even fighting hostile tribesmen, but the policing or internal control of mostly unarmed civilians, especially in India where the majority of British battalions were employed to guard against the threat of uprisings in the cities or the Indian Army. Some British Army commanders said that after a few years overseas most units were fit for little more than glittering parades and cookhouse inspections. 'We have for twenty years thought little about how to win big campaigns on land; we have been immersed in our day-to-day imperial police activities,' lamented one staff officer as German forces overran Europe in 1940.[2]

Few denied that the RAF was far from ready for war in 1939, despite frantic efforts to modernise and expand on the eve of the conflict. Nor did the air force escape the malign tendency of colonial soldiering to reinforce the amateur spirit that all too often dominated the regular British forces and portrayed war as just another sport. Flying against Arab nomads or Pathan tribes had few parallels with facing the might of the Axis powers: 'primitive' opponents had no aircraft or anti-aircraft artillery; colonial operations relied on light, often obsolete aircraft; night operations were rare and it soon became apparent that imperial service had done little to boost bombing and other vital skills. Above all, colonial campaigns tended to discourage wider, more critical thinking about aerial warfare.

Slessor said the Second World War changed such outlooks, 'the amateur status has disappeared and today it is no longer an agreeable part-time occupation for a gentleman, but a serious and very wholetime profession.'[3]

Air Control did, however, reinforce the RAF's conviction that the 'morale effect' of bombing won wars by breaking an opponent's will. In one of the few wartime references to air policing, a 1941 Air Staff paper said the bombing of Germany was 'an adaptation, though on a greatly magnified scale, of the policy of air control which has proved so outstandingly successful in recent years in the small wars in which the air force has been continuously engaged'.[4] While colonial policing may have been a poor training ground for modern global warfare, it nonetheless played a crucial part in forging the ethos that sustained the RAF in the Second World War, especially its fighting spirit, its camaraderie, outstanding airmanship and an elan which, at its best, could be indomitable.

Air Control was also crucial in blooding a generation of RAF leaders – it is remarkable how so many of the men who figure in the campaigns in Iraq, India and elsewhere as young pilots and squadron commanders rose to the highest ranks in the Second World War.

★★★

The onset of the Second World War saw the British adopt a much harsher attitude to colonial unrest. With the empire fighting for survival, there was no more talk of bloodless air blockades or limiting casualties; tribes or villages that caused trouble were bombed as ruthlessly as German or Japanese troops. Attacks by the Fakir of Ipi and other diehards on the North-West Frontier were met with devastating retaliation, employing new and far more powerful aircraft and weapons.

In just one operation, the villages of Margha and Shodiakai Punga were destroyed in June 1944 after a nearby British military post was attacked by the fakir's followers. The Indian Air Force's 3 Squadron hit Margha with a hail of seventy-six 500lb bombs, after which Shodiakai Punga was shelled by the army and then hit with twenty 500lb bombs; the attacks indiscriminately targeted all of the inhabitants.

In another punitive operation, Hurricanes of 6 Squadron riddled the village of Tahai Sari with salvos of 60lb rockets in November the same year to punish local troublemakers.[5] An approving 1945 Indian Army memo, asserting that reliance before the war on light bombs, warnings and other moderate methods had done little good, said the use of ruthless tactics and heavy bombs was far more effective:

> ... drastic air action against specified villages until they have been destroyed proved very effective ... The two main factors which contributed to success are ... naming guilty tribesmen and certain villages for destruction, and following this up by concentrated action with heavy bombs and rocket projectiles from modern aircraft.[6]

In another sign of change, air duties on the North-West Frontier were handed over almost entirely to the expanding Indian Air Force. British commanders, who might once have opposed black pilots, now praised the skill and determination with which Indian flight crews hammered Pathan villages.

★★★

Air Control was not mentioned, much less revived, by the RAF after 1945, even though Britain faced a series of colonial wars and insurgencies. The conditions facing the RAF were the exact opposite of the dilemma it faced in 1919: the air force was now revered by a country convinced that it needed a strong air defence, just as it was equally clear that the empire was a dwindling concern.

The same currents that were bringing down the curtain on the British Empire, moreover, made something like Air Control unpalatable in the face of new sensitivities about race and colonialism. Britain's new Labour Government was horrified when military commanders in Palestine asked for permission to use bombers to help put down civil unrest in 1945.[7]

Not everything changed overnight, however, and the attitudes of more than a few officials and military commanders in the colonies echoed the simplistic prejudices of earlier generations of imperialists. A 1958 War Office manual on tribal warfare read like a carbon copy of earlier guides on native peoples:

The inhabitants of tribal country are usually Moslem by religion. They are a poor, but hardy race, brought up in an atmosphere of blood[y] hereditary feuds. They are experts in the art of self-preservation and learn to handle a rifle at an early stage. They have many good qualities, among which manliness, hospitality, a sturdy spirit of independence and a good sense of humour predominate, but on the other hand they are often fanatical, cruel and treacherous, and should always be treated with suspicion.[8]

Even the hoary notion that the mere sight of a flying machine could terrify 'primitive' people lingered on in some of the more backward parts of the British military establishment. A 1949 War Office publication said:

Air action, particularly in undeveloped countries, can be the quickest, cheapest, and most convenient and humane means of imposing a sanction effectively. The severity of air action can be widely varied to suit the circumstances. A show of force alone may prove effective, but if force has to be used the required degree of accuracy and destruction may be achieved by choosing the appropriate weapon ... air power can have great moral effect on dissidents, particularly in the case of native populations to whom it may be an unknown factor.[9]

Air power would be vital in the last years of empire, only now the airmen worked closely, and mostly amicably, with their army counterparts in what were called counter-insurgency or combined operations. Ironically, the British military after 1945 remembered very little of the lessons gleaned from generations of colonial policing, and had to relearn many of the basics in conflicts from Malaya to Kenya. Indeed, the initial response in many post-war campaigns was inadequate and amateurish.

One thing that had not changed was the ability of aircraft to inflict damage on an opponent far more quickly and cheaply than ground forces, giving the British a major advantage over lightly armed insurgents. That edge was boosted further by modern jets, rockets, communications and other technology. A range of aircraft, from Lincoln heavy bombers to Hawker Hunter jets, bombed and strafed insurgents in Asia, the Middle East and Africa with varying results.

Lincoln squadrons pounded the thick forests of central Kenya, probing for Mau Mau gangs, and captured insurgents said the strikes had inflicted heavy losses and caused some of the bands to break up. The RAF made some 6,000 air strikes in Malaya between April 1949 and the end of 1950, but bombing was calculated to have inflicted just 10 per cent of the casualties suffered by communist forces.

Aden, that unflinching bastion of Air Control, saw some of the most extensive use of air power in the post-war era and the outpost's defences were still under the control of an RAF officer as late as 1957. A tribe was punished for raiding caravans in 1948, with Tempest fighter-bombers destroying their village, war towers, crops and irrigation works with 12 tons of rockets. Earlier that year, a force of Lincoln heavy bombers and Tempests hit the Bal Harith tribe with 87 tons of bombs and rockets and 3,420 20mm cannon rounds, destroying homes, waterholes, crops and livestock for defying the authority of the local ruler. 'The Bal Harithis are semi-nomadic people to whom bombing and rocket attacks on the scale of this operation are quite new. Their villages have been devastated and their crops damaged,' a Colonial Office report dispassionately noted.[10]

Ironically, forms of Air Control lived on in some newly independent colonies after the British departure. These governments, whose leaders had protested the use of aircraft for internal control in the colonial era, had few hesitations about employing their new air forces against unruly tribes. Air strikes against dissident groups often involved a severity that appalled RAF observers already forgetful of their own raids on frontier villages. Allan Perry-Keene witnessed 1948 punitive operations by the Pakistan Air Force in retaliation for attacks by the Fakir of Ipi on government forces. Villages suspected of aiding the fakir were bombed, rocketed and strafed in surprise raids. 'It is possible the action against villages did not follow the "Queensberry Rules" of the RAF which required warning to be given before bombing,' he observed.[11]

★★★

In a direct continuation of Air Control, Western military commanders and politicians still dream of employing air power to win Third World wars cheaply without risking their own land forces. The West's attempts to combat Islamic fundamentalists in Iraq and Syria in 2014 are the latest version of air policing, this time with American, European and other air forces supporting 'native' ground forces.

Air strategists in the United States have, from time to time, rediscovered and examined Air Control for lessons on modern conflicts. Some American theorists have applauded the RAF's colonial exploits as a model for controlling wild and remote regions from the air, contending that it would avoid costly and bloody ground operations.

Interest in Air Control was revived in 1948 when Colonel Raymond Sleeper of the US Air War College began studying it for lessons in fighting insurgencies. By the early 1950s more than 100 instructors and students were involved in developing ideas in the same way as their British forerunners had done at the interwar RAF Staff College. Interest in Air Control was revived again in the 1980s when a new generation of American admirers presented it as an untrammelled success, suggesting it could be applied to Third World conflicts.

This line of thinking has continued more recently, with air power theorist Carl Builder suggesting Air Control was a model for 'constabulary' or peacekeeping missions conducted entirely from the air, only now with the intriguing possibility of using satellites and other space installations. 'Could air and space power – by themselves – substantially pursue the constabulary objectives of the United States today?' he asked in a 1995 article.[12]

American officials have spoken of Unmanned Aerial Vehicles (or drones) constantly hovering over Afghan villages, showing the people below that resistance was futile – an update of the RAF's 1920s notion of a giant eye in the sky. 'It is possible to look at drones as an antiseptic weapon,' said Philip J. Crowley, a former US Air Force officer and assistant secretary of state from 2009 to 2011.[13]

While modern advocates argue that Air Control can succeed because of better technology, the airmen of today continue to face many of the same problems as their predecessors in the 1920s and 1930s. The use of drones by the United States against Islamic fundamentalists on the old North-West Frontier bears more than a slight resemblance to the RAF's mixed success against religious warlords in the same region. The men who chugged over the mountains in wooden biplanes could not have dreamed of pilotless aircraft controlled from thousands of miles away, but they would have immediately recognised the same problems of deciding who was a foe and who was not, and how and when to attack a village. They would also have recognised the overwhelming difficulties and complexities of attempting to control anarchic regions of which they had little or no understanding.

***

No monument or memorial exists to mark the RAF campaigns of the interwar years and the men who fought them, nor is it likely that one will ever be erected. Arthur Harris, who had said with his usual acerbic insight that putting down political unrest never did a soldier's career any good, would not have been surprised. And yet Trenchard's crews were, for the most part, exceptional young men – bright, courageous and idealistic – among the best of their generation. The bravery and skill they showed bombing a Pathan village was no different from the qualities needed to attack Germany or Japan a few years later. They were convinced that they were serving a just cause and protecting the vast majority of the empire's subject races. Perhaps the most fitting tribute to the colonial squadrons is to understand them by their own ideas and values, without forgetting our own.

NOTES

PROLOGUE – POLICE BOMBING

1   *Report on the Co-Operation of C Flight No 17 Squadron, Royal Flying Corps with the column operating against Darfur during May and June 1916.* Papers of P.R.C. Groves, Imperial War Museum (IWM) 69/34/1.
2   Raleigh/Jones, *The War in the Air*, vol. 5, p.175.
3   Slessor, *The Central Blue*, p.18.
4   National Archives (TNA)/Public Record Office (PRO) WO 33/757.
5   Ibid.
6   Templewood, *Empire of the Air*, p.53.
7   TNA/PRO Air 2/2051.
8   Beaumont, 'A New Lease on Empire: Air Policing 1919–1939', *Aerospace Historian*, 26 (1979), pp.84–90.
9   Templewood, p.48.
10 Orwell, 'Politics and the English Language' in *Essays*, p.963.
11 Raleigh/Jones, *The War in the Air*, vol. 1, p.6.
12 TNA/PRO Air 5/1253.
13 TNA/PRO Air 5/1287, Air 5/1322.
14 Saunders, Per Ardua: *The Rise of British Air Power 1911–1939*, p.210.

1 – SMALL WARS

1 Quoted in Gilmour, *Curzon*, p.497.
2 Graves/Hodge, *The Long Week-end*, p.70.
3 Sims, *The Royal Air Force*, p.37.
4 Dean, *The Royal Air Force and Two World Wars*, pp.33–385. TNA/PRO Cab 21/262.
5 Lawrence, *The Mint*, p.95.
6 Raleigh/Jones, *The War in the Air*, vol. 1, p.471.
7 Quoted in Hyde, *British Air Policy Between the Wars 1918–1939*, p.57.
8 Quoted in Boyle, *Trenchard*, p.95.
9 James, *The Paladins*, p.41.
10 Quoted in Morrow, *The Great War in the Air*, p.323.
11 Hansard, 15 December 1919, vol. 123, cc 137–40.
12 Callwell, *Small Wars*, p.21.
13 Raleigh/Jones, *The War in the Air*, vol. 6, p.136.
14 Moyse-Bartlett, *The King's African Rifles*, p.49.
15 Graves/Hodge, p.16.
16 Chamier, 'The Use of Air Power for Replacing Military Garrisons'.
17 R.M. Groves Memorial Essay, *RAF Quarterly*, 1923.

2 – THE CINDERELLA SERVICE

1 S.E. Towson, IWM 77/148/1.
2 Geoffrey Tuttle, IWM 3178.
3 Sydney Ubee, IWM 12893; Francis Long, IWM 4799.
4 Raleigh/Jones, *The War in the Air*, vol. 1, p.12.
5 T.C. Traill, IWM 67/264/1.
6 Quoted in Hyde, *British Air Policy Between the Wars 1918–1939*, p.141.
7 Tuttle.
8 *RAF Quarterly*, January 1930.
9 Gilbert Smith, IWM 10293.
10 Richard Brooks, IWM 4595.
11 G.V. Howard, IWM 88/9/1.
12 Sydney Sills, IWM 4601.
13 Spencer Viles, IWM 4549.
14 Smith.

15 Stanley Eastmead, IWM 4504.

16 Howard.

17 Ibid.

18 E. Brewerton, IWM Strong Room xx25.

19 John Buckley, IWM 4582.

20 Samuel Wentworth, IWM 4768.

21 Alfred Griffin, IWM 9101.

22 Gwynn, *Imperial Policing*, p.29.

23 Quoted in Boyle, *Trenchard*, p.409.

24 TNA/PRO Air 1/26/15/1/125.

3 – CRISIS OF EMPIRE

1   TNA/PRO Cab. 21/262.

2   TNA/PRO FO 848/2.

3   TNA/PRO WO 33/1004.

4   Ibid, 106/157.

5   Robson, *Crisis on the Frontier*, p.XI.

6   TNA/PRO WO 106/157.

7   TNA/PRO WO 106/157.

8   Franks, *First in the Indian Skies*, p.13.

9   Ibid, p.12.

10 Ibid, p.20.

11 TNA/PRO Air 5/1321.

12 Ibid.

13 Ibid.

14 Robson, p.53.

15 Franks, p.21.

16 TNA/PRO Air 5/1321.

17 George Carmichael, Royal Air Force Museum, B2191.

18 Ibid.

19 Ernest Haire, IWM 10401.

20 Ibid.

21 Carmichael.

22 TNA/PRO Air 5/806.

23 TNA/PRO Air 1/26/15/1/125.

24 Slessor, *The Central Blue*, p.43.

25   TNA/PRO Air 9/59.

26   TNA/PRO Air 1/2033/204/326/35.

27   F.E. Wynne, IWM P.162.

28   TNA/PRO Air 2/1097.

29   Ibid.

30   Ibid.

31   Ibid.

4 – THE CHEAPEST WAR IN HISTORY

1   Lee, *Imperial Military Geography*, p.79.

2   TNA/PRO FO 373/5/19.

3   TNA/PRO CO 535/87.

4   TNA/PRO WO 106/5975.

5   De Wiart, *Happy Odyssey*, p.48.

6   Lewis, *A Modern History of Somalia*, p.77.

7   Beachey, *The Warrior Mullah*, p.100.

8   TNA/PRO WO 32/5828.

9   Ibid.

10   TNA/PRO Air 1/36/15/1/238.

11   Boyle, *Trenchard*, p.366.

12   TNA/PRO Air 5/846.

13   Gray, 'Bombing the Mad Mullah 1920', p.43.

14   TNA/PRO Air 5/1309.

15   TNA/PRO Air 5/846.

16   Ibid.

17   TNA/PRO Air 5/1309.

18   Gray, p.46.

19   Lunt, *Imperial Sunset*, p.253.

20   Hansard, House of Commons, 17 February 1920, vol. 125, cc 722.

21   TNA/PRO Air 5/846.

5 – THE AIR SERVICE OF THE FUTURE

1   TNA/PRO Air 1/1649/204/94/44.

2   Lunt, *Imperial Sunset*, p.293.

3   TNA/PRO Air 20/680.
4   Ibid.
5   Ibid.
6   Ibid.
7   Ibid.
8   Ibid.
9   Ibid.
10 Ibid.

6 – THE MESSPOT MESS

1   G.V. Howard, IWM 88/91.
2   Longrigg, *Iraq 1900 to 1950*, p.102.
3   Ibid, p.190.
4   Victor Groom, IWM 4608.
5   Glubb, *War in the Desert*, p.77.
6   TNA/PRO Air 1/426/15/260/9.
7   Groom.
8   D.H. Allen, IWM 76/85/2.
9   Howard.
10 Ibid.
11 Carr, *You Are Not Sparrows*, p.26.
12 Charlton, *Charlton*, p.269.
13 *The Times*, 23 September 1919.
14 *Royal United Services Institution Journal*, December 1923.
15 TNA/PRO Air 9/14.
16 Ibid.
17 TNA/PRO Air 5/224.
18 TNA/PRO Air 5/168.
19 Ibid.
20 TNA/PRO WO 32/5744.
21 Gilbert, *Winston S. Churchill Companion*, vol. IV, p.1063.
22 Jeffery, *The Military Correspondence of Field Marshal Sir Henry Wilson*, p.283.
23 TNA/PRO WO 32/5225.
24 TNA/PRO Air 5/1253.
25 Allen.

26 E. Brewerton, IWM Strong Room xx 25.
27 Ibid.
28 TNA/PRO Air 5/1253.
29 Ibid.
30 Ibid.
31 TNA/PRO WO 32/5185.
32 Douglas, 'Did Britain Use Chemical Weapons in Mandatory Iraq?'
33 Haldane, *The Insurrection in Mesopotamia 1920*, p.172.
34 Brewerton.
35 Groom.
36 Carr, p.37.
37 Groom.
38 Quoted in *RAF Quarterly*, January 1934.
39 Brewerton.
40 Jeffery, p.152.

7 – 'EVERYBODY MIDDLE EAST IS HERE'

1   Catherwood, *Winston's Folly*, p.127.
2   Gilbert, *Winston S. Churchill*, Vol. 4, p.509.
3   TNA/PRO WO 32/5234.
4   TNA/PRO Air 5/476.
5   Wilson, *Lawrence of Arabia*, p.650.
6   Gilbert, p.1400.
7   Jeffery, *Field Marshal Sir Henry Wilson*, p.8.
8   TNA/PRO WO 32/5899.
9   TNA/PRO Air 5/476.
10 Jeffery, *The British Army and the Crisis of Empire*, p.69.
11 Boyle, *Trenchard*, p.406.
12 Bond, *British Military Policy between the Two World Wars*, p.27.
13 Hansard, 21 March 1922, vol. 152, cc 342–94.

8 – A NEW PLANET

1   Bell, *The Letters of Gertrude Bell*, p.165.
2   Gilbert, *Churchill Documents*, vol. 10, p.1623.

3 Quoted in Laffin, *Swifter Than Eagles*, p.133.
4 Quoted in Bowyer, *RAF Operations 1918–1939*, p.83.
5 TNA/PRO Air 23/542.
6 Keith, *Flying Years*, p.104.
7 Arthur Harris, IWM 3765.
8 Harris, *Bomber Offensive*, p.22.
9 TNA/PRO Air 23/542.
10 Ibid.
11 Ibid.
12 Ibid.
13 Quoted in Saunders, Per Ardua: *The Rise of British Air Power 1911–1939*, p.293.
14 Spencer Viles, IWM 4549.
15 TNA/PRO Air 5/1253.
16 Carr, *You Are Not Sparrows*, p.82.
17 TNA/PRO Air 5/292.
18 TNA/PRO Air 5/1253.
19 TNA/PRO Air 5/292.
20 Sims, *The Royal Air Force*, p.47.
21 TNA/PRO Air 23/542.
22 TNA/PRO Air 5/1254.
23 TNA/PRO Air 5/338.
24 TNA/PRO Air 2/611.
25 Ibid.
26 Quoted in Laffin, *Swifter Than Eagles*, p.178.
27 B.G. Amos, IWM 81/45/1.
28 TNA/PRO Air 5/1253.
29 Ibid.
30 TNA/PRO Air 5/256.
31 Ibid.

9 – DEATH AND TAXES

1 TNA/PRO Air 5/1253.
2 TNA/PRO Air 5/256.
3 TNA/PRO Air 5/1253.
4 TNA/PRO Air 1/426/15/260/9.

5   Hyde, *British Air Policy between the Wars 1918–1939*, p.96.
6   TNA/PRO Air 5/334.
7   Boyer, *RAF Operations 1919–1938*, p.89.
8   Boyle, *Trenchard*, p.101.
9   TNA/PRO Air 5/334.
10   Ibid.
11   TNA/PRO Air 5/338.
12   TNA/PRO Air 5/334.
13   TNA/PRO Air 5/1253.
14   TNA/PRO Air 5/344.
15   TNA/PRO Air 5/1254.
16   TNA/PRO Air 5/1253.
17   Haldane, *The Insurrection in Mesopotamia 1920*, p.21.
18   Cox, 'A Splendid Training Ground', p.172.
19   Gilbert, *Winston S. Churchill Companion*, vol. IV, p.797.
20   Hansard, 14 February 1924, vol. 169, cc1026-7.
21   Vincent, *Flying Fever*, p.59.
22   Richard Brooks, IWM 4595.
23   Bell, *The Letters of Gertrude Bell*, p.701.
24   TNA/PRO Air 5/256.
25   Ibid.
26   T.C. Traill, IWM 67/264/1.
27   Carr, *You Are Not Sparrows*, p.77.
28   TNA/PRO Air 5/264.
29   TNA/PRO WO 32/5184.
30   TNA/PRO Air 2/122.
31   Ibid.
32   TNA/PRO Air 5/1253.
33   Ibid.
34   Hansard, 20 March 1923, vol. 161, cc 2460.
35   Hansard, 3 July 1923, vol. 175, cc 1490-2.
36   Norman Bottomley Papers, B2234, RAF Museum.
37   Hansard, 4 July 1927, vol. 208, cc 864-5.
38   TNA/PRO Air 9/27.
39   Charlton, *Charlton*, p.240.
40   Ibid, p.271.
41   Ibid, p.271.
42   Ibid, p.277.

43 Boyle, p.511.

44 Charlton, *Charlton*, p.284.

45 Ibid, p.281.

46 Keith, *Flying Years*, p.24.

47 TNA/PRO Air 5/1253.

48 Wilfred Page, IWM 875.

49 Geoffrey Tuttle, IWM 3178.

50 Quoted in Omissi, *Air Power and Colonial Control*, p.176.

51 Ibid.

52 Omissi, p.27.

53 *The Times*, 22 April 1925.

10 – DESERT KINGDOMS

1 Thomas Traill, IWM 67/264/1.

2 Traill.

3 Lunt, *Imperial Sunset*, p.129.

4 TNA/PRO Air 5/300.

5 R.E. Penwarm, IWM 2779.

6 Samuel Wentworth, IWM 4768.

7 Ibid.

8 G.V. Howard, IWM 88/9/1.

9 Ibid.

10 Ibid.

11 Lee, *Never Stop the Engine When it's Hot*, p.11.

11 – BEFORE OSAMA BIN LADEN

1 *RAF Quarterly*, vol. 4, no 2, 1933.

2 *RAF Quarterly*, vol. 4, no 3, 1933.

3 Gibbs, *Survivor's Story*, p.47.

4 TNA/PRO Air 8/94.

5 Glubb, *War in the Desert*, p.123.

6 Richard Brooks, IWM 4595.

7 G.V. Howard, IWM 88/9/1.

8 TNA/PRO Air 8/94.

9   Ibid.
10 Ibid.
11 Ibid.

12 – DESERT PURGATORY

1   L.A. Simmons, IWM 76/92/1.
2   W.H. Lawrence, IWM 09/9/10.
3   Keith, *Flying Years*, p.4.
4   Harris, *Bomber Offensive*, p.23.
5   G.V. Howard, IWM 88/9/1.
6   Quoted in Bowyer, *RAF Operations 1918–1938*, p.258.
7   Keith, p.5.
8   Alfred Earles, IWM 4499.
9   Ronald Ivelaw-Chapman, IWM P149.
10 Howard.
11 Ibid.
12 G.A. Bolland, IWM 02/34/1.
13 John Buckley, IWM 4582.
14 Frederick Richardson, IWM 4623.
15 Bolland.
16 Howard.
17 Ernest Ford, IWM 4614.
18 Howard.
19 Ibid.
20 B.G. Amos, IWM 81/45/1.
21 Howard.
22 Ibid.
23 John Varley, IWM 4551.
24 Keith, p.248.
25 Howard.
26 Sydney Sills, IWM 4601.
27 Samuel Wentworth, IWM 4768.
28 Stanley Eastmead, IWM 4504.
29 Robert Goddard, IWM 3189.
30 Bell, *The Letters of Gertrude Bell*, p.173.

13 – THE ELUSIVE PRIZE

1   Quoted in Monroe, *Britain's Moment in the Middle East 1914–1956*, p.11.

2   Norman Bottomley Papers, B2275, RAF Museum.

3   TNA/PRO Air 5/298.

4   TNA/PRO Air 5/1321.

5   Saunders, Per Ardua: *The Rise of British Air Power 1911–1939*, p.281.

6   Arthur Harris, IWM 3765.

7   TNA/PRO Air 8/45.

8   Ibid.

9   TNA/PRO Air 2/065.

10   TNA/PRO Air 5/1321.

11   TNA/PRO Air 83/6/1.

12   Ibid.

13   TNA/PRO Air 9/25.

14   TNA/PRO Air 5/298.

15   TNA/PRO Air 5/1328.

16   TNA/PRO Air 5/298.

17   TNA/PRO Air 5/1328.

18   TNA/PRO Air 8/122.

19   Arthur Capel, IWM 3166.

20   TNA/PRO Air 5/177.

21   Omissi, *Air Power and Colonial Control*, p.166.

22   Aubrey Ellwood, IWM 3167.

23   Capel.

24   TNA/PRO Air 5/298.

25   Ibid.

26   Spencer Viles, IWM 4549.

27   TNA/PRO Air 69/73.

28   TNA/PRO Air 5/248.

29   Ibid.

30   Ibid.

31   TNA/PRO Air 8/46.

32   TNA/PRO Air 5/248.

33   Ellwood.

34   TNA/PRO Air 2/1721.

35   TNA/PRO Air 5/298.

36   Ibid.

37 TNA/PRO Air 5/298.
38 TNA/PRO Air 9/25.
39 TNA/PRO Air 10/875.
40 William Alec Coryton, IWM 3190.
41 Ellwood.
42 Harris.
43 TNA/PRO Air 10/875.
44 TNA/PRO Air 5/1331.
45 Capel.
46 W.H. Lawrence, IMW 09/9/1.
47 Wilfred Page, IWM Page 875.
48 Wilfred Anderson, IWM 4662.
49 Ackerley, *Hindoo Holiday*, p.52.
50 TNA/PRO Air 10/875.
51 Page.

14 – THE KABUL MIRACLE

1 TNA/PRO Air 23/683.
2 Ronald Ivelaw-Chapman, IWM P149.
3 S.T.Townson, IWM 77/148/1.
4 William Dickson, IWM 3168.

15 – A BRITISH AIR SERVICE

1   TNA/PRO Air 5/433.
2   Ibid.
3   TNA/PRO Air 5/563.
4   Ibid.
5   Ibid.
6   Ibid.
7   Lecture to Boys at Marlborough Public School, Norman Bottomley Papers, B2240, RAF Museum.
8   *RAF Quarterly*, vol. 3, no 4, October 1932.
9   TNA/PRO Air 5/563.
10 Ibid.

11 Ibid.
12 TNA/PRO WO 33/1121.
13 TNA/PRO Air 5/563.
14 Hansard, 25 November 1936, vol. 318, cc 430-1.
15 Wilfred Page, IWM 875.
16 TNA/PRO Air 8/122.
17 TNA/PRO Air 5/433.
18 Ibid.
19 Ibid.
20 Ibid.
21 Ibid.

16 – BOOM'S SWANSONG

1   Boyle, *Trenchard*, p.580.
2   Hansard, March 1933, vol. 275, cc 1795–1896.
3   T.C. Traill, IWM 67/264/1.
4   Aubrey Ellwood, IWM 3167.
5   Arthur Capel, IWM 3166.
6   *RAF Quarterly*, vol. 1, no 4, 1930.
7   TNA/PRO Air 2/1560.
8   *Sunday Pictorial*, 24 August 1930.
9   *Daily Telegraph*, 27 May 1930.
10 Hansard, 9 April 1930.
11 Ibid.
12 Ibid.
13 *Notes by the Air Staff on the Regulation of Air Control in Undeveloped Countries*, November 1928.
14 TNA/PRO Air 5/1422.
15 'Air Control. The Other Point of View', Norman Bottomley Papers, B2241, RAF Museum.
16 'The Conduct of Small Wars with Particular Reference to Air Control in Semi-Civilised Countries', Bottomley Papers, B2271.
17 Ibid.
18 TNA/PRO Air 23/708.
19 TNA/PRO Air 5/1323.
20 RAF Staff College 9th Course, *Small Wars*, 1932.

21 Ibid. Bottomley, B2271.
22 'Report on the Operations against Sheikh Ahmed of Barzan', Bottomley Papers, B2249, RAF Museum.
23 Ibid.
24 Ibid.
25 TNA/PRO Air 23/708.
26 TNA/PRO Air 2/611.
27 TNA/PRO Air 2/611.
28 Ibid.
29 TNA/PRO Air 69/102.
30 Hansard, 14 March 1933, vol. 275, cc 1795–1896.

17 – SWIFT AGENTS OF GOVERNMENT

1   Quoted in Killingray, '"A Swift Agent of Government": Air Power in British Colonial Africa, 1916–1939'.
2   TNA/PRO Air 9/59.
3   Ibid.
4   TNA/PRO Air 2/1460.
5   Killingray.
6   TNA/PRO Air 20/681.
7   *RAF Quarterly*, vol. 3, no. 2, April 1932.
8   S.E. Townson, IWM 77/148/1.
9   Ibid.
10 TNA/PRO Air 20/681.
11 Killingray.
12 TNA/PRO Air 2/1046.
13 TNA/PRO Air 9/59.
14 Ibid.
15 Ibid.
16 Ibid.
17 Ibid.
18 Ibid.
19 James Pelly-Fry, IWM 96/9/1.
20 TNA/PRO Air 2/1519.
21 TNA/PRO Air 9/59.
22 TNA/PRO Air 9/59.

23 TNA/PRO Air 2/1519.

24 TNA/PRO Air 2/691.

25 Ibid.

26 TNA/PRO Air 2/3805.

27 TNA/PRO Air 2/69.

28 TNA/PRO Air 1/21/15/1/01.

29 Ibid.

30 Lindqvist, *A History of Bombing,* p.107.

31 Hansard, 25 July 1922, vol. 157, cc 185-6.

32 TNA/PRO Air 1/21/15/1/01.

33 Renfrew, *Forgotten Regiments,* pp.120–121.

34 Dudgeon, *The Luck of the Devil,* p.129.

35 TNA/PRO Air 5/1322.

36 Ibid.

37 TNA/PRO WO 106/5268.

38 TNA/PRO WO 32/2526.

39 TNA/PRO Air 5/1322.

40 TNA/PRO Air 5/1322.

41 *RAF Quarterly,* vol. 1, no 4, 1930.

18 – BATTLE FOR THE RAJ

1   *Royal United Services Institution Journal,* vol. 27, issue 1, 1932, pp.59–64.

2   Lee, *Never Stop the Engine When it's Hot,* p.21.

3   Norman Bottomley Papers, B2308, RAF Museum.

4   Robert Goddard, IWM 3189.

5   TNA/PRO Air 8/125.

6   Ibid.

7   Ibid.

8   Moon, *The British Conquest and Dominion of India,* p.1042.

9   TNA/PRO Air 5/1324.

10 Ibid.

11 *Daily Telegraph,* 10 December 1930.

12 *Daily Telegraph,* 11 August 1930.

13 TNA/PRO Air 5/1322.

14 Ibid.

15 TNA/PRO Air 5/1321.

16 TNA/PRO Air 8/122.
17 TNA/PRO WO 32/3525.
18 TNA/PRO Air 5/1321.
19 TNA/PRO Air 5/1322.
20 TNA/PRO Air 5/1321.
21 TNA/PRO Air 8/119.
22 Ibid.
23 Ibid.
24 TNA/PRO Air 2/1721.
25 Ibid.
26 'Air Operations against the Mohmands August/September 1935', B2297, Norman Bottomley Papers, RAF Museum.
27 TNA/PRO Air 2/2065.
28 TNA/PRO Air 8/129.
29 TNA/PRO Air 2/1721.
30 TNA/PRO WO 32/3526.
31 TNA/PRO Air 69/12.
32 TNA/PRO Air 5/1322.
33 TNA/PRO Air 8/129.
34 TNA/PRO Air 5/1322.
35 TNA/PRO WO 32/4148.
36 Corum and Johnson, *Airpower in Small Wars*, p.22.
37 Embry, *Mission Complete*, p.41.
38. 'Notes from 12 Pilots on Operations in Mohmand 1935', B2277, Bottomley Papers, RAF Museum.
39 Slessor, IWM p.125.
40 TNA/PRO Air 5/1322.
41 Ibid.
42 TNA/PRO Air 5/1334.
43 TNA/PRO Air 23/687.
44 'Air Operations against the Mohmands August/September 1935', B2297, Bottomley Papers, RAF Museum.
45 Lee, p.15.
46 'Address by C-in-C to Staff College, Quetta', B2275, Bottomley Papers, RAF Museum.
47 TNA/PRO Air 2/1721.
48 Towle, *Pilots and Rebels*, p.42.
49 TNA/PRO Air 23/687.

50 TNA/PRO Air 5/1325.

51 Embry, p.77.

19 – 'WHAT A MESS WE HAVE MADE'

1   W.H. Lawrence, IWM 09/9/1.
2   Bond, *British Military Policy between the Two World Wars*, p.269.
3   Leo Hetherington, IWM 4838.
4   TNA/PRO Air 5/1243.
5   Ibid.
6   Ibid.
7   Ibid.
8   76/1/37 CII/9/1-15 RAF Museum.
9   TNA/PRO Air 5/1244.
10 Samuel Wentworth, IWM 4768.
11 TNA/PRO Air 5/1244.
12 Sherman, *Mandate Days*, p.109.
13 TNA/PRO Air 5/1244.
14 Sherman, p.105.
15 TNA/PRO Air 5/1244.
16 James Pelly-Fry, IWM 96/9/1.
17 Corum, 'Air Control: Reassessing the History', p.28.
18 TNA/PRO Air 5/1324.
19 Ibid.
20 TNA/PRO Air 5/1244.
21 Ernest Ford, IWM 4614.
22 Alfred Earle, IWM 4499.
23 Charles Thomas Batchelor, IWM 4607.
24 Ernest Folley, IWM 4699.
25 Folley.
26 Earle, IWM 4499.
27 Spencer Viles, IWM 4549.
28 TNA/PRO Air 5/338.
29 Ibid.
30 TNA/PRO Air 2/1385.
31 Ibid.
32 Ibid.

33   TNA/PRO Air 23/708.
34   Ibid.
35   Ibid.

20 – BOMBING FOR POLICE PURPOSES

1   TNA/PRO Air 8/145.
2   TNA/PRO Air 5/1097.
3   TNA/PRO Air 8/157.
4   TNA/PRO Air 8/145.
5   Ibid.
6   Ibid.
7   TNA/PRO Air 5/1097.
8   Ibid.
9   Ibid.
10   TNA/PRO Air 2/1721.
11   TNA/PRO Air 8/145.
12   *RAF Quarterly*, vol. 5, no 3, January 1934.
12   TNA/PRO Air 8/529.
13   Hansard, 5 July 1933, vol. 280, cc 341.
14   Hansard, 7 July 1933, vol. 280, cc 353–4.
15   Kiernan, *Colonial Empires and Armies 1815–1960*, p.200.
16   TNA/PRO Air 8/145.
17   Hansard, 13 June 1933, vol. 279, cc 22-146.
18   Ibid.
19   Gardiner, *The Thirties: An Intimate History*, p.505.
20   Overy, *The Morbid Age*, p.232.
21   Hansard, 5 July 1933, vol. 280, cc 34113.
22   Hansard, 5 July 1933, vol. 280, cc 353–4.
23   TNA/PRO Air 2/2501.
24   TNA/PRO Air 8/529.
25   Ibid.
26   Patterson, *Guernica and Total War*, p.108.
27   TNA/PRO Air 2/2501.

21 – THE LAST OF THE GENTLEMEN'S WARS

1   Caroe, *The Pathans*, p.393.
2   Warren, *Waziristan*, p.14.
3   Ibid, pp.263–4.
4   'Air Operations in Waziristan November 1936–January 1937', B2300, Norman Bottomley Papers, RAF Museum.
5   Ibid.
6   'Warning Notice to Inhabitants of Arsal Kot', B2301, Bottomley Papers, RAF Museum.
7   'Air Operations in Waziristan November 1936–January 1937', B2300, Bottomley Papers, RAF Museum.
8   TNA/PRO WO 32/4142.
9   Wilfred Randall Page, IWM 875.
10 Warren, p.184.
11 'Warning Notice to Inhabitants of Arsal Kot', B2301, Bottomley Papers, RAF Museum.
12 'Waziristan Operations February–December 1937', B2304, Bottomley Papers, RAF Museum.
13 TNA/PRO Air 2/2051.
14 TNA/PRO Air 2/1721.
15 'Waziristan Operations February–December 1937', B2304, Bottomley Papers, RAF Museum.
16 TNA/PRO Air 2/4263.
17 'Waziristan Operations February–December 1937', B2304, Bottomley Papers, RAF Museum.
18 Ibid.
19 TNA/PRO Air 2/2065.
20 TNA/PRO Air 2/1721.
21 Ibid.
22 TNA/PRO Air 8/529.
23 TNA/PRO Air 2/2051.
24 'Waziristan Operations February–December 1937', B2304, Bottomley Papers, RAF Museum.
25 TNA/PRO Air 2/4263.

22 – LEGACY

1   TNA/PRO Air 1/26/15/1/125.
2   Quoted in Hastings, *Finest Years*, p.14.
3   Slessor, *The Central Blue*, p.84.
4   Quoted in Biddle, *Rhetoric and Reality in Air Warfare*, p.83.
5   TNA/PRO Air 23/5354.
6   Ibid.
7   French, *The British Way in Counter-Insurgency 1945–1967*, p.83.
8   Ibid, p.127.
9   FTNA/PRO WO 279/391.
10 TNA/PRO CO 537/3980.
11 Perry-Keene, *No Reflected Glory*, p.98.
12 Corum, 'Air Control: Reassessing the History'.
13 Interview, *World This Weekend*, BBC Radio 4, 27 October 2013.

BIBLIOGRAPHY

Ackerley, J.R., *Hindoo Holiday* (London: Chatto & Windus, 1952).

Baden-Powell, Robert, 'How Airships are Likely to Affect War' (*Royal United Services Institution*, vol. 54, issue 387, pp.555–581, 1910).

Barker, A.J., *The Neglected War* (London: Faber and Faber, 1967).

Barnett, Corelli, *Britain and her Army* (London: Allen Lane, The Penguin Press, 1970).

Beachey, Ray, *The Warrior Mullah* (London: Bellew Publishing, 1990).

Beaumont, R.A., 'A New Lease on Empire: Air Policing, 1919–1939', *Aerospace Historian*, 26, pp.84–90 (1979).

Bell, Gertrude, *The Letters of Gertrude Bell* (Teddington, Middlesex: The Echo Library, 2006).

Bialer, Uri, *Shadow of the Bomber* (London: Royal Historical Society, 1980).

Biddle, Tami Davis, *Rhetoric and Reality in Air Warfare* (Princeton: Princeton University Press, 2002).

Bond, Brian, *British Military Policy between the Two World Wars* (Oxford: Oxford University Press, 1980).

Bowyer, Chaz, *RAF Operations 1918–1939* (London: William Kimber, 1988).

Boyle, Andrew, *Trenchard* (London: Collins, 1962).

Brandon, Piers, *The Decline and Fall of the British Empire* (London: Cape, 2007).

Brown, Judith M. and Wm. Roger Lewis (Eds), *Oxford History of the British Empire: The Twentieth Century* (Oxford: Oxford University Press, 1999).

Cady, John F., *A History of Modern Burma* (Ithaca: Cornell University, 1958).

Callwell, C.E., *Small Wars* (London: Greenhill Books, 1990).

Caroe, Olaf, *The Pathans* (Karachi: Oxford University Press, 1983).

Carr, S.J., *You Are Not Sparrows* (London: Ian Allan, 1975).

Catherwood, Christopher, *Winston's Folly* (London: Constable, 2004).

Chamier, R.A., 'The Use of Air Power for Replacing Military Garrisons', *Royal United Services Institution Journal*, 1921.

Charlton, L.E.O., *Charlton* (London: Faber and Faber, 1931).

Charlton, L.E.O., *Deeds that Held the Empire* (London: John Murray, 1941).

Churchill, Winston, *Frontiers and Wars* (New York: Smithmark, 1995).

Clayton, Anthony, *The British Empire as a Superpower 1919–1939* (Basingstoke: Palgrave, 2001).

Corum, James S., 'Air Control: Reassessing the History', *The Royal Air Force Air Power Review*, vol. 4, no 2, Summer 2001.

Corum, James S. and Wray R. Johnson, *Airpower in Small Wars* (Lawrence, Kansas: University Press of Kansas, 2003).

Cox, Jafna, 'A Splendid Training Ground', *Journal of Imperial and Commonwealth History 1985*, vol. 13, part 2, pp. 157–84.

Dean, Maurice, *The Royal Air Force and Two World Wars* (London: Cassell, 1979).

De Wiart, Adrian Carton, *Happy Odyssey* (London: Jonathan Cape, 1950).

Douglas, R.M., 'Did Britain Use Chemical Weapons in Mandatory Iraq?', *The Journal of Modern History*, 2009, vol. 81, part 4.

Dudgeon, A.G., *The Luck of the Devil*, (Shrewsbury: Airlife, 1985).

Dunsterville, L.C., *The Adventures of Dunsterforce* (East Sussex: The Naval & Military Press Ltd, 2007).

Edmonds, C.H.K., 'Air Strategy', *Journal of the Royal United Service Institution*, no. 474, vol. 69, May 1924, pp. 191–208.

Embry, Basil, *Mission Complete* (London: Methuen & Co Ltd, 1957).

Ferguson, Niall, *Empire* (London: Penguin Books, 2004).

Ferris, John, 'The Theory of a "French Air Menace"', *Journal of Strategic Studies*, vol. 10, 1987.

Franks, Norman L.R., *First in the Indian Skies* (The RAF Collection, undated).

French, David, *The British Way in Counter-Insurgency 1945–1967* (Oxford: Oxford University Press, 2011).

Gann, L.H. and Peter Duignan, *The Rulers of British Africa 1870–1914* (London: Croon Helm, 1978).

Gardiner, Juliet, *The Thirties: An Intimate History* (London: Harper Press, 2010).

Gibbs, Gerald, *Survivor's Story* (London: Hutchinson, 1956).

Gilbert, Martin, *Winston S. Churchill Companion*, vol. IV: 1917–1922 (London: Heinemann, 1975).

Gilbert, Martin, *First World War* (London: Weidenfeld and Nicolson, 1994).

Gilbert, Martin, *The Churchill Documents*, vol. 10 (Michigan: Hillsdale College Press, 2nd ed. 2008)

Gilmour, David, *Curzon* (London: John Murray, 1994).

Glubb, John Bagot, *War in the Desert* (London: Hodder and Stoughton, 1960).

Graves, Robert and Alan Hodge, *The Long Week-end* (London: Faber and Faber, 1941).

Gray, Peter W., 'The Myths of Air Control and the Realities of Imperial Policing', *The Royal Air Force Air Power Review*, vol. 4, no 2, summer 2001.

Gray, Randal, 'Bombing the Mad Mullah 1920', *Journal of the Royal United Services Institution*, December 1980.

Gwynn, Charles W., *Imperial Policing* (London: Macmillan, 1939).

Haldane, Aylmer L., *The Insurrection in Mesopotamia 1920* (London: Imperial War Museum, 1922).

Hanley, Gerald, *Warriors* (London: Eland, 1971).

Harris, Arthur, *Bomber Offensive* (Barnsley: Pen & Sword Military Classics, 2005).

Hastings, Max, *Finest Years* (London: Harper Press, 2009).

Higham, Robin, *Armed Forces in Peacetime* (London: G.T. Foulis & Co., 1962).

Higham, Robin, *The Military Intellectuals in Britain 1918–1939* (New Brunswick: Rutgers University Press, 1966).

Hyam, Ronald, *Britain's Declining Empire* (Cambridge: Cambridge University Press, 2006).

Hyde, H. Montgomery, *British Air Policy between the Wars 1918–1939* (London: Heinemann, 1976).

Ismay, Lord, *The Memoirs of General the Lord Ismay* (London: Heinemann, 1960).

Jackson, Ashley, 'British Counter-insurgency in History', *British Army Review*, 2006, no 139, pp.12–22.

James, John, *The Paladins* (London: Macdonald & Co., 1990).

James, Lawrence, *The Rise and Fall of the British Empire* (London: Little, Brown and Company, 1994).

Jeffery, Keith, *Field Marshal Sir Henry Wilson* (Oxford: OUP, 2006).

Jeffery, Keith, *The British Army and the Crisis of Empire* (Manchester: Manchester University Press, 1984).

Jeffery, Keith (Ed.), *The Military Correspondence of Field Marshal Sir Henry Wilson* (London: Bodley Head, 1985).

Jeffery, Keith, 'Sir Henry Wilson and the Defence of the British Empire 1918–22', *Journal of Imperial and Commonwealth History*, 1977, vol. 5, part 3, pp.270–93.

Keith, C.H., *Flying Years* (London: John Hamilton Ltd, c. 1937).

Kiernan, V.G., *Colonial Empires and Armies 1815–1960* (Stroud: Sutton Publishing, 1998).

Killingray, David, '"A Swift Agent of Government": Air Power in British Colonial Africa, 1916–1939', *Journal of African History*, vol. 25, no 4 (1984).

Kincaid, Dennis, *British Social Life in India 1608–1937* (Newton Abbott: Readers Union, 1974).

Korda, Michael, *Hero* (London: J.R. Books, 2011).

Lacey, Robert, *The Kingdom* (London: Hutchinson, 1981).

Laffin, John, *Swifter Than Eagles* (Edinburgh: Blackwood, 1964).

Lawrence, T.E., *The Mint* (London: Cape, 1955).

Lee, Arthur Gould, *Fly Past* (London: Jarrolds, 1974).

Lee, David, *Never Stop the Engine When it's Hot* (London: Harmsworth, 1983).

Lee, Fitzgerald, *Imperial Military Geography* (Aldershot: Sifton Praed & Co., 1925)

Lewis, I.M., *A Modern History of Somalia* (London: Longman, 1980).

Lindqvist, Sven, *A History of Bombing* (London: Granta, 2012).

Lloyd, T.O., *The British Empire 1558–1983* (Oxford: Oxford University Press, 1984).

Lloyd, T.O., *Empire, Welfare State, Europe* (Oxford: Oxford University Press, 1993).

Longrigg, Stephen Hemsley, *Iraq 1900 to 1950* (Oxford: Oxford University Press, 1953).

Lowe, Norman, *Mastering Modern British History* (London: Macmillan, 1989).

Lunt, James, *Imperial Sunset* (London: MacDonald, 1981).

Masters, John, *Bugles and a Tiger* (London: Michael Joseph, 1956).

Monroe, Elizabeth, *Britain's Moment in the Middle East 1914–1956* (London: Chatto & Windus, 1963).

Moon, Penderel, *The British Conquest and Dominion of India* (London: Duckworth, 1989).

Moreman, T.R., 'Small Wars and Imperial Policing', *Journal of Strategic Studies*, 19:4 (1996) pp.105–31.

Morrow, John H. Jr., *The Great War in the Air* (Tuscaloosa: University of Alabama Press, 2009).

Mowat, Charles, *Britain between the Wars* (London: Methuen, 1968).

Moyse-Bartlett, H., *The King's African Rifles* (Uckfield: N&M Press, no date).

Omissi, David E., *Air Power and Colonial Control* (Manchester: Manchester University Press, 1990).

Orwell, George, *Essays* (New York: Knopf, 2002).

Overy, Richard, *The Morbid Age* (London: Allen Lane, 2009).

Patterson, Ian, *Guernica and Total War* (London: Profile Books, 2007).

Perry-Keene, Allan, *No Reflected Glory* (no publisher).

Philpott, Ian M., *The Royal Air Force: An Encyclopaedia of the Interwar Years*, 2 Volumes (Barnsley: Pen and Sword Aviation, 2005).

Porter, Bernard, *The Absent-Minded Imperialists* (Oxford: Oxford University Press, 2004).

Raleigh, W. and H.A. Jones, *The War in the Air*, vols 1–6 (London: Imperial War Museum, 1998).

Renfrew, Barry, *Forgotten Regiments* (Amersham: Terrier Press, 2009).

Robson, Brian, *Crisis on the Frontier* (Stroud: Spellmount, 2007).

Roskill, Stephen, *Naval Policy between the Wars*, vol. 1 (London: Collins, 1968).

Royle, Trevor, *Glubb Pasha* (London: Abacus, 1993).

Saunders, Hilary St George, Per Ardua: *The Rise of British Air Power 1911– 1939* (Oxford: Oxford University Press, 1944).

Sherman, A.J., *Mandate Days* (London: Thames and Hudson, 1997).

Sims, Charles, *The Royal Air Force* (London: Adam & Charles Black, 1968).

Slessor, John, *The Central Blue* (London: Cassell and Company, 1956).

Sluglett, Peter, *Britain in Iraq* (London: I.B. Tauris, 2007).

Smith, Malcolm, *British Air Strategy between the Wars* (Oxford: Oxford University Press, 1984).

Spiers, Edward M., 'Gas and the North-West Frontier', *Journal of Strategic Studies*, vol. 4 (1981).

Spiers, Edward M., *The Late Victorian Army* (Manchester: Manchester University Press, 1999).

Stark, Freya, *The Southern Gates of Arabia* (London: Arrow Books, 1990).

Steiner, Zara, *The Lights that Failed* (Oxford: Oxford University Press, 2005).

Strachan, Hugh (Ed.), *Big Wars and Small Wars* (London: Routledge, 2006).

Swinson, Arthur, *North-West Frontier* (London: Hutchinson, 1967).

Taylor, A.J.P., *English History 1914–45* (Oxford: Oxford University Press, 1965).

Templewood, Viscount, *Empire of the Air* (London: Collins, 1957).

Tennant, J.E., *In the Clouds above Baghdad* (London: Cecil Palmer, 1920).

Terraine, John, *The Right of the Line* (London: Hodder and Stoughton, 1985).

Thompson, Robert, *The Royal Flying Corps* (London: Hamish Hamilton, 1968).

Towle, Philip Anthony, *Pilots and Rebels* (London: Brassey's, 1989).

Townshend, Charles, 'Civilisation and Frightfulness' in Wrigley, Chris (Ed.), *Warfare, Diplomacy and Politics* (London: Hamish Hamilton, 1986).

Toye, Richard, *Churchill's Empire* (London: Macmillan, 2010).

Trench, Charles Chenevix, *The Indian Army* (London: Thames and Hudson, 1988).

Turner, E.S., *Gallant Gentlemen* (London: Michael Joseph, 1956).

Vincent, S.F., *Flying Fever* (London: Jarrolds, 1972).

Warren, Alan, *Waziristan, The Faqir of Ipi, and the Indian Army: the North-West Frontier Revolt of 1936–37* (Pakistan: Oxford University Press, 2000).

Wilson, Jeremy, *Lawrence of Arabia* (London: Minerva, 1990).

Winstone, H.V.F., *Gertrude Bell* (London: Quartet Books, 1980).

INDEX